The Price of Assimilation

The Price of Assimilation

Felix Mendelssohn and the Nineteenth-Century
Anti-Semitic Tradition

Jeffrey S. Sposato

UNIVERSITY PRESS

2006

OXFORD
UNIVERSITY PRESS

Oxford University Press, Inc., publishes works that further
Oxford University's objective of excellence
in research, scholarship, and education.

Oxford   New York
Auckland   Cape Town   Dar es Salaam   Hong Kong   Karachi
Kuala Lumpur   Madrid   Melbourne   Mexico City   Nairobi
New Delhi   Shanghai   Taipei   Toronto

With offices in
Argentina   Austria   Brazil   Chile   Czech Republic   France   Greece
Guatemala   Hungary   Italy   Japan   Poland   Portugal   Singapore
South Korea   Switzerland   Thailand   Turkey   Ukraine   Vietnam

Copyright © 2006 by Oxford University Press, Inc.

Published by Oxford University Press, Inc.
198 Madison Avenue, New York, New York 10016

www.oup.com

Oxford is a registered trademark of Oxford University Press

Library of Congress Cataloging-in-Publication Data
Sposato, Jeffrey S.
The price of assimilation : Felix Mendelssohn and the nineteenth-century
anti-semitic tradition/Jeffrey S. Sposato.
p. cm.
Includes bibliographical references and index.
ISBN-13 978-0-19-514974-6
ISBN 0-19-514974-2
1. Mendelssohn-Bartholdy, Felix, 1809–1847—Religion.   2. Jewish Christians—
Germany—History—19th century.   3. Antisemitism—Germany—
History—19th century.   I. Title.
ML410.M5S66 2005
780'.92—dc22   2004021553

2 4 6 8 9 7 5 3 1

Printed in the United States of America
on acid-free paper

Acknowledgments

For assistance with the completion of this book, I am heavily indebted to many individuals and organizations. First and foremost, I would like to thank my dissertation advisor, Robert L. Marshall, who read and commented on both the dissertation and this volume with his characteristic attention to detail, balance, and style, and who has served as an insightful sounding board for almost a decade. I am also grateful to R. Larry Todd and Peter Ward Jones, both of whom read and responded to my manuscript—twice—with tremendous care, as well as to the anonymous readers who reviewed my proposal to Oxford University Press. Special thanks also go to Ellen Harris, whose early interest in my project and continued enthusiasm have meant a great deal to me over the years.

For financial assistance, I am grateful to the Fulbright Commissions of the United States and Germany for sponsoring an academic year of research in Berlin, and to the Spalding Trust for supporting extended research visits to the Mendelssohn archives in Oxford and Kraków. My thanks also to the Josephine de Kármán Foundation and the Brandeis University Music Department for assisting with my final year of dissertation work, and to the American Council of Learned Societies and the Andrew W. Mellon Foundation for funding a final year of research on the book. I am also indebted to the University of Pittsburgh Center for International Studies, as well as to Richard Blevins, Norman Scanlon, and Mark McColloch of the University of Pittsburgh at Greensburg, for their generous support of my presentations at national and international conferences.

Of invaluable assistance during the course of my research were the librarians and support staff at numerous institutions. I am especially grateful to the Biblioteka Jagiellońska at the Uniwersytet Jagielloński, the Birmingham (UK) Public Library, the Bodleian Library at Oxford University, the New York Public Library of the Performing Arts, and the Staatsbibliothek zu Berlin—Preussischer Kulturbesitz for access to and permission to quote from unpublished sources. My thanks as well to the Andover-Harvard Theological Library at Harvard University, the Barbour Library at Pittsburgh Theological Seminary, the Boston Public Library, the Goldfarb/Farber Library at Brandeis University, the Hillman and music libraries at the University of Pittsburgh, and the Tisch and music libraries at Tufts University.

Deserving of special mention among the many helpful librarians I worked with are James Cassaro, Vera Deak, Helmut Hell, Hans-Günter Klein, Agnieszka Mietelska-Ciepierska, Diane Ota, Michael Rogan, Darwin Scott, John Shepard, and especially Peter Ward Jones, who spent hours helping me decipher some of the more difficult passages of the handwritten libretto drafts. Also of great assistance with the libretto drafts, unpublished letters, and seemingly endless translations were Ilse Andrews, James Hill, Traute Marshall, R. Larry Todd, and Christian Schwirten.

Numerous scholars—including Leon Botstein, David Brodbeck, Clive Brown, Eric Chafe, Marcia Citron, John Michael Cooper, Stephen Crist, Don Franklin, Helen Greenwald, Monika Hennemann, Marion Wilson Kimber, Robin A. Leaver, Ralph Locke, Roberta Marvin, Peter Mercer-Taylor, Jessie Ann Owens, Nancy Reich, Siegwart Reichwald, Christian Martin Schmidt, Douglass Seaton, and Michael P. Steinberg—were kind enough to discuss my research with me and, in some instances, to allow me access to their unpublished works. I am also grateful to the panelists and conference participants at the 1997, 1999, and 2001 National Meetings of the American Musicological Society, the Twelfth Biennial International Conference on Nineteenth-Century Music, the Christian Theological Seminary and Indianapolis Symphonic Choir Symposium "The Majesty of Mendelssohn's Music and the Origin of *Elijah*," and the Musicology Forums of Brandeis University, New England Conservatory, and the University of Pittsburgh, where earlier versions of my ideas were presented. My thanks also to the staff at Oxford University Press—especially Kimberly Robinson, Eve Bachrach, Stacey Hamilton, Marie Milton, Bob Milks, Norm Hirschy, and Maribeth Payne—for their patience, assistance, and support.

Many friends and colleagues—including Fernando Álvarez, Ivy Chen, Silvio Dos Santos, Michael Ellison, Patrick Fairfield, Sayre Greenfield, Wendy Heller, Kimberly Jew, Robert Matsuoka, John McDonald, Elliott McKinley, Christopher Mossey, David Nichols, Bill Owens, Scott Phillips, Géza Schenk, Cathy Schmidt, Margie Vinkler, Laura Voight, and Hugh Wilburn—have also been very supportive and willing to listen and react to my ideas. I am, of course, deeply grateful to my parents, Frank and Judith Sposato, and to the rest of my family, for both their love and their willingness to wait for what must have seemed like a very long time. I would particularly like to thank my grandmother Molly Cohen, who shared with me her insights into Jewish history and tradition, both general and familial. Finally, and most important, I want to thank my partner, Peter F. Cohen, who provided love, encouragement, and support, who served as both reader and conscience, and to whom, in many ways, this book owes its existence.

Sections of chapter 1 of this book previously appeared in "Creative Writing: The [Self-]Identification of Mendelssohn as Jew," published in *The Musical Quarterly*, 82 (Spring 1998); a short section of chapter 4 appeared as "Mendelssohn, *Paulus*, and the Jews: A Response to Leon Botstein and Michael Steinberg," in *The Musical Quarterly*, 83 (Summer 1999). Finally, an earlier version of chapter 3 appeared as "'For You Have Been Rebellious Against the Lord': The Jewish Image in Mendelssohn's *Moses* and Marx's *Mose*," in *Historical Musicology: Sources, Methods, Interpretations*, edited by Stephen Crist and Roberta Marvin (University of Rochester Press, 2004). I am grateful to all parties involved for their permission to reprint this material.

Contents

Abbreviations

Bd.   *Band* (volume)

D-Bsb   Staatsbibliothek zu Berlin—Preussischer Kulturbesitz, Berlin, Germany

D-F   Stadt- und Universitätsbibliothek, Frankfurt, Germany

GA   *Gesamtausgabe* (published score from the complete edition of Mendelssohn's works, edited by Julius Rietz, published 1874–77)

GB-Bp   City Archives, Birmingham Public Library, Birmingham, UK

GB-Ob   Bodleian Library, Oxford University, Oxford, UK

MA   *Mendelssohn Archiv* (Staatsbibliothek zu Berlin)

MN   *Mendelssohn Nachlass* (Staatsbibliothek zu Berlin, Biblioteka Jagiellońska)

PL-Kj   Biblioteka Jagiellońska, Uniwersytet Jagielloński, Kraków, Poland

US-NYp   New York Public Library of the Performing Arts, Music Division (Astor, Lenox and Tilden Foundations), New York, NY, USA

The Price of Assimilation

Introduction

In THE EARLY NINETEENTH CENTURY, Jews living in German-speaking lands began to view themselves not as the shunned aliens of the past, but as Jewish Germans, a result of their emancipation and increased acculturation, as well as the secularization of their countrymen. Christian rationalists, in particular, tended to share this view, defining Jewish otherness as merely a difference in religion (as opposed to culture) and accepting Jews into their social circles. But despite this shift in enlightened perception, as well as Jewish efforts to assimilate through superficial changes in clothing, speech,[1] and gesture, the general populace—and indeed the law itself—continued to see the Jews as adherents to what Kant had called a "useless, true-religion-displacing old cult," and refused to grant them any more than partial entry into German society.[2] This circumstance led many Jews who had given up the ritual law (either under the influence of rationalism or because they wished to better assimilate), and were therefore Jews in name only, to separate themselves from Judaism altogether and to accept what poet Heinrich Heine had called the "admission-ticket to European culture"—baptism.[3] But far from being a simple bill of admittance, baptism was a virtual Pandora's box, filled with paradoxes and contradictions, the most demoralizing of which was surely the continued distrust Jews faced from the non-Jews who had originally called for their conversion.

From early childhood onward, composer and conductor Felix Mendelssohn Bartholdy had to contend with the reality that, despite his conversion from Judaism to Protestantism at age seven, the public display of his Christian faith through his sacred music, and his claims (reflected in his private correspondence) of both German pride and discipleship to noted Protestant theologian Friedrich Schleiermacher, many continued to see him as both religiously and culturally Jewish—or, at the very least, as having a strong personal connection to his Jewish heritage.[4] Such suspicions were common with respect to the so-called New Christians (*Neuchristen*),[5] many of whom had, admittedly, converted for purely opportunistic reasons.[6] In fact, such attitudes often originated from sources close to home, as was true in Mendelssohn's case. When the young Felix asked to see a J. S. Bach prelude owned by his organ teacher, August Wilhelm Bach, in the early 1820s, Bach purportedly asked one of his other charges, "Why does the young Jew need to have everything? He has enough anyway; don't give him the fugue."[7] Similarly, in 1821, Mendelssohn's composition teacher, Carl Friedrich Zelter, commented regarding his twelve-year-old pupil that "it would be a truly rare thing,[8] if the son of a Jew (*Judensohne*) were to become an artist."[9] Such remarks were hardly restricted to Mendelssohn's childhood, however. In 1840, for instance, Mendelssohn's friend the composer Robert Schumann re-marked to his wife, Clara, in their marriage diary:

> Clara told me that I seemed different toward Mendelssohn; surely not toward him as an artist—you know that—for years I have contributed so much to promoting him, more than almost anyone else. In the meantime—let's not neglect ourselves too much. Jews remain Jews; first they take a seat ten times for themselves, then comes the Christians' turn. The stones we have helped gather for their Temple of Glory they occasionally throw at us. Therefore do not do too much [for them] is my opinion.

To which Clara replied:

> First I must tell you, my dear husband, that I agree with you completely in regard to the above statement, and that I have sometimes, silently, had simi-lar thoughts, but out of great admiration for Mendelssohn's art have again and again adopted the old excessive attentiveness toward him. I will take your advice and not degrade myself too much before him, as I have done so often.[10]

After his death in 1847, the tendency to see Mendelssohn as Jewish intensified with the continuing rise of anti-Semitism. Indeed, Richard Wagner's notorious essay *Judaism in Music*, in which he attacked the music of Jews (Meyerbeer) and perceived Jews (Mendelssohn), appeared in print less than three years later.[11] The trend reached its apex in the twentieth century with the passage of the 1935 Nazi "Nuremberg Laws," which, with their new definition of who was a Jew under the law, wiped away any and all attempts by Jews at assimilation—including conversion, even of the family two generations before.[12] From that moment on, Jewish Germans—both living and dead, both converted and nonconverted—were now Jews alone in the eyes of the state. The consequences for Mendelssohn of this official reclassification included the destruction of his memorial statue outside the Gewandhaus concert hall in Leipzig on the night of November 10, 1936, the prohibition of performances of his music, and his elimination from any prominent position in written music history. Nineteenth-century anti-Semites (such as Richard Wagner), followed by the Nazis, saw Mendels-sohn's Jewish heritage as a badge of shame—one that could not be washed away with baptismal water or covered up with a large pile of Christian sacred music.

For most German-speaking Jews, the collapse of the Nazi regime meant little in terms of a change in their self-identification. The transformation from Jewish Ger-mans into Jews alone (albeit now with German passports) was irreversible—the possibility of anything else being, at best, a distant memory.[13] The transformation was just as complete for Mendelssohn, who, in many biographies written since the war, has been described as a person of Jewish, rather than German, "solidarity," to use Eric Werner's term, and as a man who, to use Wulf Konold's term, expressed "pride" in his Jewish heritage.[14] Perhaps out of a need to compensate for the Nazi defamation campaign or perhaps because challenging Mendelssohn's Jewishness would have been seen as furthering that campaign, Mendelssohn's mark of shame was refashioned as a badge of honor—but the presence of the badge itself has rarely been questioned. Moreover, Mendelssohn is assumed to have experienced this pride throughout his life, ignoring the possibility that the views of a man with such a complicated religious history and who lived in such a volatile era might have varied over time. This book seeks to challenge the monolithic postwar assessment of this aspect of Mendelssohn's biography by demonstrating that the composer's relationship to his Jewish heritage was far more complex than generally assumed and, more important, changed over the course of his life. By far the most prominent agent for change in this regard was Felix's father, Abraham, who strongly encouraged his son to separate himself from Judaism. Abraham's death in 1835, however, was equally significant, since it—coupled with the establishment of Felix's career on firm footing in Leipzig that same year—represented a turning point in Mendelssohn's attitude toward Judaism, one that allowed him eventually to stop repudiating his birth religion so vehemently.

Despite the claims of writers such as Eric Werner to the contrary, evidence of Mendelssohn's attempt to disassociate himself from Judaism appears in both the composer's carefully worded correspondence and the memoirs of his colleagues. However, these sources only imperfectly relate the evolution of Mendelssohn's attitudes, since, on the whole, the composer rarely discussed matters relating to Judaism, especially in the years following his father's death. Of greater relevance—and far more revealing of the composer's character—is how he wanted himself to be regarded by the public. Any inquiry into Mendelssohn's relationship to his Jewish heritage must therefore begin with his sacred choral works—compositions that not only were addressed to the public but that also grapple with Jewish topics and themes. For indeed, Mendelssohn considered his compositions confessional documents, a realization to which he apparently came as early as July 1831, writing that month in letters to both his cousin Henriette von Pereira Arnstein and his close friend actor Eduard Devrient:

> I take music in a very serious light, and I consider it quite inadmissible to compose anything that I do not thoroughly feel. It is just as if I were to utter a falsehood; for notes have as distinct a meaning as words, perhaps even a more definite sense.[15]

> I look upon it as my duty to compose just how and what my heart indites, and to leave the effect it will make to Him who takes heed of greater and better

things. As time goes on I think more deeply and sincerely of that,—to write only as I feel, to have less regard than ever to outward results, and when I have produced a piece that has flowed from my heart—whether it is afterwards to bring me fame, honours, orders, or snuff-boxes, does not concern me.[16]

These statements, while significant, should not be used to justify overinterpretation of Mendelssohn's works, lest we claim, for example, that the composer's *Ave Maria* shows a clandestine desire to convert to Catholicism or *The First Walpurgis-Night* (*Die erste Walpurgisnacht*) an affection for Druid rites! They do, however, clearly demonstrate that Mendelssohn was aware that his music served as one pillar of his public persona.

In considering the sacred works and their reflection of this persona, we must move beyond titles and subjects and examine in detail the texts themselves, as well as the circumstances surrounding the composition of the works. A failure to do so in the past has resulted in the construction of a pair of commonly held beliefs about Mendelssohn that have worked together in a circular manner to support the postwar assessment of the composer: that is, Mendelssohn set subjects and texts significant to Judaism, therefore he was strongly attached to his Jewish heritage; Mendelssohn was strongly attached to his Jewish heritage, therefore he set subjects and texts significant to Judaism. Mendelssohn's oratorio *Elias* and his psalm motets and cantatas are used as evidence in many such discussions, but generally that testimony begins and ends with the titles or Old Testament subject matter of the works themselves.[17] Closer examination of the pieces, their history, and their cultural context quickly reveals the flaws of this approach, however. Since *Elias* receives a chapter-length discussion later, Mendelssohn's psalm settings will serve as an example for the moment.

In the first edition (1880) of his *Dictionary of Music and Musicians*, George Grove remarked of Psalm 114, *When Israel Went Out of Egypt* (*Da Israel aus Ägypten zog*), "The Jewish blood of Mendelssohn must surely for once have beaten fiercely over this picture of the great triumph of his forefathers."[18] Grove did not claim Mendelssohn made such a statement, nor did he argue that the Psalm was of a quality greatly superior to the rest of Mendelssohn's oeuvre or that it was any less Christian than his other sacred music. Nevertheless, Grove's comment remains the most cited assessment of Mendelssohn's Psalms, and he is often quoted in an effort to link the composer with his heritage.[19] More important, Grove's statement has caused commentary on Mendelssohn's many Psalms to focus on this single piece, has led to the expansion of Grove's assessment to encompass all of Mendelssohn's endeavors in this area,[20] and has helped to foster the belief that—despite the genre's rich history—Mendelssohn's composition of psalm motets and cantatas was unusual and stemmed from a desire to bridge Judaism and Christianity.[21]

While Felix unquestionably understood the importance of the Psalms to both Judaism and Christianity, past assumptions that he attempted to make a statement through his settings dissolve when their historical and functional contexts are considered, a process that allows the pieces to be sorted into four groups:

1. *The juvenilia (Psalms 19, 46, 66, and 119)*.[22] Mendelssohn composed these Psalms while under Zelter's watchful eye in the months after October 1, 1820, at which time Felix and Fanny joined Berlin's leading institution for choral music, the Singakademie, where Zelter served as director. Although Zelter deemed Psalm 19 sufficiently advanced to warrant performance by the Singakademie on September 18, 1821, these early Psalms were essentially exercises in which Felix demonstrated his ability to compose, among other things, a variety of different kinds of fugues.[23] They were not professions of his faith.

An interesting aside to the juvenilia is Mendelssohn's choice to use his grandfather Moses Mendelssohn's translation over Martin Luther's for Psalm 119. As shall soon be seen, the composer's descent from the celebrated philosopher and Jewish reformer was frequently remarked upon, even during Felix's lifetime, and was the root of the unique assimilation difficulties he and his family faced, even after their conversion to Protestantism. It is therefore tempting to view Felix's use of his grandfather's translation as a gesture of Jewish solidarity. But given Mendelssohn's age (about twelve years old), the fact that the piece was simply an exercise, and that it represents his only surviving work based on his grandfather's writings, care should be taken not to read too much into the choice. Family pride was no doubt a factor, as was Felix's youthful lack of understanding of the dynamics of assimilation (the complexities of which his father would not explain until their trip to Paris in 1825).[24]

2. *Music for the Berlin Cathedral Choir (Psalms 91, 98, and 100 [1844], the three op. 78 Psalms, and the harmonizations of seven melodies from the Lobwasser Psalter)*. At the other end of Mendelssohn's career were the Psalms written as part of his responsibilities as *Generalmusikdirektor für kirchliche und geistliche Musik* in Berlin, a position to which the Prussian monarch Friedrich Wilhelm IV officially appointed him on November 22, 1842.[25] The king had originally brought Mendelssohn to Berlin in 1841 on the counsel of Christian Karl Josias von Bunsen (who later wrote a libretto for what posthumously became known as *Christus*) in an attempt to reenergize musical life in the city, first in the concert hall (for which Mendelssohn received the title of *Kapellmeister*) and then, the following year, in the church.[26] As part of the latter effort, the king revised the Prussian liturgy to—among other things—increase the prominence of Psalms.[27] All the Psalms Mendelssohn composed during this period were designed to satisfy this liturgical assignment (with each custom-written for a specific Sunday of the church year).[28] Again, nothing here suggests an attempt on Mendelssohn's behalf to demonstrate his solidarity with Judaism.

3. *Commissions (Psalms 5, 13, 31, 55, 100 [1847], and possibly a lost setting of Psalm 24)*. Between 1839 and 1847, Mendelssohn wrote a group of Psalms on commissions from various individuals and institutions, most of which specified—and often supplied—the texts they wanted set. Nearly all these commissions came from English

sources, including individuals (Charles Bayles Broadley [Psalm 13] and William Bartholomew [Psalm 55]) and publishers (Coventry & Hollier [Psalms 5 and 31] and Ewer & Co. [music for the Anglican Morning Service, including Psalm 100]).[29] The only commission not from England arrived in late 1843 from Dr. Maimon Fränkel of the New Israelite Temple of Hamburg. Fränkel suggested several possible Psalms— including 24, 84, and 100—to celebrate the temple's twenty-fifth anniversary. Eric Werner suggested that Mendelssohn sent his 1844 *a cappella* setting of Psalm 100 to fulfill the commission,[30] but as R. Larry Todd has noted, Psalm 100 was stylistically and textually inappropriate for the temple; moreover, two of Fränkel's letters (March 29 and April 12, 1844) indicate that he patiently awaited a setting of Psalm 24, which, if composed at all, is now lost.[31] As with Mendelssohn's early Psalm 119 setting, little should be read into this possible work for the temple, as Mendelssohn regularly composed sacred music for traditions outside his own, including Anglican (as seen here) and Catholic, neither of which appear to have especially appealed to him on a spiritual level.

4. *The Psalm Cantatas of the 1830s* (*Psalms 42, 95, 114, and 115*). Because they bear no dedication and were not specifically commissioned, the works in this group (especially Psalm 114) lend themselves most to the argument that Mendelssohn's Psalms reflect his desire to make connections between Judaism and Christianity.[32] A closer examination reveals, however, that all these pieces contain elements that orient them toward a Christian audience. This is most obvious in Psalm 115, which Mendelssohn composed in 1829 and 1830, in the months leading up to and during his Italian journey. In addition to setting the Latin Vulgate text of the Psalm, Mendelssohn incorporated several chorale-like melodies, including one nearly identical to the ubiquitous passion chorale, *O Haupt voll Blut und Wunden*.[33] Mendelssohn did not compose another psalm cantata until 1837, by which point he was living in Leipzig and serving as director of the Gewandhaus. Psalms 42, 95, and 114 were all composed within the next two years, with each receiving its public premiere there under Mendelssohn's baton. This suggests that Mendelssohn may have composed the pieces specifically for his Lutheran Leipzig audience, a likelihood that increases substantially when the final choruses of Psalms 42 and 114 and the second chorus of Psalm 95 are brought into the equation. Both Psalms 42 and 114 close with texts taken from outside the Psalms that are analogous to the call for eternal praise in the Doxology, the acclamation traditionally added to Psalms when they appear in a Christian liturgical context ("Glory be to the Father, and to the Son," etc.).[34] As for Psalm 95, it too incorporates a melody reminiscent of the *O Haupt* passion chorale in the canon at the end of its second movement. Once again, then, the fact that these works draw on Old Testament subject matter fails to adequately explain the religious intentions behind them.

But while the Psalms provide little useful evidence of Mendelssohn's feelings toward his Jewish heritage, other sacred works—especially his oratorios—do. Here, the problem lies in the fact that scholars have looked at the oratorios in their published versions only, while it is in the evolution of their texts that we can best observe Mendelssohn grappling with such issues. Most of Mendelssohn's shorter sacred works—including the Psalms—reveal no such development, since they are usually based on a single biblical passage. On the other hand, Mendelssohn's oratorio texts—namely, *Moses* (a libretto he wrote for his friend Adolf Bernhard Marx), *Paulus* (*St. Paul*), *Elias* (*Elijah*), and the unfinished *Christus* (*Christ*)—were assembled from disparate passages found throughout the Bible and therefore required careful selection and extensive drafting, a process that usually lasted years and often necessitated outside help. Most of these textual drafts, as well as a wide variety of musical sketches and scores, survive in the collections of the Bodleian Library in Oxford, the Staatsbibliothek zu Berlin, and the Biblioteka Jagiellońska in Kraków. Until recently, however, only a small fraction of these texts had been examined or transcribed from their original manuscripts.[35] My book focuses on this neglected resource, analyzing passages culled from the stages of development of each oratorio. These demonstrate, on the one hand, Mendelssohn's often fervent attempt to prove the sincerity of his Christian faith by participating in an anti-Semitic musical tradition, one that encouraged portrayals of Jews in sacred works that reflected contemporary stereotypes. But the texts also demonstrate the gradual softening of this attitude (as well as Mendelssohn's subsequent attempts to depict the Jews with greater sympathy) beginning with the published version of *Paulus*. Likewise, the discussion offered here of Mendelssohn's edition of Bach's *St. Matthew Passion*, which the composer prepared in connection with its Berlin revival in 1829, demonstrates that his editorial choices for this arguably anti-Semitic work represent—especially when compared with other contemporary performing editions—an early attempt to overcompensate, as it were, for his background.

Needless to say, in an era of growing anti-Semitism, Abraham Mendelssohn was not the only influence driving his son away from his Jewish heritage, nor was he the sole stimulus for the anti-Semitic characterizations found in the oratorios. As mentioned earlier, contemporary musical developments played an important role in shaping Felix's attitudes, as did the oratorio composers he both respected and knew personally (Louis Spohr and Carl Loewe) and the contributors to his oratorio libretti (especially Pastor Julius Schubring). The compositions of Spohr and Loewe reveal that anti-Semitic characterizations were common in the New Testament–based oratorios of the first half of the nineteenth century. This stance was, as we shall see, partially the result of a widespread German belief that Christianity in Germany derived not from Judaism but from Heathenism, a position most prominently codified in the seminal work of the era's most eminent theologian, *The Christian Faith* (*Der christliche Glaube*) by Friedrich Schleiermacher. (In addition to being Schleiermacher's disciple, Mendelssohn was also his personal friend.) Such views strongly affected contemporary oratorio composition by introducing what could be called a philosophy of "philo-Heathenism," a glorification of the German Gentile past that led, among other things, to the popularity of oratorios on the subject of the so-called German Apostle, St. Boniface, and on the missionary archetype St. Paul. Oratorios setting Old Testament subjects were also heavily influenced by a doctrine codified by Schleiermacher and other prominent theologians: namely, that the Old Testament's value lay in what it revealed about the New. As a result, Old Testament oratorios, such as those by Loewe, were expected to find some way of orienting themselves toward the New Covenant, typically by including Messianic prophesy or some other form of Christological imagery. The impact of all these influences is clearly discernible in the development of each of Mendelssohn's oratorio libretti.

A discussion of the depiction of the Jews in Mendelssohn's oratorios raises an issue of terminology. In short, is it accurate (or fair) to describe Mendelssohn's negative depictions as "anti-Semitic"? Since being coined by Wilhelm Marr sometime around 1873, the term "anti-Semitism" has been commonly used to describe hostility toward Jews of any kind and at any time. Recently, however, efforts have been made—notably by Gavin Langmuir—to refine the definition of anti-Semitism and to separate from it anti-Judaism, which Langmuir defines as "a total or partial opposition to Judaism—and to Jews as adherents of it—by people who accept a competing system of beliefs or practices and consider certain genuine Judaic beliefs and practices as inferior."[36] This limits anti-Semitism to that hostility against Jews that is not based on considered religious disagreement but which is instead either socially based or founded upon irrational or uninformed beliefs about the faith.[37] Thus, as Langmuir argues, it was anti-Judaism, not anti-Semitism, that predominated in the first millennium of the Christian era, as the critics of Jews focused on the perceived defects of their faith and their refusal to accept the divinity of Christ. That which he defines as anti-Semitism emerged later, when Christians began to feel that the Jews in some way positively and even physically threatened Christian beliefs. In response, these anti-Semites devised fantasies of bizarre anti-Christian rituals, such as the murder of Christian children (the so-called blood libel), the destruction of the consecrated host of the Eucharist, cannibalism, and the poisoning of wells.

The emergence of cultural anti-Semitism led to its slow intertwining with traditional religious anti-Judaism and to the development of a mutually reinforcing relationship between the two. I would argue that this trend continued to intensify, to the point that by the early nineteenth century, the two were virtually inseparable, at least in Germany. To demonstrate this, consider the two most significant aspects of Mendelssohn's depictions that might, upon initial consideration, appear to be critiques of the Jewish faith alone and therefore examples of Langmuir's anti-Judaism: the implication that the Jews are incapable of true faith, and their obsession with the letter of the law. The notion that the Jews are incapable of true faith is implied extensively in *Moses* and in some versions of the *Elias* libretto. On the surface, this accusation appears anti-Jewish as opposed to anti-Semitic, since it is a religious one, hearkening back to Paul's condemnation of the

Jews for their adherence to the letter of the law over its spirit, as well as for their unwillingness to accept Jesus as the Messiah. It is inconceivable, however, that the evocation of this image in nineteenth-century Germany would not also have had a social dimension, readily calling to mind those Jewish converts whom Christians may have praised for accepting Christ, while simultaneously admonishing (and distrusting) them for so readily abandoning their faith. The image also would have evoked other converts who lacked faith of any kind or who secretly retained their Jewish beliefs, but had converted for opportunistic reasons. Likewise, the depiction of the Jews in *Paulus* as obsessed with the letter of the law, while taken from Paul's notorious anti-Jewish rhetoric, would also have resonated with contemporary German-Christian perceptions of both the stubbornness of the Jews for their refusal to fully integrate with their surroundings, and their alleged attempt to exist as a separate state within their state.

As these examples show, those elements of Mendelssohn's negative Jewish characterizations that might theoretically appear to be a theologically motivated anti-Jewish critique are inevitably anti-Semitic in their social impact, even if the author may have intended them otherwise. In addition, there are elements of Mendelssohn's depictions that adhere more straightforwardly to Langmuir's definition of anti-Semitism, such as those segments of *Moses* that conform with contemporary stereotypes of the Jews as parasitic and engaging in barbaric ritual.[38] Therefore, I have decided—in most cases—to refer to the elements of Mendelssohn's negative depictions as anti-Semitic, rather than anti-Jewish, throughout this volume.

As a child of one Jewish and one Catholic parent, born into a family that included several cantors, I naturally heard of Mendelssohn "the great Jewish composer" while growing up. In choosing to examine Mendelssohn's relationship to his Jewish heritage, I had neither the intention nor desire to refute that image, but as a long-time devotee of the composer's choral music, I could not help but be struck by the manifest contradiction posed to that image by works such as *Paulus*, with its seemingly blatant attacks on the Jewish people. Later, as I began to read biographies of Mendelssohn in which the composer's Jewish heritage was discussed (as well as more general literature on the Jewish situation in Germany in the early nineteenth century), I became increasingly suspicious that the highly positive assessment of Mendelssohn's attitude toward his Jewish heritage was in error. I was particularly skeptical of the seemingly universal conclusion that both the composer's religious beliefs and his relationship to his Jewish heritage remained constant throughout his short life. As a person born into a religiously diverse situation, who has grappled with and changed his views on religion time and time again, it seemed unlikely to me that Mendelssohn, whose situation was even more complex and who was born into an era of growing religious polarization, did not experience similar crises as a young man. My subsequent delving into both the published and unpublished sources would eventually convince me that my suspicions were well founded.

While trying to strip away the layers of interpretation saddled on Mendelssohn over the last 150 years, first by friends, then by the anti-Semites, then by the post-war scholars, I have been most shocked by the lengths to which commentators have gone either to include or exclude the composer from the ranks of a particular group. Mendelssohn's nephew Sebastian Hensel, for example, wrote in his indispensable family history in 1880 of his desire to chronicle a "good, German, middle-class fam-ily," complete with all of the careful editing such a depiction implies.[39] Writing in 1941, on the other hand, Georg Schünemann attempted to discount Mendelssohn's importance to German music by claiming in his egregiously anti-Semitic history of the Berlin Singakademie that Mendelssohn—a name he either followed with "Jd." (*Jude*) or identified as Jewish in some other manner—played only a minor role in the revival of the Bach *St. Matthew Passion*. With no evidence to support him and a fair amount against, Schünemann wrote that it was only because the family had in-vested such a substantial sum that Mendelssohn was permitted to conduct two of the performances.[40] As chapter 1 demonstrates, however, postwar biographies have, until quite recently, engaged in a different kind of revisionism, one that has attempted to compensate for past slander by arguing for Mendelssohn's proud self-identification as a Jew. But this claim, first made by Eric Werner, was based on the incorrect tran-scription and, indeed, partial falsification of one of the composer's letters, as well as the misreading of several other crucial documents.

Considering the outrageous slanders and defilements the Mendelssohn legacy endured during the Nazi regime, it is only natural that enthusiasts of his music, along with other fair-minded people, would want to see the situation rectified. Recasting Mendelssohn into yet another version of something he was not does not, however, do him or us any favors in the long run. The efforts of postwar scholars (and, ironi-cally enough, the anti-Semites as well) to depict Mendelssohn as a man of strong Jewish allegiance may have temporarily cloaked him in the mantle of "great Jewish composer," but that image has already begun to fade. Many Jews today no longer see Mendelssohn as a hero, but rather as a turncoat and apostate who, along with his family, abandoned his faith; indeed, some have even gone so far as to prohibit the playing of the *Midsummer Night's Dream* wedding march at their marriage cere-monies for this very reason.

The best way, in my opinion, to "save" Mendelssohn is to try to see him as he was, free—or at least as free as possible—of our own projections and agendas. We must remember too that he was a Mendelssohn, bearer of a name that (to quote his father, Abraham) held "enduring significance" to German Jews and that represented "Judaism in its transitional period."[41] For this reason alone, Mendelssohn could not simply leave his heritage behind at the baptistery. In order to be accepted socially outside of the Berlin intelligentsia in which his family circulated, and, more impor-tant, to succeed professionally as a Christian musician on an international stage, Mendelssohn would have to prove not only the sincerity of his Christian faith, but also his complete separation from his Jewish roots. Only after Mendelssohn's goals of social acceptance and professional success had been achieved (as signified by his receiving the directorship of the Gewandhaus in Leipzig), could he then consider living a less-guarded existence. As the works examined here will show, however, Mendelssohn never actively embraced his Jewish heritage in the manner described by many postwar authors, and, given the sharp rise in anti-Semitism after his death in 1847, it seems unlikely that he would ever have been able to do so had he lived longer. These facts may not conform to our heroic visions of a great composer. But rather than variously celebrate or condemn Mendelssohn as the proud or lapsed Jew, or the true or false Christian, we should instead attempt to better understand his situation and see him not as a hero or symbol, but as he was—talented, sensitive, ambitious (socially and artistically), a man with an unusually complex background living in a difficult era.

New Christians

Felix was . . . determined to avoid recalling his heritage.

—*Eduard Devrient*

As MENDELSSOHN AND MENDELSSOHN STUDIES have enjoyed something of a resurgence in recent years, much discussion has centered around elements of the composer's identity. Exactly how Mendelssohn responded to one of those elements—his Jewish heritage—has been of particular interest. The prevailing view of Mendelssohn in this regard has been of a man who expressed pride in his Jewish lineage; indeed, it is a view so pervasive it has become a cornerstone of what could be termed the "postwar Mendelssohn interpretation." Much of the rationale behind it derives from the largely unspoken assumption that the composer was immersed in Judaism from the moment of his birth on February 3, 1809, until his baptism seven years later, and that, even after his conversion to Protestantism, the home in which he was raised was firmly rooted in Jewish tradition.[1] Consider, for instance, Jack Werner's concept of a "Mendelssohnian cadence"—a descending arpeggiated minor triad that appears frequently in Mendelssohn's works (especially *Elias*) and that, in Werner's view, resembles the final cadence of the rabbi's blessing sung at the end of festival services (ex. 1.1).[2] Writing several years later in 1963, Eric Werner saw a similar connection between Mendelssohn's chorus "Behold, God the Lord passed by" (*Der Herr ging vorüber*, GA 34) in *Elias*, and a High Holy Day chant sung in synagogues since the fifteenth century (ex. 1.2).[3] In 1980, with little supporting evidence, Rainer Riehn interpreted the opening "curse" solo of *Elias* as "a kind of confession that Elijah=Mendelssohn" and described Mendelssohn's use of chromaticism in the aria "Is not His word like a fire" (*Ist nicht das Herrn Wort wie ein Feuer*, GA 17) as sounding "foreign, Jewish."[4] More recently, in response to some of my earlier publications on this subject, Michael P. Steinberg and Leon Botstein have argued that Mendelssohn's oratorio *Paulus* promotes, to use Botstein's phrase, a "notion that Protestantism could become a legitimate synthesis of Western Christianity and Judaism"—in other words, that Mendelssohn could simultaneously exist as both Christian and Jew.[5]

That Mendelssohn identified in part as Jewish is beyond question. How could he not have, with queens, princes, fellow musicians, and friends all, to a greater or lesser

EXAMPLE 1.1. *Jack Werner's illustrations of the "Mendelssohnian Cadence" in* Elias, *GA 2 (mm. 51–53) and its supposed point of origin, the closing blessing chanted on Jewish feast-days. (J. Werner, "Mendelssohnian Cadence," 17–18.)*

extent, seeing him as such? But to identify as Jewish and to embrace that identity are two very different things. I would maintain, in fact, that for Mendelssohn to have embraced Judaism in the manner postulated by the above scholars (as well as many nonmusicologists, including members of my own family) requires that we accept the idea of a precocious child immersed in the Jewish faith during his formative years. Strangely, however, this idea stands in sharp contrast to Abraham Mendelssohn's own descriptions—all long known and frequently cited in print—of the home environment he attempted to create for his family. The first appears in the letter Abraham wrote to his daughter Fanny in 1820 on the occasion of her confirmation, in which he suggests that the children did not receive any religious instruction until after baptism. Furthermore, the letter depicts what would seem to be a very secular and rationalist household,

EXAMPLE 1.2. *Eric Werner's comparison of the melodies of* Elias, *GA 34 (mm. 6–9) and the "Thirteen Divine Attributes" sung in German synagogues on the High Holy Days. (E. Werner, Neuer Sicht, 498.)*

with its head professing his belief in a philosophy firmly rooted in Immanuel Kant's concept of a "universal religion" based on a shared moral code.[6] Abraham writes:

> Does God exist? What is God? Is He a part of ourselves, and does He continue to live after the other part has ceased to be? And where? And how? All this I do not know, and therefore I have never taught you anything about it. But I know that there exists in me and in you and in all human beings an everlasting inclination towards all that is good, true, and right, and a conscience which warns and guides us when we go astray. I know it, I believe it, I live in this faith, and this is my religion. . . . We have educated you and your brothers and sister in the Christian faith, because it is the creed of most civilised people, and contains nothing that can lead you away from what is good, and much that guides you to love, obedience, tolerance, and resignation.[7]

A letter Abraham wrote to Felix nine years later while his son was in London further clarifies Abraham's rationalist belief system and confirms that the children were raised without religious instruction until after baptism:

> I had learned, and until my last breath will never forget, that the truth is one and eternal; its forms, however, are many and transitory; and so I raised you, to the extent that the constitution under which we then lived permitted it, free from any religious form, which I wished to leave to your own convictions, should they demand it, or to your choice, based on considerations of convenience. That was not to be, however, and I had to choose for you. Given the scant value I place on all [religious] forms, it goes without saying that I felt no inner calling to choose for you the Jewish, the most obsolete, corrupt, and pointless of them [all]. So I raised you in the Christian, the purer [form] accepted by the majority of civilized people, and also confessed the same for myself, because I had to do myself what I recognized as best for you.[8]

But can we, or should we, take Abraham at his word on this matter, especially in light of so many arguments to the contrary? Fortunately, we do not have to, for tracing Abraham's movements over the course of his life exposes a carefully orchestrated plan to create and sustain an existence that was independent of the Jewish community and that was as privileged as any Christian's. Moreover, evidence suggests that Abraham worked diligently to ensure that such freedom and privilege would be enjoyed by his progeny as well, the key to which was to separate himself and his children from Judaism—first through isolation from the faith and community, then later, as circumstances dictated, through baptism.

THE MENDELSSOHNS AND THE SYNAGOGUE

Abraham Mendelssohn's livelihood never depended on the Jewish community; in fact, in each of the cities he lived—Berlin, Paris, and Hamburg—he was guaranteed most of the same rights and privileges as any Christian, enabling him to conduct business with the entire population and to associate with any elements of society he wished. As his upbringing, his travels, his letters, and the state synagogue records suggest, Abraham took full advantage of this freedom, befriending those who shared his enlightenment ideals and avoiding strong connections to the synagogue and its community. In so doing, he was able to raise his children in a true enlightenment atmosphere—one in which rationalism prevailed.

While the children were certainly aware of their heritage, then, their exposure to Judaism was superficial at best, with no formal or informal instruction in religion of any kind until their conversion in 1816. Conversion, in fact, proved essential to the rationalist program. As Abraham, like many German Jews, would discover, a rationalist, assimilationist worldview was insufficient for full acceptance into German culture. To be Jewish and a rationalist was still to be a Jew; to be Christian (rationalist or not) was to be a German.[9]

Paradoxically, it may have been Abraham's own illustrious father, Moses Mendelssohn, who set him on the path that would eventually lead to a rejection of Judaism and an embrace of contemporary rationalist philosophies. Because of his father's many Christian-rationalist associates (some of whom came regularly to his home),[10] Abraham grew up surrounded by the influence of rationalism and was able to observe the benefits of membership in the Christian community. Abraham's own religion tutor, Herz Homberg, may also have had a hand in moving him toward a more secular and nationalist philosophy, since Homberg advocated (both in print and in conversations with Abraham's father, with whom he disagreed) a nationalist philosophy that allowed the laws of the state to supersede those of faith.[11]

Once Abraham reached adulthood, the influences he absorbed during his youth led him to pursue a lifestyle in which his status as a Jew would not stand in the way of a successful career. In order to accomplish this, he made it a point to live only in those cities in which he would enjoy rights on par with those of Christian businessmen, and where he would be permitted to live apart—both physically and socially—from the Jewish community. Abraham's unwillingness to accept nothing less than what was allowed Christians undoubtedly stemmed from the fact that he began his career having inherited such privileges from his father. Moses had been granted "General Privileges" by the Prussian government for his service to the state, and these rights were passed on to his widow and children shortly after his death.[12] As long as Abraham continued to live in Prussia, he was freed from the restrictions placed on most of the kingdom's Jews that limited their rights to marry, buy property, or conduct business.[13] As a result, he was also released from any kind of economic or social dependence on the Jewish community, a rare privilege that allowed him to explore and strengthen his rationalist leanings. But since these freedoms would not follow him when he left the kingdom, Abraham made certain that he always settled in places where Jews were granted rights similar to those he had enjoyed in Berlin.

The first such place was Paris, where Abraham moved in 1797, taking a position as a cashier at Fould's Bank.[14] He quickly became a devout Francophile, no doubt in part due to the freedoms he and other Jews enjoyed there. (The French had granted all Jews citizenship in 1791.)[15] When Abraham married Lea Salomon in 1804, he returned briefly to Berlin for the wedding. Since Lea did not wish to live in Paris and since her family was adamantly opposed to her marriage to a mere clerk, Abraham joined his brother Joseph in the banking business, with the two opening a new bank (*J. & A. Mendelssohn*) in Berlin that same year, and, a year later, a second branch (*Gebrüder Mendelssohn & Co.*) in Hamburg, where both brothers settled.[16]

The Mendelssohns' choice of Hamburg is particularly revealing of Abraham's attitudes toward Judaism because of the mixed reputation the city had in terms of Jewish tolerance. As far as trade and living conditions were concerned, the situation was more than favorable in many respects. Since the Hamburg senate had passed the *Judenreglement* almost a century earlier, the Jews in Hamburg had much greater freedom than those living in most other German states.[17] Unlike in Prussia, for example, Jews were not required to pay any taxes in excess of those expected from Christians, they were free to practice nearly any trade they wished, and no restrictions were placed on where they could live. The Hamburg Jewish community was also quite wealthy, since the community was taxed as a unit, and poorer Jews who could not pay their fair share were discouraged from joining it. The one provision of the *Judenreglement* that interfered with this comfortable state of affairs was that Jews were permitted to worship only in private. This, of course, meant that Hamburg itself did not have any synagogues—a situation that remained unchanged until the middle of the nineteenth century. The nearest one was in neighboring, Danish-controlled Altona, which also had an emancipated Jewish community, but one whose privileges included public worship. As a result, many Jews who worked in Hamburg chose to live in Altona and make the daily three-kilometer commute into the city.[18] Abraham, however, chose to set up his family's primary residence at Große Michaelisstraße 14, just down the street from his bank, in the heart of faith-hostile/ trade-hospitable Hamburg: an odd choice for a religiously observant family, but a logical choice for a secular, rationalist one. In fact, the Mendelssohn brothers chose to move to Hamburg, even though their mother, Frommet, was already living in Jewish-friendly Altona.[19] While the Mendelssohns did purchase an attractive summer cottage near Neumühlen (a district of Altona) in 1805, that they elected to spend most of the year in Hamburg despite the familial and religious (not to mention aesthetic) attractions of Altona suggests their greater dedication to their trade and to mainstream society than to their faith.[20]

While she and Abraham lived in Hamburg, Lea gave birth to three of their four children: Fanny in 1805, Felix in 1809, and Rebecka in 1811. (Paul would be born in Berlin in 1812.) The records—or lack thereof—surrounding these births are particularly enlightening regarding the family's interaction with the Jewish community. For as Jacob Jacobson and Rudolf Elvers have discovered, no listings appear for any of the children in the birth registers of the Jewish congregation of Altona and Hamburg, despite their inclusion of a listing for another Große Michaelisstraße 14 resident, Ferdinand David, who was born in 1810 and who would later serve as Mendelssohn's concertmaster at the Leipzig Gewandhaus.[21] In the case of Felix, we can be certain that the missing entry is no mere clerical error. As Elvers points out, the lack of an entry is supported by a newly published version of the Zelter-Goethe correspondence, in which Felix's composition teacher, Carl Friedrich Zelter, indicates in a letter written during his travels with his twelve-year-old pupil that Abraham, "with great sacrifice, did not allow his sons to be circumcised."[22] Had the Mendelssohns been involved with the Jewish community, it would have been difficult to keep the birth of their children a secret, and, more significant, it would have been remarkable not to have their son circumcised.

When the Mendelssohns were forced to flee Hamburg in the summer of 1811 and hastily returned to Berlin (they may have been involved in smuggling goods to England in violation of Napoleon's "Continental Ban"), Abraham found himself in possession not only of the General Privileges inherited from his father, but also of full citizenship, a result of his marriage to Lea, who was a granddaughter of Daniel Itzig. Due to both his position at the pinnacle of the Berlin Jewish community and his service to the king, Itzig had been able in 1791 to obtain a patent granting citizenship for himself and the members of his extended family, up to Lea's generation.[23] That limitation meant, of course, that the Mendelssohn children would not have enjoyed this status, nor would they have been protected by the privileges granted Moses Mendelssohn, since these encompassed only the immediate family. Indeed, all that protected the children's rights was the citizenship extended them by the French laws that came into effect when Napoleon occupied Prussia, an occupation Abraham hoped would be temporary (and whose end he even helped finance).[24] As a result, Abraham and Lea were once again motivated to keep themselves separate from the Jewish community, so that should more drastic steps (such as baptism) become necessary to retain their children's rights, any backlash—social or otherwise—would be minimal. Physical separation began shortly after their arrival, with the Mendelssohns settling at Markgrafinstraße 48 (on the Gendarmenmarkt), across town from the city's Jewish quarter (see fig. 1.1).[25] They remained there until 1820, at which point they moved into the apartment above Lea's mother, Bella, at Neue Promenade 7, a building that, while closer to the Jewish quarter, was situated in a diverse neighborhood that included many Christians and converted Jews.[26] However, in 1825 (shortly after Bella's death on March 9, 1824), Abraham left the quarter far behind, moving his family to the palatial Leipzigerstraße 3 at the far western edge of the city.

As in Hamburg, the Mendelssohns' separation from the Jewish community in Berlin appears to have been as much social as it was physical, with no evidence to suggest that the family ever attended synagogue. Had they been in regular attendance, it would have been customary, for example, to note in the congregation's records their surname change to "Mendelssohn Bartholdy," which Abraham began using

❶ Mendelssohn residence at Markgrafinstraße 48   ❸ Mendelssohn residence at Neue Promenade 7
❷ Jerusalems-Kirche   ❹ Mendelssohn residence at Leipzigerstraße 3

FIGURE 1.1. *The Mendelssohn residences, the Jerusalems-Kirche, and the Berlin Jewish Quarter (Map: D.G. Reymann,* Neuester Grundriss von Berlin. Berlin: Simon Schropp & Co., 1830). *For more on the location and nature of Berlin's Jewish quarter, see Lowenstein,* Berlin Jewish Community, *16–18.*

unofficially as early as 1812 and which the entire family officially adopted shortly after the parents' conversion in 1822.[27] Jacob Jacobson finds the lack of any mention in the synagogue records of the "Bartholdy" addition odd, since conversions and name changes were fairly common and did not generally lead to total separation from the Jewish community.[28] If little contact between the Mendelssohns and the synagogue existed in the first place, however, the omission is less surprising.

Despite his effort to separate himself from the majority of the Berlin Jewish community, Abraham was not averse to associating with other Jews who embraced ideals similar to his own. His chief connection to this select segment of the community was through his life-long membership in the Society of Friends (*Gesellschaft der Freunde*), a men's organization founded by, among others, his brother Joseph (a nonconvert) in 1792.[29] Its members were like Abraham in that they followed and promoted enlightenment principles—to the point that after the first few years, they refused to discharge the sizable number of society members (including Abraham) who converted, and eventually even permitted Christian members to take on leadership positions.[30] (Felix's younger brother, Paul, in fact, presided over the organization from 1849 to 1856.[31]) Indeed, when the group commemorated its fiftieth anniversary in 1842, religion was not even a consideration in commissioning works for the celebration, which included a memorial painting by Fanny's husband, Wilhelm (a life-long Protestant), and a piece by Felix himself (*Die Stiftungsfeier*).[32] Although founded to further enlightenment ideals and curb the power of the Jewish orthodoxy (which the Society felt discriminated against freethinkers), the *Gesellschaft* did not accomplish much in the end: it had no concrete program and as a result was little more than an organization for mutual help and a club for friends to interact and relax.[33]

The Mendelssohn family's return to Berlin and Abraham's knowledge that his children's rights there depended upon a French occupation he personally despised undoubtedly caused him to think seriously about baptizing them. While Abraham likely saw Prussian chancellor Karl von Hardenberg's 1812 "edict concerning the civil status of Jews within the Prussian state" (which granted all Jews living legally in Prussia the status of "native residents and Prussian citizens")[34] as a positive development, he and the heads of many other elite Jewish families in Berlin found it insufficient to quell their concerns. Steven Lowenstein notes that although the number of conversions declined for a couple of years after the edict, the dip was relatively minor and was soon replaced by a sharp rise that caused the number of baptisms to quickly exceed those performed before the edict had been issued. In fact, the highest number during this particular wave of conversions (starting in 1800 and continuing through 1820) took place in 1816, the year the Mendelssohn children were baptized.[35] The general increase in conversions in the years after the edict can probably be attributed to a rise in anti-Semitism, which itself sprang (at least in part) from a rise in German nationalism and anti-French sentiment: as Germans began to consolidate a national identity, being Christian became a fundamental component, while hating the French meant hating everything they had brought with them—including Jewish emancipation.[36]

What made 1816 a final breaking point for so many Jews was likely the Congress of Vienna, which in June 1815 ratified a constitution for the newly formed German Confederation. This document had a significant impact on the legal status of Jews living within the confederation's nearly forty states. The issue of Jewish status was raised at the Congress by those states that had Jewish emancipation thrust upon them by the French, and that were now, in the face of Napoleon's defeat, hoping to see those laws reversed. Prussia's ambassador to Vienna, Abraham's friend Wilhelm von Humbolt, and Chancellor Hardenberg, whose emancipation edict had been issued independent of any French legislation, attempted to negotiate a uniform emancipation code similar to Prussia's that would apply to the entire confederation. The resistance from many of the smaller states was considerable, however, and the effort failed. Instead, the French laws were declared invalid, and individual states were permitted to make their own decisions as to how to proceed, with most returning to the pre-Napoleonic laws, some of which dated back to the early seventeenth century. Some city-states did not wait for the Congress: immediately after ousting the French in 1813, Bremen and Lübeck repealed the French laws, and a year later Hamburg reinstated its *Judenreglement* and began enforcing many of the less-enlightened clauses that had slowly come to be ignored in the century since its original passage. The situation in Prussia itself was by far the most complex. The state had been granted additional territories by the Congress, but King Friedrich Wilhelm III decided that the 1812 edict would apply only to those lands that were part of the old Prussia. Like the rest of the confederation, the new territories were authorized to abolish any French edicts and reinstate their old laws regarding the Jews.[37] As we have already seen, the Mendelssohn children were separated from Judaism and raised without religion from the day they were born.[38] But with Abraham's former home of Hamburg choosing to return to a more conservative interpretation of its hundred-year-old law and with the rights of his children no longer guaranteed in all corners of the Prussian kingdom, the time must have seemed right—as it was for so many that year—for him to take action on his children's behalf and convert them.

The conversion itself took place on March 21, 1816, in Berlin's own Jerusalems-Kirche.[39] Sebastian Hensel implies that the children's baptism was conducted in complete secrecy, and, indeed, it seems clear that the family wished to conceal the event from Lea's mother.[40] (Judging by her temporary disownment of her son Jacob Bartholdy upon his conversion,[41] Bella Salomon apparently felt strongly about remaining steadfast to one's cultural heritage, even while living an otherwise secular life, as she thought her children and grandchildren were doing.) However, a truly secretive baptism—such as those in which many Jewish converts engaged to avoid embarrassment or the disapproval of friends and family—would have taken place outside the city of residence.[42] No such effort seems to have been made in the case of the Mendelssohn children, as their baptisms were performed by their own landlord (Pastor Johann Jakob Stegemann)[43] in a reasonably prominent church located in the center of an open square only blocks away from their home (again, see fig. 1.1). The situation appears to have been quite different for Abraham and Lea themselves, however, who chose to be baptized on October 4, 1822, while in distant Frankfurt am Main.[44] This level of secrecy on the parents' behalf may be attributable simply to their living in Lea's mother's building at the time of their conversion.[45] However, it is also possible that even though Abraham had succeeded in keeping his children separate from the Jewish community, he himself had developed sufficient ties since his return to Berlin to warrant some discretion on his part.[46] Most of these ties were likely business related, since he was, until ten months before his conversion, a partner in the bank that bore the legendary Mendelssohn name and which handled the accounts of many Jews.[47]

The gap between the baptismal dates of the children and adults of the Mendelssohn household was not an uncommon circumstance: many Jewish parents chose to have their children baptized while themselves remaining Jews because of social pressures. And while carrying the name Mendelssohn added certain unique elements to their situation, the Mendelssohns' story has, for the most part, a great deal in common with that of other wealthy Jewish families who chose to convert, especially those in Berlin. Like the Mendelssohns, many of these families moved out of the Jewish quarter several years before conversion, with a number settling, as the Mendelssohns did, in the streets immediately surrounding Unter den Linden.[48] It was also not uncommon for the adults in these families to begin adopting rationalist philosophies in an effort to justify (if only to themselves) their abandonment of the faith, nor was it uncommon for those families (even those in which the adults remained Jewish) to speak of Protestantism as the logical successor to Judaism and thus the proper faith in which to raise their children.[49] It is this particular attitude that Michael P. Steinberg and Leon Botstein attribute to Felix Mendelssohn. But those who held this belief were of the *preceding* generation, the generation that made the decision to baptize— in the case of the Mendelssohn family, Abraham's generation. For the members of the generation raised in the new faith—Felix's generation—Judaism was a part of their history, but it was a history that was seldom discussed openly.[50] For Felix, Fanny, Rebecka, and Paul, that history was a particularly nebulous one, both because there was near silence on the matter and because that silence began—as but a single component of a complicated program for assimilation—long before they were born. As mentioned earlier, this does not mean that these children did not—despite their parents' best efforts—identify as Jewish: they were Mendelssohns, members of a family whose name symbolized, as Abraham put it, "Judaism in its transitional period."[51] But as shall soon be seen, to identify as Jewish did not necessarily translate into pride in one's Jewish past. In fact, a careful reexamination of those documents in which Felix appears to break the silence on this issue only serves to further bear this hypothesis out.

REINVENTING MENDELSSOHN

In the first two decades after the fall of the Third Reich, a handful of documents was brought to light to help support the new postwar Mendelssohn interpretation—namely, that the composer felt a strong, positive attachment to his Jewish lineage. Eric Werner was responsible for the majority of this work, which he published piecemeal in articles in 1955 and 1961, and then comprehensively in his 1963 Mendelssohn biography, *Mendelssohn: A New Image of the Composer and His Age,* and its 1980 German revision. Significantly, Werner had a tendency to mistranscribe and misinterpret these documents, and as a result to overstate the composer's sense of Jewish self-identification.[52] In reexamining the documents afresh, however, one discovers not only that they do not support this "new image," to borrow from Werner's title, but also that they often reveal a man who saw himself as enlightened, rationalist, and, in many ways, a typical German *Neuchrist,* or New Christian.

One aspect of this overstatement of Mendelssohn's Jewish identity has been the scholarly assessment of the anti-Semitic acts committed against him. While Mendelssohn clearly encountered anti-Semitism during his lifetime, even from close personal and professional associates, the level of intensity was different, and indeed less virulent, than that faced by nonbaptized German Jews, and especially that faced by the predominantly ghettoized Eastern Jews. In the postwar interpretation, however, Mendelssohn has been seen as a member of these more marginalized groups, which is more in keeping with a mid-twentieth-century sense of German-Jewish identification, and which denies the unique status of the nineteenth-century converted Jew.

One such incident whose postwar interpretation has already been challenged involved the Berlin Singakademie, whose directorship the twenty-three-year-old Mendelssohn was denied in 1833, despite having been promised the post by one of the directors more than a year earlier.[53] William Little takes issue with Werner's assessment that anti-Semitism was solely responsible for the composer's rejection in favor of Carl Friedrich Rungenhagen. Werner, Little demonstrates, read selectively when investigating this incident, focusing on anti-Semitism—something mentioned only in Eduard Devrient's reminiscences of the composer—and ignoring numerous other documents (including the Devrient reminiscences themselves) which discuss the Singakademie's more central concerns. These included Mendelssohn's youth, his apparent *Wanderlust* (he had just completed more than three years of nearly continuous travel), and his rival's thirty-two-year association with the Singakademie (including many as assistant director).[54]

An earlier incident, which Werner originally exposed and which has since been greatly stressed by many Mendelssohn biographers, occurred during the so-called Hep-Hep riots (or *Judensturm*) of 1819, during which Jewish businesses were plundered throughout Germany and Jews themselves were assaulted physically and with taunts of "Hep-Hep" when recognized in public.[55] According to Karl August Varnhagen von Ense (an author and diplomat, as well as the husband of Rahel Levin, one of the pillars of the Jewish salon community), ten-year-old Felix Mendelssohn was among those taunted in Berlin. As Werner, citing the Varnhagen von Ense account, reports in both editions of his Mendelssohn biography, "On a bright spring day in 1819 a royal prince of Prussia stopped Felix Mendelssohn, then ten years old, on the street, spat at his feet, and exclaimed: 'Hep hep, Jew-boy!'"[56] But according to the original diary entry, the incident, while reprehensible, may not have been as brutal as Werner describes: "With the acts of violence was mixed foolish teasing, a desire for mischief; a royal prince laughingly cried to the boy Felix Mendelssohn on the street 'Hep, Hep!'"[57] Even in its actual form, the episode remains undeniably anti-Semitic. But Werner's additions of the prince's spitting and use of the derogatory "Jew-boy" (*Judenjung*) have clearly added a level of virulence not present in the original.

According to Werner, Mendelssohn endured a second anti-Semitic attack in August 1824, this time accompanied by his sister Fanny:

> Another incident occurred in 1824, when Felix was fifteen. The family spent its vacation in Dobberan [*sic*], a then much frequented watering place on the Baltic. This time both Felix and his beloved sister Fanny were insulted by street urchins, who shouted "Jew-boy" and similar epithets and finally threw stones at them. Felix defended his sister vigorously and staunchly, but seems to have collapsed afterwards. His tutor J. [*sic*] L. Heyse writes tersely about the incident: "Felix behaved like a man, but after he had returned home could not conceal his fury about the humiliation, which in the evening broke out in a flood of tears and wild accusations."[58]

While the violence of this episode would seem to support Werner's implication that Mendelssohn was in fact subject to the same intense anti-Semitism as nonconverts or Eastern Jews, its authenticity remains doubtful. At the very least, Werner's date and location are wrong: as Felix's correspondence with Fanny and Paul clearly demonstrates, Fanny was in Berlin, not Doberan, in August 1824.[59] Moreover, Werner does not cite a source for the account in his 1963 edition, nor did he when he recounted the story in an article in 1955, where Mendelssohn's tutor is correctly identified as "K[arl] L[udwig Wilhelm] Heyse."[60] In the 1980 German revision of his biography, Werner reveals the source as an excerpt from the unpublished diary of a "Dr. Heyse" (no initials are provided), which was "earlier in the possession of the deceased Prof. Joachim Wach, the great-grandson of Felix, who allowed me to see these and many other reminiscences and documents of the family."[61] Nonetheless, this source remains elusive. The estate of Joachim Wach ended up—apparently without the diary—at the University of Chicago. Likewise, the diary was neither submitted to the collections of Heyse's writings at either the Bayrische Staatsbibliothek in Munich or the Staatsbibliothek zu Berlin, nor, according to Mendelssohn descendant Thomas Wach, is it in the possession of the Mendelssohn family.[62]

Several other sources Werner cites as part of his argument that Mendelssohn— and his siblings—retained a strong attachment to their Jewish heritage are equally elusive. Among these is Felix's letter of July 17, 1829, to his sister Rebecka, in which he supposedly chastises her for an anti-Semitic comment she made in her letter to him of June 23, 1829.[63] But while both a letter from the family in Berlin (including Rebecka) to Felix in London dated June 23 and a reply from him dated July 17 exist, neither letter includes the comments Werner mentions (nor do those from the surrounding days).[64] Also a mystery are the letters in which, according to Werner, Rebecka signed her name "Rebecca Mendelssohn *meden* (Greek for never) Bartholdy."[65] In addition to Werner's failing to mention the specific dates and locations of these letters, the number of times he claims that Rebecka did this varies, beginning with "often" in a 1955 article and "frequently" in the 1963 English edition of his biography, and ending with a significantly more conservative "twice" in the biography's 1980 edition. Moreover, the spelling of Rebecka's name changes in each of Werner's quotations, from "Rebecca" in the English versions to "Rebekka" in the German. Neither spelling, however, appears to have been used by Felix's sister, who either signed her letters as "Rebecka" or "Beckchen."

Mendelssohn's "pride in the family and in the name," as Wulf Konold put it, has also been interpreted as implying pride in his Jewish heritage, yet this argument too faces documentation problems.[66] On July 8, 1829, Abraham Mendelssohn wrote to his son in London, angered by his use of the name "Mendelssohn" on his concert programs there, as opposed to "Bartholdy" or "M. Bartholdy."[67] He noted that because of the fame of Felix's grandfather, "a Christian Mendelssohn is as impossible as a Jewish Confucius. If your name is Mendelssohn, you are *eo ipso* a Jew, and that is of no benefit to you, because it is not even true."[68] Writers who have discussed this letter, which Werner rescued from obscurity, have almost unilaterally adopted his position: "[T]he facts speak for themselves. In the four [London] concerts conducted by Felix after that letter was sent, his name appears as Mendelssohn, in open contradiction to his father's wishes."[69] But a close examination of the dates involved here does not support this conclusion. As table 1.1 shows, with the exception of the final concert, all the London concerts occurred *before* Abraham wrote the letter. The last concert, on July 13, did occur after the letter was written, but according to Felix's reply on July 16, before the letter was received.[70]

Werner describes a draft of Felix's lengthy reply (the whereabouts of which remain unknown) as apologetic, "cool," and not addressing the heart of the matter, a fact he uses to further support what he sees as Felix's act of filial defiance.[71] The letter Felix actually sent, however, addresses the matter quite directly, with Felix claiming that he implored the Philharmonic Society to use the name "Mendelssohn Bartholdy," but that they felt it too long to fit on a program. Felix responded with numerous alternatives, but they urged him to at least leave the name "Mendelssohn" intact since so many were familiar with his grandfather. Felix apologized to Abraham for misunderstanding his wishes and promised to be more vigilant about the matter in the future (a promise that he kept through a permanent return to "Mendelssohn

TABLE 1.1. Timetable of Mendelssohn's performances with the Philharmonic Society in London and correspondence with his family on the name issue.

21 April	Arrival in London.
25 April	Mendelssohn conducts a performance of his c-minor symphony (op. 11).
30 May	Mendelssohn plays in Weber's f-minor *Konzertstück für Klavier und Orchester*.
24 June	Mendelssohn conducts his *Midsummer Night's Dream* Overture.
8 July	Mendelssohn's father, Abraham, writes regarding his displeasure in his son's use of the name "Mendelssohn" on London concert programs. His sister Fanny also writes a private letter to him on this same issue.
13 July	Final London concert: a benefit, in which Mendelssohn again conducts his *Midsummer Night's Dream* Overture and plays in his Concerto for Two Pianos and Orchestra in E-major.
14 July	Abraham Mendelssohn's letter arrives in London.
16 July	Mendelssohn replies to Abraham's letter.
End of July	Trip to Scotland and the Hebrides. Fanny's letter arrives shortly before his departure.
11 August	Mendelssohn replies to Fanny's letter.

Ranft, *Lebenschronik*, 19–20, with letter dates inserted.

Bartholdy").[72] According to Fanny, Abraham was pleased by his son's response; although he did not share the private letter with his daughter, she heard that it was "supposed to be divine."[73]

That Felix chose to obey his father's wishes does not necessarily indicate a lack of interest in maintaining the Mendelssohn name. In fact, a private letter[74] from Fanny to Felix on this very matter (and written the same day that Abraham wrote his letter) would seem to indicate the opposite. She writes:

> It's suddenly come to Father's attention that your name was mentioned merely as Felix Mendelssohn in several English newspapers. He thinks he detects an ulterior motive in this fact and wants to write you today about it. . . . I don't know now whether or not he will still carry it out, but last night Hensel and I decided to write you this letter in any case. . . . I know and approve of your intention to lay aside someday this name that we all dislike [i.e., Bartholdy], but you can't do it yet because you're a minor, and it's not necessary to make you aware of the unpleasant consequences it could have for you. Suffice it to say that you distress Father by your actions. If questioned, you could easily make it seem like a mistake, and carry out your plan later at a more appropriate time.[75]

But as Felix's reply (again a private letter) makes perfectly clear, maintaining the integrity of the Mendelssohn name was not a high priority. He writes:

How grateful I am for the dear private letter that you wrote me, and almost as grateful because it wasn't necessary. . . . [A]nd it touched me doubly how you had spoken in such a precautionary and conciliatory manner, especially since it didn't require conciliation. For it would never in my life occur to me to want to oppose Father's will, and over such a trifle! No, believe me, it doesn't enter my mind.[76]

That Felix truly believed this matter to be "a trifle" is quite plausible, given that from as far back as 1823, he always signed his name as "Felix," "Felix M.B.," "Felix Mendelssohn Bartholdy," or "F.M.B." in both his private correspondence and music manuscripts.[77]

The most significant document for the postwar Mendelssohn interpretation is unquestionably the family letter that Mendelssohn wrote from London on July 23, 1833, in which he reports on the Jewish Civil Disabilities Act that had just passed the House of Commons. Eric Werner first discovered the letter and published it several times between 1955 and 1980.[78] In its most recent incarnation,[79] the relevant segment of the letter reads as in examples 1.3a and b.

The "miserable Posen statutes" Mendelssohn mentions were a series of laws handed down by Prussia's King Friedrich Wilhelm III on the rights and responsibilities of Jews in the recently acquired Polish duchy of Posen (Poznań). The laws, as reported in the July 17, 1833, London *Times*, introduced general education and trade training requirements, established marriage restrictions, and, most significant,

EXAMPLE 1.3a. *Letter of July 23, 1833, as published in Eric Werner,* Mendelssohn: Leben und Werk in neuer Sicht, *p. 64. Bracketed expression in line 7 is Werner's. Formatting altered to match the manuscript transcription in Ex. 1.4a. Emphasis added.*

1. Heute früh haben sie
2. die Juden emanzipiert, **das macht mich stolz**, zumal
3. da vor ein paar Tagen Eure lumpigen Posener Ordnungen
4. hier runtergemacht worden sind, nach Recht und Billigkeit! Die
5. Times fühlte sich vornehm, und meinte, in England
6. **sey es doch besser für uns**, und nachdem gestern eine Menge Juden[-]
7. hasser: Mr. Finn und Mr. Bruce, und der *Rohsche* [judendeutsch «Bösewicht»] Inglis
8. gesalbadert hatten, schloß Robert Grant, der die Bill
9. einbringt, indem er fragte, ob sie glaubten, daß sie da
10. seyen, um die Prophezeiungen zu erfuellen (denn darauf stützen
11. sie sich), und sagte er hielte sich an das Wort: «Glory to
12. God and good will to men»,
13. und darauf waren ayes 187 und noes 52. Das ist ganz nobel
14. und schön **und erfüllt mich mit Dankbarkeit gegen den Himmel** . . .

EXAMPLE 1.3b. *Translation of 1.3a.*

1. This morning they
2. emancipated the Jews, **which makes me proud**, especially since,
3. a few days ago, your miserable Posen statutes
4. were attacked here, just as they deserve! The
5. *Times* felt noble and was of the opinion that in England
6. **it is certainly better for us**. Yesterday, after a bunch of Jew-
7. haters (Mr. Finn, Mr. Bruce, and that *Rohsche* [Yiddish for 'villain'] Inglis)[80]
8. babbled, Robert Grant, who introduced the bill, concluded
9. by asking if they believed themselves to be there
10. to fulfill the prophecies (for they rely on that)
11. and said that he himself followed the words "Glory to
12. God, and good will to men,"
13. and then the ayes were 187 and the noes 52. That is completely noble
14. and good **and fills me with gratitude to heaven** . . .

severely limited the rights of nonnaturalized Jews.[81] In the same issue of the *Times* appeared, as Mendelssohn mentions, a strong attack on the statutes from an anonymous staff writer, who notes that

> [w]ith us [the English] the Jew is admitted to the enjoyment of civil rights as an individual citizen, distinguished only by his particular creed. . . . We impose no more restraints upon him than upon any other subject for the civil rights which we confer. . . .
>
> By the ordinance of the Prussian Government, it would appear that Frederick William, the new lawgiver of the Jews, with probably no chance of being reckoned their second Moses, has read his legislative duties differently. He has marshaled the Jews into corporations, where he makes them responsible for each other. He keeps them, even by law, a separate people.[82]

Coincidentally, five days later and after months of debate, the British House of Commons passed the Jewish Civil Disabilities Act, which was designed to remove the last civil restrictions placed on Jews, including the prohibitions on voting and serving in public office. Summaries of the MP's comments were printed in the next day's *Times*, including, as Mendelssohn read, Charles Bruce's and George Finch's ("Mr. Finn" in Mendelssohn's letter) remarks that they believed it incongruous for a Jew to serve in the Parliament of a Christian country, especially one that legislated the church; Sir Robert Inglis's assertion that, on the whole, "Jews should not be admitted into a participation of civil rights in this country"; and, finally, Robert Grant's trouncing "good will to men" argument.[83] (As Abraham, who was with Felix in London, predicted, however, the bill later failed to pass in the House of Lords, where the archbishop of Canterbury—much to Abraham's surprise—cited Moses Mendelssohn as an example of the Jews' intellectual talent before arguing that Parliament was not an appropriate forum for its display.)[84]

As mentioned, several scholars have pointed to the July 23 letter in making arguments for Mendelssohn's Jewish self-identification. Drawing on Werner's transcription, Wulf Konold noted the "pride in the tradition of his family and his heritage" that Mendelssohn's letter shows.[85] Likewise, Mendelssohn's proclamation of "thankfulness to heaven" led Eric Werner himself to claim that the composer's "sympathy for the Jewish people was infused with religious ardor."[86] And, most important, Mendelssohn's use of the words "for us" when referring to the Jews' situation enabled Leon Botstein to postulate that Heinrich Heine's "mistrust of Mendelssohn's . . . self-image as Jew may . . . have been misplaced."[87] But however relevant these comments may appear in the light of the published text does not alter the fact that not a single one of the statements on which they are based appears in the original manuscript letter (reproduced in fig. 1.2, followed by a transcription and translation [ex. 1.4a, b]).

In comparing the German transcription of the manuscript to Werner's text in the previous example, three important differences are visible. The first appears in line 2, where Werner transcribes "which amuses me greatly" (*das amüsirt mich prächtig*)

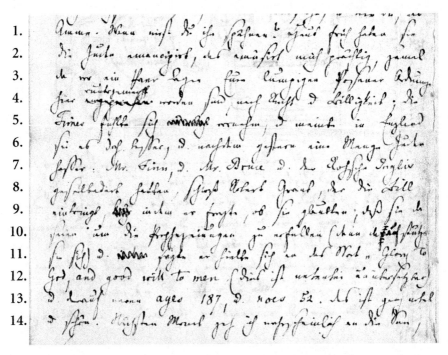

FIGURE 1.2. *Letter of July 23, 1833, ms, folio 1 verso* (*US-NYp, *MNY++, no. 165*).

EXAMPLE 1.4a. *Transcription of figure 1.2. Italicized text represents Latin script.*

1. Heut früh haben sie
2. die Juden emancipiert, das amüsirt mich prächtig, zumal
3. da vor ein Paar Tagen Eure lumpigen Posener Ordnungen
4. hier ~~{unreadable}~~ runtergemacht worden sind, nach Recht und Billigkeit; die
5. *Times* fühlte sich ~~{unreadable}~~ vornehm, und meinte in *England*
6. sei es doch besser, und nachdem gestern eine Menge Juden[-]
7. hasser: *Mr. Finn,* und *Mr. Bruce* und der Rohsche *Inglis*
8. gesalbadert hatten, schloß *Robert Grant,* der die Bill
9. einbringt, ~~{unreadable}~~ indem er fragte, ob sie glaubten, daß sie da
10. seien um die Prophezeiungen zu erfüllen (denn darauf stützen
11. sie sich) und ~~indem~~ sagte er hielte sich an das Wort „*Glory to*
12. *God, and good will to men*" (dies ist nebenbei unübersetzbar)
13. und darauf waren *ayes* 187, und *noes* 52. Das ist ganz nobel
14. und schön. Nächsten Monat geh ich . . .

EXAMPLE 1.4b. *Translation of 1.4a.*

1. This morning they
2. emancipated the Jews, which amuses me greatly, especially since,
3. a few days ago, your miserable Posen statutes
4. were attacked here, just as they deserve; the
5. *Times* felt noble and was of the opinion that in England
6. it is certainly better. Yesterday, after a bunch of Jew-
7. haters (Mr. Finn, Mr. Bruce, and that villain Inglis)
8. babbled, Robert Grant, who introduced the bill, concluded
9. by asking if they believed themselves to be there
10. to fulfill the prophecies (for they rely on that)
11. and said that he himself followed the words "Glory to
12. God, and good will to men" (this is, incidentally, not translatable)
13. and then the ayes were 187 and the noes 52. That is completely noble
14. and good. Next month, I'm going . . .

as "which makes me proud" (*das macht mich stolz*). Then in line 6, Werner adds the words *für uns* after *sei es doch besser* to create "in England it is certainly better *for us.*" And finally, Werner's conclusion to the sentence in line 13, "and fills me with gratitude to heaven" (*und erfüllt mich mit Dankbarkeit gegen den Himmel*) is nowhere to be found in the entire letter.

In contrast to Werner's version, the actual text negates the stated and implied claims of both Werner and those who unwittingly built on his research that this letter represents clear evidence of Mendelssohn's self-identification as a Jew. In the original there is no expression of Jewish pride, but rather amusement at the irony that five days after the Prussian government should issue an edict restricting the rights of Jews, the English government should vote to emancipate them. There is certainly no infusion of "religious ardor," and, most significant, no assertion of Jewish self-identification. The statement "in England it is certainly better" does invite the possibility of implied text (e.g., "than in Prussia"), but there is nothing in the passage to suggest that the text should be "for us"—quite the contrary, in fact. In the preceding text, the Jews are consistently referred to as a separate group, with no indication that Mendelssohn included himself among them.

Clearly the letter does show Mendelssohn's interest in, and approval of, the Jewish Civil Disabilities Act, as well as his distaste for the Posen statutes. And certainly, some of this interest may have stemmed from a concern for his Jewish friends in London and the nonconverted members of his extended family (such as his uncle Joseph), as well a recognition of his own heritage.[88] This, however, is far from the level of self-identification that Werner's "for us" addition implies. Moreover, a distaste for persecution based on religious ideals, and consequently a desire to see the instruments of that persecution eliminated, were at the heart of the enlightened rationalist's philosophy. Abraham's rationalist leanings have already been noted at length, and indeed the entire Mendelssohn family lifestyle, with its strong interaction with the predominantly Christian public is a clear indicator of their identification with this group of cultural elite. That Felix himself adhered to a liberal, rationalist agenda is demonstrated both in this letter and in one written on December 23, 1834, to his sister Rebecka:

> Reform is what I desire and love in all things, in life, and in art and in politics and in street-pavement and God knows where else; for reform is only a negative against corruption and only discards what stands in the way.[89]

It is therefore likely that in the July 23 letter, Mendelssohn expressed his views on the Jewish situation out of a sense of justice and joy on behalf of his friends, and not, as Werner contends, to demonstrate that he was becoming "aggressively conscious" of his Jewish heritage.[90]

Because of biased interpretations and mistranscriptions, the documents described here have always stood apart from the remaining examples of Mendelssohn's writings, from the reminiscences of his contemporaries, and even from his creative output. Reevaluated, they blend with their surroundings, which as a whole depict Mendelssohn as one who, despite his interest in the ultimate political fate of the Jews, by and large remained detached from his heritage. In a letter he wrote on February 8, 1831, from the Roman Festival, for example, Mendelssohn reported on the Jews' annual Papal appeal for permission to live in the ghetto for another year, but his only comment was that the event was "very boring."[91] Likewise, two weeks later, he dispassionately reported on a holy-week ceremony depicting the conversion of the nonbelievers—Heathens, Jews, and Muslims—each group of which was represented by a trembling child, who was baptized and given first communion.[92] Finally, in describing to Zelter a performance of Victoria's *St. John Passion* heard during the Good Friday mass, Mendelssohn commented on the "very tame Jews" of the crowd (*turba*) choruses, adding that during the prayer ceremony that followed, no one kneeled or said "Amen" during the prayers for the Jews, which was not the case with the prayers for other groups.[93] But again, aside from Mendelssohn's mentioning the facts, both incidents pass without comment, and the composer never gives any indication of membership in or even solidarity with the slighted group.

In fact, beyond the instances discussed so far, Mendelssohn mentions Jews very rarely in his published correspondence, and when he does, they are always referred to in the third person. One particularly striking reference appears in his family letter of April 14, 1829, in which he describes a concert he heard the previous evening with the Hamburg Singing Society (*Singverein*):

> The Singverein was quite good last night; Spohr's last [i.e., most recent] works were sung. . . . But the composition was simply disgraceful, people here mistake boredom and dullness for edification, and find the music sacred; in fact it is profane, and a sinful play of trifles. They hang Jews for poisoning fountains; but music is just as valuable as a fountain, I hope, and therefore Spohr will have to die.[94]

Mendelssohn's flippant, dispassionate attitude toward the atrocities faced by Jews demonstrates the degree of detachment he had from Jewish culture at that time, and which, as shall be seen in the next chapter, he further demonstrated in his performances of Bach's *St. Matthew Passion* only weeks earlier.

Despite his father's rationalist outlook toward religion, complete with its Kantian overtones, Felix developed a genuinely religious faith. As his friend Pastor Julius Schubring commented in his reminiscences of the composer, Mendelssohn demonstrated the most important component of this—faith in God himself—with the initials for one of two short prayers that appear on the first version manuscript of nearly every piece he ever wrote: "L.e.g.G." (*Laß es gelingen, Gott* ["Let it succeed, God"]) or "H.D.m." (*Hilf Du mir* ["Help Thou me"]).[95] Mendelssohn also made frequent declarations of gratitude to God throughout his private correspondence, with expressions which included "Thank God" (*Gott sei Dank*) or the more religious "I thank the Lord" (*Ich danke dem Herrn*).[96] Robert Schumann even remarked on Mendelssohn's deep commitment to his faith (*Religiosität*) in the sketches for his unfinished reminiscences of the composer, and also noted Mendelssohn's remarkable knowledge of the Bible and the vigor with which he fulfilled his responsibilities to both God and man.[97]

Although he appears not to have attended services regularly, Mendelssohn's specific adherence to Protestantism was frequently remarked upon by friends and acquaintances, including Hector Berlioz, who after spending some time with Mendelssohn in Rome, wrote that "[Mendelssohn] has one of those clear, pure souls that one does not often come across: he believes firmly in his Lutheran creed, and I'm afraid I shocked him terribly by making fun of the Bible."[98] One of the more detailed accounts comes again from Pastor Schubring:

> Mendelssohn's character had a deep feeling of religion for its basis. That this wanted the specifically church colouring is a fact on which we disputed a great deal in our earlier years. As an unconditional Schleiermacherite, I was then almost incapable of recognizing Christianity in any other shape, and, consequently, wronged Felix. . . . When I recollect, however, with what a serious religious feeling he pursued his art, the exercise of it always being, as it were, a sacred duty; how the first page of every one of his compositions bears impressed on it the initial letter of a prayer; . . . how the very best touches in his oratorios result from his delicate tact—for instance, the words for the air of Paul during the three days of his blindness, when he had just been converted before Damascus, for which Mendelssohn, dissatisfied with everything proposed to him, himself hit upon the 51st Psalm, that seems as though it had been written on purpose; moreover, when I call to mind everything connected with my beloved friend, . . . religion and veneration were enthroned in his countenance; this was why his music possessed such a magic charm. On one occasion, he expressly said that sacred music, as such, did not stand higher in his estimation than any other, because every kind of music ought, in its peculiar way, to tend to the glory of God.[99]

And while, as Schubring notes, Mendelssohn may not have been interested in the teachings of the foremost Protestant theologian of the time (Friedrich Schleiermacher) during his youth, that position would change, as we shall see, in the late 1820s.

Mendelssohn's Evolving Relationship with Judaism

The image of Mendelssohn's attitude toward his Jewish heritage presented in these and other letters is one of relative indifference, but the actual situation was considerably more complicated. As the analyses of the oratorios in the following chapters demonstrate, Mendelssohn's attitudes changed significantly over time. Indeed, Mendelssohn experienced periods in which he distanced himself from his family's Jewish roots much more actively than the letters and reminiscences presented here suggest, and other periods where he felt less need to deliberately separate himself from his religious heritage.

During his boyhood years, Felix knew little of the politics surrounding the life of the converted Jew or of the need to disassociate himself from anything related to Judaism.[100] Such ignorance on Felix's part is hardly surprising, since there was little in his surroundings that would have suggested a need for caution: his family never lived in the Jewish quarter, they were financially successful, and they interacted regularly with Christians. Moreover, Abraham Mendelssohn, as noted earlier, enjoyed the same rights and privileges of any Christian businessman (indeed, his service to the city of Berlin during the war against Napoleon even earned him the title of City Counselor [*Stadtrath*]).[101] Thus, the possible repercussions of Felix's use of his grandfather's psalm translations for two of his earliest sacred works (the pair of verses from Psalm 119 he set during the summer of 1821) was something that most likely never entered the twelve-year-old's mind.[102] (Significantly, this would be the last time he would ever use Moses Mendelssohn's translations in his music, relying instead almost exclusively on Martin Luther's.)

Abraham, however, knew better. He understood well the complexities of the life of the Jew in Europe (both converted and nonconverted), and especially the added factors associated with being a descendant of such a noted figure in German-Jewish history. If the textual source of the Psalm 119 settings was unknown to Abraham, Felix's nonchalance regarding the family's precarious social position must have surfaced while the two journeyed to Paris in March 1825, at which time Felix inquired about the rationale behind their adoption of the name "Mendelssohn Bartholdy."[103] (It was around this time that Felix was preparing to write his confirmation confession, a process that no doubt stirred up issues of identity.)[104] Since silence on the subject of Judaism and Jewish culture was an integral part of the successful assimilation of the converted Jew, it is indeed possible that this subject had never been raised before. Now that it finally had, Abraham took the opportunity to make the realities of their situation known to Felix, and from that time forward, he remained alert for signs that his son was not taking his words to heart. As we have seen, such a sign appeared (in Abraham's mind at least) during Felix's 1829 London trip, in the form of missing "Bartholdy"s in the London concert programs. To Abraham, it looked as though Felix's youthful nonchalance was beginning to reassert itself in the more tolerant British Isles (where his relationship to the great philosopher Moses was highly celebrated), an attitude Abraham wasted no time quashing by reiterating the details of their earlier discussion:

> On our trip to Paris, the day after that neck-breaking night, you asked me about the reasons for our change of name, and I explained them to you at length. If you have forgotten them, you could have asked me about them again; if they did not seem compelling to you, you should have offered better reasons to the contrary. I wish to believe the former, since I cannot find any of the latter, and will therefore repeat my reasons and views to you.
>
> My father's father was named Mendel Dessau. When his son, my father, went out into the world, when he began to become known, when he made the noble decision—which can never be praised enough—to pull himself and his brethren up from the deep wretchedness into which they had sunk by spreading a higher learning, he felt that as "Moses Mendel Dessau" it would be too difficult to develop the necessary close relationships with those who

then possessed this higher learning: so he called himself "Mendelssohn," without fearing that this would displease his father. The change was as insignificant as it was decisive. As "Mendelssohn" he severed himself irrevocably from an entire class—the best of which he raised up along with himself —and joined a different community. The tremendous influence he then exerted most nobly and brilliantly through word, writ, and deed—and which continues to this day to grow and spread—gave not only great weight, but also an enduring significance to his adopted name. A Christian Mendelssohn cannot be, for the world does not acknowledge one, and moreover it should not be because he himself did not wish to be one. "Mendelssohn" is and will forever belong to Judaism in its transitional period.[105]

As we have already seen, Abraham's worries here would prove unwarranted, for in the years since the 1825 trip to Paris, Felix had fully embraced his father's way of thinking. As the chapters that follow demonstrate, Felix's new attitude would be reflected in the larger sacred works he composed and edited during his father's lifetime. It would also be visible in his attitude toward his grandfather's works, which—with the exception of reading *Phaedon* while in Naples in 1831[106]—he does not appear to have consulted again until several years after his father's death. Indeed, Felix seems not to have discussed his grandfather's writings (at least in his letters) until 1840, when Heinrich Brockhaus approached him to propose undertaking a new complete edition of Moses Mendelssohn's works. On February 20, 1840, Felix wrote about the proposal to his uncle Joseph Mendelssohn, who—after implying that Felix had not written in some time and chastising him for not including updates about his family—gave his enthusiastic permission for the project.[107] At that point, Felix served as an intermediary between his uncle and Brockhaus for at least a couple of months, after which Joseph began working with Brockhaus directly (all the while sending periodic progress reports to his nephew).[108]

Felix's assistance with the production of the new Moses Mendelssohn edition clearly demonstrates an interest and pride in his family history, as well as some lessening of the need he felt to disassociate his name with Judaism—at least privately. The private aspect of this matter is significant: as Joseph's last letter to Felix on this subject demonstrates, Felix never sought any mention or recognition in the edition, either as the grandson of the subject or as an agent of its publication.[109] More significant, Joseph did not mention Felix or his siblings in the biography of Moses he wrote for the edition, perhaps not wishing to call public attention to an ancestry that they had worked so hard to leave behind.[110] It should be emphasized, however, that Felix's work on the publication of his grandfather's writings in the 1840s does not demonstrate, as some have suggested, a life-long fascination with these works, nor does it imply that he was at all versed in the works (with the exception of *Phaedon*). Indeed, a letter written in February 1842—in which he noted that he did not possess "a single page of his [Moses Mendelssohn's] writing"—would seem to indicate the opposite.[111] Nor, as discussed earlier, should it be inferred that Felix's interest in his family constituted an interest in the Jewish faith or culture.

Nevertheless, this private involvement with a major Jewish figure clearly represents one of Felix's first steps toward a more comfortable stance toward his heritage. Additional private and semiprivate steps would follow, such as his composition of a piece for the *Gesellschaft der Freunde's* fiftieth anniversary celebration in 1842 and his attendance of the event itself.[112] More public steps would come soon afterward, in the form of his oratorios of the mid-1840s. All of this, however, would remain impossible until after Abraham's death and the firm establishment of Felix's career. Once both of these events transpired in late 1835 (just months before the premiere of *Paulus*), Mendelssohn could begin to take the kinds of small steps that he was unwilling to risk at the outset of his career. But as the preceding discussion has demonstrated and the sacred works will show, he never embraced Judaism in the active manner suggested by Werner and the other architects of the postwar interpretation.

The St. Matthew Passion *Revival*

And [to think] that it must be an actor and a Jew-boy (*Judenjunge*)
who restore to the people the greatest Christian musical work!
— *Felix Mendelssohn Bartholdy* (*attributed*)

IN WHAT COULD BE DESCRIBED as a moment of youthful indiscretion,
twenty-year-old Felix Mendelssohn Bartholdy spoke the above words to his close
friend, the actor Eduard Devrient, as the two began the final preparations for the
first public performance of J. S. Bach's *St. Matthew Passion* in about eighty-seven
years.[1] Assuming we can trust Devrient's recollection, the statement constitutes
the only known occasion in which Mendelssohn identified himself as a Jew.[2] Even
Devrient, who recorded the episode in his reminiscences of the composer, remarked on the singularity of the outburst, noting that Felix was "carried away by
his striking observation and joyful mood" and "was otherwise determined to avoid
recalling his heritage."[3] Little reading between the lines is required, however, to
realize that Mendelssohn was being facetious. As the context of his comment and
his use of the derogatory "Jew-boy" (*Judenjunge*) over the less hostile "Jewish boy"
(*jüdische Junge*) implies, Mendelssohn was undoubtedly speaking in an ironic, self-
deprecating sense, rather than attempting to proudly assert his Jewish identity.
Devrient's reaction confirms this, as indeed do all of the documents and anti-
Semitic episodes examined in the previous chapter. Nevertheless, Mendelssohn's
comment clearly reveals his awareness that, despite his baptism and Protestant
upbringing, many continued to see him as a Jew. This fact strongly affected the
composer's first sojourn into large-scale sacred music, the *St. Matthew Passion*.
Mendelssohn adapted Bach's masterpiece as he believed any other Christian conductor would, thereby creating a work that was theologically and musically accept-
able to an early nineteenth-century Christian audience.

JUDICIOUS CUTS

As Devrient chronicles, Mendelssohn's association with Bach's "Great Passion" was
extensive, with his earliest exposure taking place in the late 1810s or early 1820s at
the private rehearsals conducted in his teacher Carl Friedrich Zelter's home. These
rehearsals were in part designed to explore great choral works (especially those of

Bach) that Zelter deemed too difficult or inappropriate for performance by the Singakademie. By 1824, Felix's partiality toward Bach's Passion was sufficiently obvious that his grandmother Bella Solomon (still unaware of Felix's baptism) felt moved to fulfill his desire for a copy of the score.[4] A few years later, Felix's interest in the Passion surfaced again, leading him in the winter of 1827 to begin his own series of private rehearsals, for which he recruited a small choir of friends.[5] Among them were Devrient and his wife, Therese, who recorded her experiences at one of the rehearsals in 1828, just as the group was beginning its study of the *St. Matthew Passion*. Therese also chronicled Felix's heartfelt desire to perform the work, and his awareness of what seemed to be insurmountable obstacles to such an undertaking:

> It was on an October evening [in 1828], that a small gathering had assembled at the Mendelssohns, who had been invited to get acquainted for the first time with some of Sebastian Bach's Passion-Music. . . .
>
> Felix sat down pale and excited at the piano, we singers stood around him so that he would always have us in his sight and could help us, which was absolutely necessary, since it was going miserably! We didn't just have difficulty sight-singing this music, it was also almost impossible to read the very illegible notes and text; nonetheless we were deeply shaken and felt as though we were transported into a new musical world.
>
> In the evening, Felix often said that for a musician, it would be the greatest thrill to release this work with full chorus and orchestra and present it to the world, but believed it to be impossible due to all the complications and difficulties. It was different with Eduard, who fully resolute and with firm resolve set out towards this lofty and lovely goal. He went to Felix the next morning to share his plan with him, which was already completely worked out. He asked him to prepare a performable score, while he promised him to put together an orchestra and chorus.[6]

Eduard Devrient himself described his epiphany and his subsequent visit to the somewhat hesitant Felix on that "next morning":

> One evening in January 1829, after we had sung through the whole first part of the work, . . . and we had all gone home profoundly impressed, a sleepless night gave me the idea as to how a performance might be brought about. I waited impatiently for the late winter's day to dawn; Therese encouraged me with my plan, and so I set forth to see Felix. . . .
>
> I now told him straight-out that during the night I had decided that the Passion had to be performed in the next few months—before his intended journey to England—at the Singakademie.
>
> He laughed. "And who is going to conduct it?"
>
> "You!"
>
> "The devil I am!". . .

"At the moment, no one but you can successfully undertake the performance, and so you have to do it."

"If I were sure I could bring it off, then yes!"[7]

Despite Felix's trepidation, Devrient continued to outline his plan, eventually win-
ning Mendelssohn's support. In a letter to Hanoverian diplomat and family friend
Karl Klingemann, Fanny described the appeal the men subsequently made to the
directors of the Singakademie:

> Felix and Devrient had been talking for a long time of the possibility of a per-
> formance, but the plan had neither form nor shape; one evening at our house
> it acquired both, and the two walked off the next morning in newly bought
> yellow gloves (which they believed very important) to the directors of the
> [Sing]akademie. They approached softly and asked modestly whether they
> could be allowed the use of the hall for a charitable purpose. They would then,
> since the music was likely to be well-received, give a second performance for
> the benefit of the [Sing]akademie.
>
> But the gentlemen thanked them politely and preferred to take a fixed
> honorarium of fifty thalers, leaving the receipts to the disposal of the concert
> givers. . . . [Singakademie director Carl Friedrich] Zelter had no objections,
> and so the rehearsals began the following Friday.[8]

The performance took place at the Singakademie on March 11 and was a phenom-
enal success; so much so, in fact, that despite the directors' initial rejection of a second
performance, one was immediately arranged for March 21 (Bach's birthday).[9] This
too was insufficient to satisfy public demand, and the work was performed yet again
on the liturgically appropriate Good Friday (April 17), in place of the Singakademie's
traditional presentation of Carl Heinrich Graun's *The Death of Jesus* (*Der Tod Jesu*).[10]
(Since Mendelssohn was on his way to England by this point, Zelter conducted the
performance.) The ability of Bach's work to hold its own against Graun's caused the
St. Matthew Passion to become a holy-week tradition at the Singakademie in future
years.[11]

The primary concerns for all parties involved in the *St. Matthew Passion* revival
were practical ones: accessibility and length. Therese Devrient, as quoted above, made
some reference to this when she commented on how difficult the piece was for the
group to sight-sing, and noted that Felix, too, believed the piece all but impossible
to perform. Therese also revealed the source of these difficulties when she recalled
feeling as though she had been "transported into a new musical world." Indeed, for
most of the performers and listeners in 1829, the *St. Matthew Passion*—with its complex melodies and counterpoint, archaic harmonic idiom, formalistic designs, and
Pietistic theology—was something completely outside their experience. Even before
he raised with Felix the idea of a performance, Eduard was greatly concerned with
this fact:

[H]ow would the public receive a work so utterly strange to them? In sacred concerts, a short movement by Bach may have been accepted now and then as a curiosity, bringing pleasure to only a few connoisseurs (*Kenner*); but now how would it be for an entire evening to hear nothing but Sebastian Bach, who was known to the public as unmelodious, mathematical (*berechnend*), dry, and unintelligible? That would seem to be an audacious undertaking.[12]

Devrient was not alone in his assessment of Bach. As Julius Schubring wrote, "I once said to him [Felix], lamentingly, that I found it difficult to conceive Bach's music as aught but a dry arithmetical sum."[13]

The solution to the issues of both accessibility and length was to make, as Fanny described it, "a few judicious cuts."[14] Devrient elaborates:

Many times we sat down together to think about the shortening of the score for the performance. It could not be a question of presenting the work—which was in so many ways influenced by the taste of its time—in its entirety, but rather of conveying an impression of its greatness. The majority of arias would have to be omitted, while from others only the introductions, the so-called *accompagnements*, would be retained; also from the gospel text everything had to be removed that did not belong to the passion story. Quite often we had conflicting views, for it was a matter of conscience; but what we finally settled upon seems to have been correct, since it was later adopted for most performances.[15]

As both of his statements make clear, Devrient's paramount concern was that the public would not accept the *St. Matthew Passion* in its original form and that a carefully reduced version of the work was the best solution. The second passage also states that the producers wished to preserve "an impression of its [the Passion's] greatness." These two ideas, in combination with Devrient's remark that "from the gospel text everything had to be removed that did not belong to the passion story" suggest that the goal was to present a sampling of the Passion. Everything they thought unnecessary, unimportant, outmoded, or repetitious would be removed for the sake of brevity (which, in their minds, was intrinsically linked to the idea of accessibility). Devrient's charge that the heart of the narrative be preserved, however, indicates one of the underlying concerns behind the reduction process: dramatic continuity. Indeed, it was the dramatic aspect of the work, in the form of the operatic assignment of one character per voice, that sparked Devrient's initial interest in the piece.[16]

Devrient implies that cutting for the sake of brevity and rapid dramatic motion was most apparent in the evangelist's recitatives, which present the gospel story, and an examination of Mendelssohn's score and the textbook printed for the premiere reveals this to be the case.[17] On the whole, the deleted passages present material unnecessary to, or often a hindrance to, the dramatic argument of the work. My interpretation here calls into question Michael Marissen's argument that Mendelssohn focused on eliminating texts that "ran the risk of being perceived as anti-Jewish,"[18] a thesis that, if true, would have important implications concerning Mendelssohn's feelings toward his religious heritage. But Marissen's analysis of the primary sources is incomplete, in part because he evaluated the deleted segments in isolation from the surrounding material. When they are considered in context, however, anti-Semitism becomes an unlikely basis for their removal, since in most cases the anti-Semitic sentiment of the longer passage remains intact even without the deleted text.

Mendelssohn's deletions in the gospel recitatives divide readily into three groups: simple repeated material, repetitious connections to Old Testament prophesy, and scenes involving minor characters (notably women). For the sake of clarity and dramatic coherence, however, the cuts are best reviewed in roughly the order of their appearance.

The first edited gospel recitative (no. 31 in the *Neue Bach Ausgabe* numbering system) demonstrates quite clearly the principles of brevity/accessibility and dramatic continuity that Mendelssohn followed.

Die aber Jesum gegriffen hatten, führeten ihn zu dem Hohenpriester Kaiphas, dahin die Schriftgelehrten und Ältesten sich versammlet hatten. ~~Petrus aber folgete ihm nach von ferne bis in den Palast des Hohenpriesters und ging hinein und satzte sich bei die Knechte, auf daß er sähe, wo es hinaus wollte.~~ Die Hohenpriester aber und Ältesten und der ganze Rat suchten falsche Zeugnis wider Jesum, auf daß sie ihn töteten, und funden keines.[19]	Then those who had seized Jesus led him to the high priest Caiaphas, where the scribes and the elders had gathered. ~~But Peter followed him at a distance, as far as the palace of the high priest, and went inside and sat with the servants, so that he would see how it would end.~~ But the high priests and the elders and the whole council sought false testimony against Jesus, that they might kill him, and found none.[20]

Since recitative no. 38a (*Petrus aber saß draußen im Palast*) mentions Peter's presence outside the palace just before the mob confronts him, the deletion of the passage chronicling Peter's trip to the palace in no. 31 not only eliminates repetitious material, but also allows for Peter's introduction at the most dramatically appropriate time: the moment of his confrontation, just before his denial of Christ.

Keeping the last sentence of the preceding passage in mind makes the next cut in no. 33 almost self-explanatory.

~~Und wiewohl viel falsche Zeugen herzutraten, funden sie doch keins.~~ Zuletzt traten herzu zween falsche Zeugen und sprachen:	~~And though many false witnesses came forward, they still found none.~~ At last came forward two false witnesses and said:

Since Mendelssohn also deleted the chorale (no. 32) that normally separated these passages, this duplication of what became the immediately preceding sentence had to be avoided.

Because of its length, no. 43 needs to be broken in two parts and each considered separately.

Sie hielten aber einen Rat und kauften einen Töpfersakker darum zum Begräbnis der Pilger. ~~Daher ist derselbige Akker genennet der Blutakker, bis auf den heutigen Tag. Da ist erfüllet, das gesagt ist durch den Propheten Jeremias, da er spricht: "Sie haben genommen dreißig Silberlinge, damit bezahlet ward der Verkaufte, welchen sie kauften von den Kindern Israel, und haben sie gegeben um einen Töpfersakker, als mir der Herr befohlen hat."~~ Jesus aber stund vor dem Landpfleger; und der Landpfleger fragte ihn und sprach:	So they took counsel, and bought a potter's field with them for the burial of pilgrims. ~~Therefore that same field has been called the Field of Blood to this day. Thus was fulfilled what had been spoken by the prophet Jeremiah, when he said: "They took thirty pieces of silver, and with them was paid the price of the one who was sold, whom they bought from the children of Israel, and they gave them for a potter's field, as the Lord directed me."~~ Now Jesus stood before the governor; and the governor asked him and said:

In this first part, Mendelssohn cut various forms of superfluous material. He retained the main idea of the recitative (i.e., that the high priests held counsel and used the thirty silver pieces Judas returned to buy a burial site for pilgrims), but removed inconsequential details such as the field's name and Jeremiah's Old Testament prophesy of this act—neither of which adds anything to the passion story. While the removal of the reference to Judas' betrayal of Christ for money could be interpreted as an attempt to temper the narrative's anti-Semitic content, as Marissen viewed it,[21] such an interpretation ignores Mendelssohn's retention of Judas' initial betrayal of Jesus for the thirty silver pieces (no. 7), Jesus' identification of Judas as the betrayer (nos. 11 and 26), and Judas' remorse and return of the silver pieces (no. 41).

A desire to lessen repetition is also at the heart of the cuts made to the second part of no. 43, where the latter (deleted) half of the recitative repeats, in essence, the first (retained) half, since both mention the clamor of the priests and elders, and Jesus' refusal to speak.

Pilatus Bist du der Jüden König?	*Pilate* Are you the King of the Jews?
Evangelist Jesus aber sprach zu ihm:	*Evangelist* Jesus said to him:
Jesus Du sagests.	*Jesus* You have said so.
Evangelist Und da er verklagt war von den Hohenpriestern und Ältesten, antwortete er nichts. ~~Da sprach Pilatus zu ihm:~~	*Evangelist* And when he was accused by the high priests and elders, he made no answer. ~~Then Pilate said to him:~~

Pilatus
Hörest du nicht, wie hart sie dich
verklagen?

Evangelist
Und er antwortete ihm nicht auf
ein Wort, also, daß sich auch der
Landpfleger sehr verwunderte.

Pilate
Do you not hear how severely they
testify against you?

Evangelist
And he answered not even a
single word, so that the
governor wondered greatly.

In addition to needing deletions because of its repetitious content, recitative 45a is the first to require cuts to eliminate references to and by an inconsequential character: Pilate's wife (*Uxor Pilati*).

Evangelist
Auf das Fest aber hatte der Landpfleger
Gewohnheit, dem Volk einen Gefangenen
loszugeben, welchen sie wollten. Er hatte
aber zu der Zeit einen Gefangenen, einen
sonderlichen vor andern, der hieß
Barabbas. Und da sie versammlet waren,
sprach Pilatus zu ihnen:

Evangelist
Now at the feast the governor had the
custom of releasing to the people any one
prisoner whom they wanted. And they
had at that time a prisoner,
who was notorious, called
Barabbas. And when they had gathered,
Pilate said to them:

Pilatus
Welchen wollet ihr, daß ich euch losgebe?
Barabbam oder Jesum, von dem gesaget
wird, er sei Christus?

Pilate
Whom do you want me to release to you?
Barabbas or Jesus, of whom it is said,
is Christ?

Evangelist
Denn er wußte wohl, daß sie ihn aus Neid
überantwortet hatten. Und da er auf dem
Richtstuhl saß, schickete sein Weib
zu ihm und ließ ihm sagen:

Evangelist
For he knew well that it was out of envy
that they had delivered him. And as he
sat on the judgment seat, his wife
sent word to him, and had him told:

Uxor Pilati
Habe du nichts zu schaffen mit diesem
Gerechten; ich habe heute viel erlitten
im Traum von seinetwegen!

Pilate's Wife
Have nothing to do with this
righteous man, for today I have suffered
much in a dream for his sake!

Evangelist
Aber die Hohenpriester und die Ältesten
überredeten das Volk, daß sie um
Barabbas bitten sollten und Jesum
umbrächten. Da antwortete nun der
Landpfleger und sprach zu ihnen:

Evangelist
But the chief priests and the elders
persuaded the people that they should
ask for Barabbas and kill Jesus.
Then the governor answered
and said to them:

Pilatus
Welchen wollt ihr unter diesen zweien,
den ich euch soll losgeben?

Pilate
Which of these two do you want
that I should release to you?

Evangelist	*Evangelist*
Sie sprachen:	They said:
Chorus	*Chorus*
Barabbam!	Barabbas!

The repetition in this recitative is fairly self-evident, as Pilate asks the mob twice whom they wish to see released. The bulk of the deletion, however, seems aimed at excising the character of Pilate's wife. Mendelssohn made similar cuts toward the end of the Passion (nos. 63c and 66a), removing all mention of the two Marys at the crucifixion and burial. Combined, the cuts suggest that Mendelssohn considered the role of women in the story relatively unimportant from a dramatic and, possibly, theological standpoint. (A notable exception is the evangelist's report of Mary Magdalene's anointing of Jesus' feet in no. 4c, an event critical to the passion story as it spurs Judas' betrayal.) While Marissen may be correct that the composer held a patriarchal attitude that factored into this decision[22] (an argument we can extend to the general downplaying of the role of women in Lutheran theology), by almost any reckoning Pilate's wife and the two Marys do little to advance the narrative.

The only remaining gospel recitative Mendelssohn edited is no. 58a, which, like the first part of no. 43, includes Old Testament prophesy among the other repetitious material Mendelssohn removed.

~~Und da sie an die Stätte kamen mit~~	~~And when they came to a place~~
~~Namen Golgatha, das ist verdeutschet~~	~~called Golgotha, which means the~~
~~Schädelstätt, gaben sie ihm Essig zu~~	~~place of skulls, they gave him vinegar to~~
~~trinken mit Gallen vermischet; und da~~	~~drink, mingled with gall; and when~~
~~er's schmeckete, wollte er's nicht trinken.~~	~~he tasted it, he would not drink it.~~
Da sie ihn aber gekreuziget hatten, teilten	And when they had crucified him, they
sie seine Kleider, und wurfen das Los	divided his garments, and cast lots for
darum, ~~auf daß erfüllet würde, das gesagt~~	them, ~~that might be fulfilled the word~~
~~ist durch den Propheten: "Sie haben~~	~~spoken by the prophet: "They divided~~
~~meine Kleider unter sich geteilet, und~~	~~my garments among themselves, and~~
~~über mein Gewand haben sie das Los~~	~~for my clothing cast lots."~~
~~geworfen." Und sie saßen allda und~~	~~And they all sat down there and~~
~~hüteten sein. Und oben zu seinem~~	~~kept watch over him. And over his~~
~~Häupten hefteten sie die Ursach seines~~	~~head they put the reason for his~~
~~Todes beschrieben, nämlich: "Dies ist~~	~~death, which read: "This is Jesus,~~
~~Jesus, der Jüden König."~~ Und da wurden	~~the King of the Jews."~~ And there were
zween Mörder mit ihm gekreuziget, einer	two murderers crucified with him, one
zur Rechten und einer zur Linken. Die	on the right and one on the left. Those
aber vorübergingen, lästerten ihn und	who passed by derided him, and
schüttelten ihre Köpfe und sprachen:	shook their heads and said:

The offering of vinegar to Jesus, also deleted, reoccurs in no. 61c, where it stands between two exclamations from the chorus about Jesus' supposed cry to Elijah, a far more dramatic setting. And since Mendelssohn chose to retain the alto arioso *Ach, Golgatha*, its mention here as well is also unnecessary, as is Jesus' title "King of the Jews" (*Jüden König*), which appears earlier in nos. 43 and 53b. Thus, as with the alterations to the other gospel recitatives, none of the changes here suggest an attempt to lessen the Passion's anti-Semitic content; rather, Mendelssohn's goal appears to have been to condense the work and quicken its dramatic pace.

THE *ST. MATTHEW PASSION* CHORALES AND THE BERLIN HYMN TRADITION

As with the gospel recitatives, the decisions behind which chorales to remove were based on Mendelssohn's desire to make the Passion accessible and dramatically continuous through brevity. But since the chorales are essentially hymns that provide modern-day communal reflection on the story, they are by their nature not essential to the narrative; as a result, the criteria for their removal or retention were more complex than simply eliminating repetitious material (in this case, repeated hymn tunes). In fact, a chorale that used a melody already heard in the work could not be categorically deleted because of the structural purpose the melodies sometimes served. Moreover, even had Mendelssohn chosen to remove all the duplicate chorales, he still would have had to remove some whose melody appears only once if he wanted to keep the overall length of the Passion manageable. Mendelssohn therefore had to take into account both the needs of the music and the public's familiarity with the hymns in creating a work that was accessible and structurally sound.

Despite these complications, Mendelssohn's pattern of removing repetitious material remained part of his decisions regarding the chorale cuts: any chorale that used a melody already heard in the Passion was removed, so long as it served no critical structural purpose. Only two chorales could be deleted for this reason, however: no. 37, "Who has struck You so" (*Wer hat dich so geschlagen*), which uses the same melody as no. 10, "It is I, I should repent" (*Ich bin's, ich sollte büßen*), and no. 46, "How wondrous indeed is this chastisement" (*Wie wunderbarlich ist doch diese Strafe*), which uses the same melody as no. 3, "Beloved Jesus" (*Herzliebster Jesu*).[23]

The only remaining repeated melody is "O head full of blood and wounds" (*O Haupt voll Blut und Wunden*)—better known in English as "O sacred head, sore wounded"—an exception that helps prove the rule. This chorale melody appears a total of six times over the course of the work, making it by far the most heard in the Passion. A reflection of Luther's "Theology of the Cross," the chorale acts in a leitmotiv-like manner to focus the work on the central sacrificial act and is the most significant (and most obvious to the typical listener) structural feature of the piece.[24] As such, Mendelssohn could not simply delete its repetitions outright. Indeed, the structural function of *O Haupt*, and resulting sacrificial focus of the work, stems from its appearance at relatively regular intervals throughout the Passion. However, not all the appearances of the melody are critical to either the piece's structure or its focus

on the crucifixion, and Mendelssohn did delete these less central references. Specifically, there are two occasions where the melody appears in very close proximity to itself, making the second instance less structurally critical: no. 17, "I would stand here
beside You" (*Ich will hier bei dir stehen*), which follows fast on the heels of no. 15, "Recognize me, my protector" (*Erkenne mich, mein Hüter*), and the second verse within
the setting of the original *O Haupt* hymn text itself (no. 54). It comes as no surprise,
therefore, that Mendelssohn eliminated these duplications in his performances.

Another factor in Mendelssohn's decision to retain most of the appearances of
the *O Haupt* chorale may have been its extreme familiarity to his audience. In 1829,
O Haupt was a canonical hymn in churches throughout Berlin.[25] Mendelssohn demonstrated his awareness of that fact by subtly changing the no. 54 text to match that
traditionally sung in these churches (specifically, by changing "adorned" [*gezieret*]
to "crowned" [*gekrönet*] and "scolded" [*schimpfieret*] to "mocked" [*verhöhnet*]).[26]
These alterations are typical of the kind one might see when comparing hymnals
from different regions—no significant theological changes, just a simple matter of
word preference. That Mendelssohn bothered to make these alterations (the only
ones in the entire Passion text) suggests, however, that he wished to present the
chorale in the form most familiar to his audience.

Audience familiarity (or lack thereof) seems to have also been the deciding factor in the deletion of those chorales that appear only once in the unedited Passion,
many of which are noticeably absent from the majority of Berlin hymnals before or
at the time of the revival.[27] For instance, no. 32, "The world has judged me deceit-
fully" (*Mir hat die Welt trüglich gericht't*)—based on Adam Ruesner's *In dich hab ich
gehoffet, Herr*—does not appear in any Berlin hymnal printed through 1829. And
although no. 40, "Though I have strayed from thee" (*Bin ich gleich von dir gewichen*)—
based on Johann Rist's *Werde munter, mein Gemüte*—appeared in many hymnals
up until 1829, it had apparently fallen out of favor (or had not been regularly sung),
as it was not included in the *New Berlin Hymnal* (*Neue Berliner Gesangbuch*) of that
same year. The hymn also never appeared in the Dieterich *Gesangbuch*, a popular
hymnal first printed in 1765 for Berlin's Marienkirche and adopted by thirty-two other
local congregations by 1806.[28]

Perhaps the most compelling evidence of audience familiarity playing a substantial
role in Mendelssohn's chorale decisions comes from a review of another Prussian performance of the Passion that took place in Breslau (Wrocław) on April 3, 1830, under
the direction of Johann Theodor Mosewius. Mosewius—an avid Bach enthusiast, head
of Breslau's Singakademie, and music director at its university—kept apprised of the
preparations for the Passion's Berlin premiere as reported in the newspapers, and then
attended the Good Friday performance under Zelter. In his own performance,
Mosewius adopted nearly all of Mendelssohn's changes, writing that he even made
several dynamic and orchestration alterations "following Mendelssohn's example."[29]
Indeed, a surviving textbook from the performance indicates that, in terms of content, Mosewius followed Mendelssohn's model precisely, with the exception of no. 6,

"Repentance and remorse" (*Buß und Reu*), which Mendelssohn kept but Mosewius did not.[30] A review of the performance by Johann Gottfried Hientzsch prominently mentions the Passion's "very well-known, splendid chorales," whose familiarity allowed for the possibility of the congregation singing along (although that does not seem to have occurred during the performance). Because of this, Hientzsch thought it best to perform the Passion in a church whenever possible.[31]

THE *ST. MATTHEW PASSION* AND THE THEOLOGY OF FRIEDRICH SCHLEIERMACHER

With accessibility and brevity still his foremost concern, Mendelssohn's knife cut deepest in the category of arias and nongospel recitatives (ariosos), in part because the prevailing nineteenth-century view of oratorio held that arias and ariosos were too closely tied to opera and detracted from the genre's choral focus.[32] For Mendelssohn to delete all of them out of hand, however, would have left his audience with an incomplete impression of the Passion's greatness. But since the arias and ariosos were neither familiar nor critical to the presentation of the narrative, the criteria used in choosing which to retain proved even more sophisticated than those applied to the gospel recitatives or the chorales. Aesthetics was one possible factor, with Mendelssohn retaining those movements he believed his audience would find the most pleasing or impressive; another was his plan to present a well-rounded sampling of the work, perhaps by retaining arias and ariosos representative of those found throughout the Passion. A third possibility, however, is that, having recently immersed himself in the teachings of the era's most prominent theologian, Friedrich Schleiermacher, Mendelssohn sought theological justification for his choices. Marissen first made this connection, noting that Schleiermacher's "communal theology" (*Gemeindetheologie*) may have influenced Mendelssohn's choices regarding some of the arias.[33] As the following discussion will demonstrate, this influence may have had an even greater impact than Marissen himself realized, affecting Mendelssohn's decisions regarding all of the arias and ariosos.

Mendelssohn's declaration of being a "follower (*Anhänger*) of Schleiermacher" appears in his letter of November 18, 1830, to Pastor Julius Schubring (a long-time Schleiermacher disciple),[34] although it seems likely that his acquaintance with Schleiermacher's theology began some years earlier. While on his European tour, which extended from April 10, 1829—a few days after the second *St. Matthew Passion* performance—to late June 1832, Mendelssohn had little German reading material available to him. ("I'm limited to the Goethe poems [Franz] Hauser gave me [in Vienna]," he wrote to his family from Naples in May 1831.)[35] This suggests Mendelssohn became acquainted with Schleiermacher's writings before his departure, at the time of the *St. Matthew Passion* performances at the very latest.

More than a mere theologian, Schleiermacher had achieved a kind of hero's status in Berlin in 1813, when he roused the student population against Napoleon. In the years that followed, students from the University of Berlin—an institution Schleiermacher helped establish and where he served as Theology Chair—would pack into the Trinity church to hear his sermons.[36] Mendelssohn may have joined this group of devout followers upon entering the university in 1827; at the very least, within a few months of his matriculation, he was able to recognize the eminent theologian by sight and thought highly enough of him to include him in a list of prominent University scholars.[37] Schleiermacher also attended the Singakademie Passion premiere,[38] but it remains unknown if he came on his own initiative or by Mendelssohn's invitation. That Mendelssohn and Schleiermacher developed a strong personal relationship at some point is clearly indicated in the composer's correspondence. In a letter to his mother written shortly after the theologian's death on February 12, 1834, Mendelssohn reflected on Schleiermacher's interest in his music and on the kindness and friendship Schleiermacher had shown him over the past year.[39] Fanny too knew of their closeness, stating plainly, "[i]n Schleiermacher you also lost a friend."[40]

As a follower of Schleiermacher, Mendelssohn would have been familiar with the fundamental tenets of his theology, as carefully laid out in what was the most well-known and influential theological treatise of the period, *The Christian Faith* (*Der christliche Glaube*). This mammoth volume, based on Schleiermacher's lectures and sermons, presented a new, unifying theology for the recently united Prussian Church (a fusion of the Lutheran and Reformed churches), and was by far the largest systematic treatise on Protestant theology to appear since the publication of John Calvin's *Institutes of the Christian Religion* in 1536.[41] One of the basic theological concepts Schleiermacher explains in the book is what has become known as "communal theology" (*Gemeindetheologie*), which, as the name implies, stresses the importance of the Christian community over the individual. To quote from Schleiermacher's overview, "The Christian Church . . . is in its purity and integrity the perfect image of the Redeemer, and each regenerate individual is an indispensable constituent of this fellowship." As he later elaborates, every individual brings positive Christian elements to the church, and over the course of time (from the origin of the church until the Last Judgment), those elements accumulate so that the body of the church grows to more closely resemble its archetype, Christ. The significance of the individual lies in those unique Christian elements he or she brings to the church—elements which, were the person not to exist or not be a part of the community, might require many other persons to replicate. Thus, the individual possesses elements of the archetype but is incapable of approaching the level of Christ's perfection—only the community, the church as a whole throughout the ages, can achieve that.[42]

Examining the arias and ariosos of the *St. Matthew Passion* in light of *Gemeindetheologie* enables one to divide them into two groups: those that focus on first-person reflections by a single, present-day observer (which Mendelssohn cut), and those that do not (which he retained). In this latter group belong the following movements:

5. Alto [Soprano[43]] Arioso: "Thou dear savior, when your disciples foolishly bicker" (*Du lieber Heiland du, wenn deine Jünger töricht streiten*)

6. Alto [Soprano] Aria: "Repentance and remorse grind the sinful heart in two" (*Buß und Reu knirscht das Sündenherz entzwei*)

19. Tenor Arioso with chorus: "O sorrow! . . . Ah, my sins have struck Thee" (*O Schmerz! . . . Ach, meine Sünden haben dich geschlagen*")

20. Tenor Aria with chorus: "I will stand watch by my Jesus" (*Ich will bei meinem Jesu wachen*)

27. Soprano/Alto Duet with chorus: "So now my Jesus has been captured" (*So ist mein Jesus nun gefangen*)

30. Alto Aria with chorus: "Ah, now my Jesus is gone" (*Ach! nun ist mein Jesus hin!*)

39. Alto [Soprano] Aria: "Have mercy" (*Erbarme dich*)

48. Soprano Arioso: "He has done good to all of us. To the blind he gave sight" (*Er hat uns allen wohlgetan. Den Blinden gab er das Gesicht*)

51. Alto Arioso: "Have mercy, God! Here the savior stands bound" (*Erbarm es Gott! Hier steht der Heiland angebunden*)

59. Alto Arioso: "Ah, Golgotha" (*Ach, Golgatha*)

64. Bass Arioso: "In the evening, when it was cool" (*Am Abend, da es kühle war*)

67. Quartet Arioso with chorus: "Now the Lord is brought to rest" (*Nun ist der Herr zur Ruh gebracht*)

Each of these retained movements either elaborates upon the narrative (nos. 5, 27, 30, 39, 48, 51, 59, 64, and 67) or offers reflection by the entire community or by an unidentified person speaking for the community (6, 19, and 20). By contrast, each of the deleted arias and ariosos is deeply immersed in Pietist theology and its focus on an intimate one-on-one relationship with the redeemer (an unfashionable concept in early nineteenth-century Berlin and one incompatible with *Gemeindetheologie*). As a result, these deleted movements consist mainly of personal reflection by present-day observers, something readily apparent in most of their textual incipits:

8. Aria: "Bleed only, dear heart" (*Blute nur, du liebes Herz*)

12. Arioso: "Although my heart swims in tears" (*Wiewohl mein Herz in Tränen schwimmt*)

13. Aria: "I will give You my heart" (*Ich will dir mein Herze schenken*)

22. Arioso: "The savior falls before his father. Thereby He raises me and everyone" (*Der Heiland fällt vor seinem Vater nieder. Dadurch erhebt er mich und alle*)

23. Aria: "Gladly will I submit myself" (*Gerne will ich mich bequemen*)

34. Arioso: "My Jesus remains silent before the falsehoods" (*Mein Jesus schweigt zu falschen Lügen stille*)

35. Aria: "Patience! When the false tongues sting me" (*Geduld! Wenn mich falsche Zungen stechen*)

42. Aria: "Give me back my Jesus!" (*Gebt mir meinen Jesum wieder!*)
49. Aria: "My savior will die out of love" (*Aus Liebe will mein Heiland sterben*)
52. Aria: "If the tears on my cheeks can achieve nothing" (*Können Tränen meiner Wangen nichts erlangen*)
56. Arioso "Yes, the flesh and blood in us is willing" (*Ja, freilich will in uns das Fleisch und Blut*)
57. Aria: "Come, sweet cross . . . help me to carry it myself" (*Komm, süßes Kreuz . . . so hilfst du mir es selber tragen*)
60. Aria with chorus: "Behold, Jesus has extended His hand to take hold of us" (*Sehet, Jesus hat die Hand uns zu fassen ausgespannt*)
65. Aria: "Cleanse yourself, my heart" (*Mache dich, mein Herze, rein*)

The case for theology as the overriding factor in the choice of the aria and arioso movements is certainly not airtight. Some of the movements could, in fact, easily fit into multiple categories: *Gebt mir meinen Jesum wieder,* for example, could conceivably be seen as either elaboration on the narrative (describing, in this case, Judas' throwing down of the thirty silver pieces) or Pietistic reflection, as could *Aus Liebe will mein Heiland sterben* and *Mache dich, mein Herze, rein.* Theological concerns also cannot unequivocally explain the deletion of *Blute nur* (no. 8), an aria that clearly builds on the betrayal narrative ("Ah, a child that you raised, that nursed at your breast, threatens to murder its guardian"). (In this case, length may have been a factor, since Mendelssohn cut all of the Passion's *da capo* arias, except no. 6, *Buß und Reu,* which he shortened.) Indeed, Mendelssohn most likely reflected on many factors when making his choices for the aria and arioso cuts, and while theology may not have been the paramount issue in every case, it certainly seems to have been a consideration.

OTHER PERFORMANCES OF THE *ST. MATTHEW PASSION*

Following the Berlin revival, numerous performances of the Passion took place throughout Germany, with the vast majority of conductors adopting Mendelssohn's changes. In terms of content, the third 1829 Berlin performance under Zelter, Johann Theodor Mosewius's 1830 performance in Breslau, and an 1835 Berlin performance (most likely under Zelter's successor at the Singakademie, Carl Friedrich Rungenhagen) were identical to Mendelssohn's, while an 1844 Berlin performance (also probably under Rungenhagen) reinstated the arioso *Wiewohl, mein Herz in Tränen schwimmt* as its only change. Two other Berlin performances, in 1830 and 1831 (probably under Zelter), also observed Mendelssohn's cuts precisely but reorganized the work's two parts so that the no. 27b chorus "Has lightning, has thunder vanished in the clouds?" (*Sind Blitze, sind Donner in Wolken verschwunden?*) became the new, highly dramatic finale to Part I, and the chorale fantasy "O man, bewail your great sin" (*O Mensch bewein dein Sünde groß*) replaced the aria "Ah, now my Jesus is gone" (*Ach, nun ist mein Jesus hin*) as the opening for Part II.[44]

That so many conductors—all of whom were Christians, and only some of whom had any personal or professional association with Mendelssohn—chose to follow the example Mendelssohn set in his performances furthers the likelihood that his primary editorial concern was pleasing his audience, and not, as Marissen suggests, protecting the Jewish image. Of these performances, Zelter's are the most significant, since his anti-Semitic leanings—even with regard to his favorite pupil—are well documented in his letters of October 21, 1821, and November 2, 1830, to his close friend, the eminent poet Johann Wolfgang von Goethe:

> Tomorrow morning I'm traveling with my Doris and a lively twelve-year-old boy, my student, the son of Herr Mendelssohn, . . . a good, attractive boy, sprightly and obedient. He is, to be sure, the son of a Jew, but not a Jew [himself]. The father, with great sacrifice, did not allow his sons to be circumcised and has raised them properly; it would be a truly rare thing (*eppes Rores* [mock-Yiddish]) if the son of a Jew were to become an artist.[45]

> Felix is probably in Rome now, about which I am very happy, since his mother was always against Italy, where she perhaps feared that the last skin of Judaism would be stripped off him.[46]

Given his condescending attitude, it seems likely that Zelter would have reedited the Passion for his Good Friday performance, or even forbidden Mendelssohn to produce the work in the first place, had he felt that his pupil was operating under some kind of hidden, philo-Semitic agenda.

Among the other (Christian) conductors to direct the Passion in Germany in the wake of the Berlin revival were two who, working independently of Mendelssohn, not only made most of the same cuts he did, but pruned the work still further: Johann Nepomuk Schelble, who performed the work on May 29, 1829, in Frankfurt, and Karl Heinrich Sämann, who directed the work on May 1, 1832, in Königsberg (Kaliningrad).[47] (Although Schelble was a long-time friend of Mendelssohn's and likely obtained his copy of the Passion score by copying Felix's, he had begun planning a performance of the work at least as early as February 1827; Sämann does not appear to have had any contact with Mendelssohn.[48]) The majority of the additional cuts made by these two conductors were to the gospel narrative, some of which appear to have been justified by applying Mendelssohn's philosophy with greater rigor. For although Mendelssohn based most of his editorial decisions on either approachability or because he believed certain passages to be of little dramatic or theological significance, he never did anything categorically—there were always exceptions. This tended not to be the case with Schelble and Sämann. For example, while Mendelssohn readily removed repetitive passages such as the mob's second call for Barabbas, or the first of two descriptions of the search for false witnesses, he was keenly aware of the theological necessity of leaving Jesus' three pleas for God's mercy at Gethsemane intact. Schelble, on the other hand, deleted the third plea, while Sämann removed both the first and the third. Likewise, while Mendelssohn deleted what he believed to be theologically or dramatically insignificant references to women throughout the passion narrative, he left Mary Magdalene's appearance in no. 4 in place, probably because it sparks Judas' betrayal. Sämann, however, removed all the references to women, including this one.

That these two Christian conductors, working independently, adapted Bach's work in a manner similar to that of Mendelssohn strongly suggests that Mendelssohn made editorial choices consistent with the expectations of his audience. But, significantly, Schelble's and Sämann's more systematic editorial policy also allowed them to remove segments that included anti-Semitic material, something the self-conscious Mendelssohn was unable to do.

The first and largest set of Sämann's and Schelble's additional deletions are the references to the betrayal of Jesus for money, a highly anti-Semitic theme in the passion narrative and one that reinforced long-entrenched stereotypes about Jews.[49] Both conductors removed references to this act, with Sämann cutting all of them and Schelble cutting all but one. The first and most significant reference to the betrayal and the payment appears in gospel recitative no. 7, which both directors cut in its entirety, but which Mendelssohn left fully intact.

Evangelist	*Evangelist*
Da ging hin der Zwölfen einer mit Namen Judas Ischarioth zu den Hohenpriestern und sprach:	Then went one of the twelve, who was called Judas Iscariot, to the high priests and said:
Judas	*Judas*
Was wollt ihr mir geben? Ich will ihn euch verraten.	What will you give me? I want to betray him to you.
Evangelist	*Evangelist*
Und sie boten ihm dreißig Silberlinge. Und von dem an suchte er Gelegenheit, daß er ihn verriete.	And they offered him thirty pieces of silver. And from then on he sought an opportunity to betray him.

Both Sämann and Schelble then edited gospel recitative no. 26 and removed the first of two references to the betrayer, as well as Jesus' description of the mob (i.e., Jews) as "the hands of sinners."

Evangelist	*Evangelist*
Und er kam und fand sie aber schlafend, und ihre Augen waren voll Schlafs. Und er ließ sie und ging abermal hin und betete zum drittenmal und redete dieselbigen Worte. Da kam er zu seinen Jüngern und sprach zu ihnen:	And he came and again found them sleeping, and their eyes were heavy with sleep. And he left them and went away again and prayed for the third time, and said the same words. Then he came to his disciples and said to them:
[deleted by Sämann only]	

Jesus
~~Ach! wollt ihr nun schlafen und ruhen?~~
~~Siehe, die Stunde ist hie, daß des~~
~~Menschen Sohn in der Sünder Hände~~
~~überantwortet wird. Stehet auf, lasset uns~~
~~gehen; siehe, er ist da, der mich verrät.~~
[deleted by Sämann and Schelble]

Jesus
~~Ah! Do you wish to sleep and rest now?~~
~~Behold, the hour is at hand that the~~
~~Son of Man will be turned over to the~~
~~hands of sinners. Arise, let us~~
~~go; behold, he who betrays me is here.~~

Evangelist
Und als er noch redete, siehe, da kam
Judas, der Zwölfen Einer, und mit ihm
eine große Schar, mit Schwertern und mit
Stangen von den Hohenpriestern und
Ältesten des Volks. Und der Verräter
hatte ihnen ein Zeichen gegeben und
gesagt: "Welchen ich küssen werde, der
ist's, den greifet."

Evangelist
And as he was still speaking, behold, Judas
came, one of the twelve, and with him
a great crowd with swords and with
clubs, from the high priests and
the elders of the people. And the betrayer
had given them a sign and
said: "The one I shall kiss,
it is he, seize him."

While a second reference to the betrayer (*Verräter*) remains in Sämann's and Schelble's final versions, it is quick and fleeting, as it appears in the middle of an extended statement from the Evangelist. The first reference, however, stands out prominently, as it appears at the cadence of Jesus' solo, where he sings the word "betrays" (*verrät*) on a strongly accented appoggiatura (ex. 2.1).

Sämann alone removed the entire final recitative that refers to betrayal in the Passion (no. 41a–c), in which Judas expresses his remorse and returns the thirty silver pieces. This particular mention of the betrayal and payment is perhaps the most offensive of the three, as it establishes the Jewish authorities as the real criminals of the passion story and acknowledges their payment of blood money (*Blutgeld*) to Judas.

Judas
Ich habe übel getan, daß ich unschuldig
Blut verraten habe.

Judas
I have sinned, for I have betrayed
innocent blood.

Evangelist
Sie sprachen:

Evangelist
They said:

Chorus
Was gehet uns das an, da siehe du zu!

Chorus
What is that to us? See to it yourself!

Evangelist
Und er warf die Silberlinge in
den Tempel, hub sich davon, ging hin,
und erhängete sich selbst. Aber die
Hohenpriester nahmen die Silberlinge
und sprachen:

Evangelist
And he threw down the pieces of silver in
the temple, departed, went
and hanged himself. But the
high priests took the pieces of silver
and said:

Pontifex 1, 2
Es taugt nicht, daß wir sie in den
Gotteskasten legen, denn es ist Blutgeld.

High Priests 1, 2
It is not lawful for us to put them into the
sacred treasury, for it is blood money.

EXAMPLE 2.1. St. Matthew Passion (*Bach original*), no. 26, mm. 13–15

More significant than Schelble's and Sämann's removal of these references to the betrayal is the latter's deletion of the scene that includes chorus 50d, "His blood be upon us and our children" (*Sein Blut komme über uns und unsre Kinder*). This scene (no. 50a–e), beginning with the mob's cry for Jesus' crucifixion and ending with the Jews' acceptance of responsibility for Jesus' death in perpetuity, is, without question, the most anti-Semitic of any in the passion narratives.[50] Sämann's deletion and Mendelssohn's retention of this scene are revealing on a number of interrelated fronts. The fact that Mendelssohn did not delete the scene removes the possibility that his editorial choices were based on a desire to eliminate the Passion's anti-Semitic content. Surely, were that his intent, he would have begun here. Furthermore, had he wished to make such a cut, Sämann's version demonstrates that he could have done so without damaging the structure of the work, both from a narrative standpoint (the first call for the crucifixion remains, which ties the sections around it together) and a musical one (the section is tonally closed, beginning and ending in e minor).

Schelble's and Sämann's removal of these passages does not, of course, indicate that they were purposely attempting to purge anti-Semitic content from their *St. Matthew Passion* performances. But their motivation does not concern us here. Of import is their demonstration that such passages were indeed removable, and that, based on contemporary reviews, their removal went completely unnoticed.[51] Indeed, that Mendelssohn reduced the work in so many other ways raises the question as to why he did not—at the very least—delete the most overt anti-Semitic references, namely, the betrayal of Jesus by a Jew for money and the *Sein Blut* chorus.

Why did Sämann and Schelble make these cuts and not Mendelssohn? In a word, exposure. While Christian-born conductors could make such deletions without so much as a raised eyebrow from the public, Mendelssohn—who, as we saw in the introduction and preceding chapter, faced the same (if not greater) suspicion as most *Neuchristen* of having lingering ties to Judaism—could have faced accusations that he had removed these sections in order to make the Passion more "Jewish-friendly," or that he harbored some other philo-Semitic agenda. Indeed, Mendelssohn may have felt that removing the *Sein Blut* chorus would have left him particularly vulnerable to such accusations, not only because of the text's central position in anti-Jewish and anti-Semitic rhetoric but also because of the importance accorded it in

EXAMPLE 2.2. *Graun,* Der Tod Jesu, *no. 12, mm. 1–12 (the* Sein Blut *arioso) and textual excerpts from the entire recitative.*

Jerusalem voll Mordlust
ruft mit wildem Thon:
"Sein Blut komm über uns,
und unsre Söhn' und Töchter!"

Jerusalem, filled with murderous desire,
cries with furious tone:
"His blood be upon us,
and our sons and daughters!"

EXAMPLE 2.2. (*continued*)

Du siegst Jerusalem,	You are victorious, Jerusalem,
und Jesus blutet schon;	and Jesus bleeds already;
in Purpur ist er schon	in purple is he already subject
des Volkes Hohngelächter. . . .	of the people's derision. . . .
Des Mitleids Stimme,	The voice of compassion, from
von Richtstuhl des Tyrannen, spricht:	the tyrant's judgment seat, speaks:
"Seht, welch ein Mensch!"	"Behold the man!"
Und Juda hört sie nicht,	And Judah does not hear it,
und legt dem blutenden	and lays upon the bloody one—
mit unerhörtem Grimme den Balken auf,	with unheard of wrath—the beams
woran er langsam sterben soll.	on which he will slowly die.

the work traditionally performed at Passiontide in Berlin, Graun's *Der Tod Jesu.* There, in the midst of a highly anti-Semitic recitative, Graun not only repeats the text several times, he gives it added prominence by setting it as an arioso (ex. 2.2). Graun's work (completed in 1755) is fairly typical of passion settings of the classical and early romantic eras, in that it is only loosely based on the gospel narratives, which enables it (and other passion oratorios from these periods) to be significantly more anti-Semitic than the New Testament itself. Indeed, these works were no doubt instrumental in establishing the anti-Semitic tradition in nineteenth-century oratorio, a tradition that, for the time being at least, Mendelssohn felt incapable of challenging.

Moses

For you have been rebellious against the Lord for as long as I have known you.

—*Deuteronomy 9:24, as quoted in Mendelssohn's* Moses *libretto*

Aᴅᴏʟꜰ ʙᴇʀɴʜᴀʀᴅ ᴍᴀʀx first considered composing a work based on the subject of Moses and the Exodus at the age of fifteen, but was unable to find the time and means to tackle what he called his "old pet project" until 1832—seventeen years later. This new effort would not, however, be the two-part opera he envisioned in his youth, but rather a piece that would "have the outward form of an oratorio, and the Bible would have to provide the text." That summer, he confided this new oratorio plan to his friend of many years Felix Mendelssohn Bartholdy, who in response mentioned that he too was planning an oratorio based on biblical texts. Marx excitedly replied, "That is a wonderful coincidence! . . . I was afraid that the business of looking for the text would take away the freshness from composing; now we are both saved. You put my libretto together for me, and I will do yours for you, and we shall both have a fresh start with our work." Mendelssohn happily agreed, despite some opposition from Marx when he requested a text on St. Paul, and quickly began assembling the libretto that was to catalyze the destruction of their friendship.[1]

The work on the libretto for Marx's oratorio *Mose* began as something of a joint effort, with Marx having already laid out an overall plan for the oratorio (Text I in table 3.1) and begun construction of a prose draft (Text II). Once Mendelssohn agreed to take on the project, Marx handed these materials over; Mendelssohn then used them in writing the libretto he called *Moses* (Text IV), a copy of which he delivered to Marx sometime after its August 21, 1832, completion date. (In the interest of clarity, *Moses* will here refer to the libretto Mendelssohn assembled for Marx, and *Mose* to Marx's finished oratorio.) But although Mendelssohn carefully modeled his libretto after Marx's own partially completed draft and covered most of the points listed in Marx's overall plan, Marx was greatly disappointed:

Now I held in my hands the text which my comrade in art assembled for me.

As I read it through and read it again, I felt as though I was thunderstruck.

"This, this then is *Mose!* of which you have for so long dreamed . . . and now

TABLE 3.1. The *Moses* Texts

Text	Library Sigla	Author(s)	Date	Comments
I	GB-Ob MS. M. Deneke Mendelssohn d. 30, no. 216a, fol. 413v	Marx, Mendelssohn	ca. early 1832	A hastily written, often illegible outline of the three-part work in Marx's hand. Mendelssohn later added some biblical citations to Part III.
II	GB-Ob MS. M. Deneke Mendelssohn d. 30, no. 216a, fol. 412r–416v (except 413v)	Marx, Mendelssohn	ca. July 1832	A prose libretto draft begun by Marx, and edited and completed by Mendelssohn. Marx had written up to and including the beginning of Part II before turning the draft over to Mendelssohn.
III	GB-Ob MS. M. Deneke Mendelssohn d. 30, no. 216a, fol. 411r–411v	Mendelssohn	ca. August 1832	Mendelssohn's first attempt to write a presentation copy of the libretto; aborted after the first scene of Part I. The text is nearly identical to that in Text IV.
IV	D-Bsb MA MS 76	Mendelssohn	August 21, 1832	Final libretto. The manuscript appears to have been a presentation copy, but Mendelssohn made some last-minute changes. He then wrote out a pristine copy for Marx (now lost).*

*Detailed descriptions and complete transcriptions of all these texts are available in Sposato, "The Price," 1:146–52, 2:7–46. The final version of the libretto has also been published (albeit with minor errors) in Kellenberger, "Mendelssohn als Librettist," 127–33.

you stand cold, emotionless before it! no heartbeat quickens for it, no vision dawns!"

I felt, with true terror, that I could not compose the work. . . . Finally, though, I had to say to myself that . . . I would have to let the text fall. . . .

Now it was clear to me how far our separate ways had drifted apart, my friend and I. Certainly, . . . he had worked for me with loyalty and total conviction. He created the text as before us so many had been created, and as had been accepted by the greatest masters without reservation. The combination of narrative, lyrical outpouring, and dramatic elements was the standard form of Handel and Bach; our favorite work, the [Bach] *St. Matthew Passion*, had the same design. Mendelssohn, therefore, was completely beyond reproach. If someone was deserving of reproach, it was I. Why had I neglected or been unable to clearly show him the new form that was so important to me?[2]

Marx continued by explaining that this "new form" centered around a sense of "living realism" (*lebendiger Wahrhaftigkeit*), which attempted to bring oratorio as close to opera as possible. (Indeed, Gebhard von Alvensleben, a critic writing about the 1841 Breslau [Wrocław] premiere of *Mose* for the *Neue Zeitschrift für Musik*, described the piece as "a new star" in the history of the oratorio, with music so dramatic that one could easily envision "the changing of the scenes and people entering and exiting," and which—to his excitement—contained no narration or "delays from little moments of feeling."[3])

Mendelssohn must have been equally disappointed by Marx's decision not to use his libretto, especially given the pride Mendelssohn evinced in the work (referring to it in his letters to Karl Klingemann as a "beautiful" text with which he was "exceptionally pleased").[4] Indeed, Mendelssohn's dismay at Marx's rejection presents itself unmistakably on the former's copy of the libretto, whose cover page bears the inscription "*Moses | componiert | von | A. B. Marx*," with the deletions so thorough as to make the underlying text barely readable.[5]

With Marx's rejection of the *Moses* libretto began a slow but steady breakdown in the relationship between the two composers, with written evidence of a change in Mendelssohn's attitude (in addition to the dedication page alterations) appearing as early as an August 1834 letter to Julius Schubring, in which Mendelssohn noted for the first time that he "exceedingly disapprove[d]" of Marx's compositions.[6] The libretto was as much of a turning point in the relationship for Marx, who later proclaimed it the source of their "inner division."[7] Like Mendelssohn, Marx was now convinced that the two were destined to pursue different compositional paths, with the libretto itself serving as the final conclusive proof.

In the years that followed, Marx and Mendelssohn maintained the outward appearance of friends and continued to meet whenever Mendelssohn visited Berlin.[8] But this superficial display came to an abrupt end in 1839, when Marx approached Mendelssohn, the newly completed *Mose* in hand, to ask him to perform the work. Marx's widow, Therese, later recounted the incident:

> It was now, 1839, when Marx was finally able to realize the dream of his youth, which he had carried with him his entire life. With jubilant, high spirits, he wrote his oratorio, *Mose*. His first thought after its completion was of his friend. He alone could help pave the way into the world for this child born of such painful labor.
>
> Filled with hope and anticipation, Marx traveled to Leipzig and visited Mendelssohn. If he performed his work there, then—as Marx, perhaps wrongly, but definitely assumed—success was assured.[9]
>
> With the plea: Help me, my work is finished, he approached his friend.
>
> Both sat down at the piano and Marx played and sang the first part of the work from the score.
>
> After completing it, Mendelssohn rose and said coolly: "Don't be angry with me, but there is nothing I can do for this work."
>
> Marx, his hopes dashed, his confidence injured, did not waste another word; he closed the score and left. . . .
>
> Marx returned from this failure very cross. The hopes, which he had set at first solely upon Mendelssohn's help were destroyed, the last bond of friend-

ship broken. For a long time this pain echoed in him; in fact he never got over it for the rest of his life.[10]

Shortly after Marx returned from Leipzig, he and Therese went for a walk in Berlin's Tiergarten, where from the Marschallsbrücke he tossed a packet full of Mendelssohn's letters into the water.[11]

As Marx's memoirs and Mendelssohn's comments to Schubring suggest, the two composers had built their relationship around the understanding that they comprehended and respected each other's styles and goals and could therefore go through life as professional partners, each helping the other as need be. With Marx's rejection of the *Moses* libretto, however, both men began to suspect that this mutual comprehension and respect did not really exist, a situation that chilled their relationship and finally led to Mendelssohn's total withdrawal of support from Marx.

The documents cannot be telling the whole story, however. For in Marx's account of his dissatisfaction with Mendelssohn's libretto he never mentioned that he himself had written a great deal of the first two of the oratorio's three parts (thereby establishing a model for Mendelssohn to emulate). In fact, Marx's prose draft (Text II) contained most of Part I (Moses' call to service)—with some segments left blank where inspiration had not yet struck him—and the beginning of Part II (Moses and Pharaoh). Consider the following examples:

Marx's prose draft (Text II), fol. 414r

Mose aber hütete die Schafe Jethor, seines Schwähers, des Priesters in Midian, und trieb die Schafe hinein in die Wüste und kam an den Berg Horeb. Und der Engel des Herrn erschien ihm in einer feurigen Flamme aus dem Busch. Und er sahe, daß der Busch mit Feuer brannte und ward nicht verzehrt. Und sprach: ich will dahin und besehn dies große Gesicht, warum der Busch nicht verbrennet.	Now Moses was keeping the flock of Jethro, his father-in-law, the priest of Midian; and he led his flock into the wilderness, and came to mount Horeb. And the angel of the Lord appeared to him in a fiery flame out of a bush. And he saw that the bush burned with fire and was not consumed. And said: I will go and see this great sight, why the bush does not burn up.
Da aber der Herr sahe, daß er hinging zu sehen, rief ihm Gott aus dem Busch und sprach: Mose! Mose!	When the Lord saw that he went to see, God called to him out of the bush and said: Moses! Moses!
Er antwortete: Hier bin ich.	He answered: Here I am.
Er sprach: Tritt nicht herzu, ziehe deine Schuhe aus von deinen Füßen, denn der Ort darauf du stehest, ist ein heiliges Land.	He said: Do not come near; remove your shoes from your feet, for the place on which you stand is holy ground.
Und sprach weiter: ich bin der Gott deiner Väter.	And he spoke further: I am the God of your fathers.

Mendelssohn's final text (Text IV), p. 4

Mose aber hütete die Schafe Jethor, seines Schwähers und trieb die Schafe tiefer hinein in die Wüste und kam an den Berg Gottes Horeb. Und er sahe[,] daß der Busch mit Feuer brannte und ward doch nicht verzehrt. Und er sprach: Ich will dahin und besehn dies große Gesicht, warum der Busch nicht verbrennet?	Now Moses was keeping the flock of Jethro, his father-in-law and he led his flock deeper into the wilderness, and came to Horeb, the mount of God. And he saw that the bush burned with fire and was not consumed. And he said: I will go and see this great sight, why the bush does not burn up?
Da aber der Herr sahe, daß er hinging zu sehn, rief ihm Gott aus dem Busch und sprach: Mose, Mose!	When the Lord saw that he went to see, God called to him out of the bush and said: Moses! Moses!
Er antwortete: Hier bin ich.	He answered: Here I am.
Er sprach: Ich bin der Gott deiner Väter.	He said: I am the God of your fathers.

As the partial transcription of the libretto draft in the first example reveals, the narrative formula that Marx complained of in his memoirs—complete with extensive scenic descriptions and monologue prefaces such as "He said" (*Er sprach*)—stands at the core of his own draft's structure. In assembling *his* version of the libretto, Mendelssohn followed this model, elaborating upon some of Marx's less-developed ideas before writing a coherent text for Part II and sketches for Part III (the journey in the wilderness). As the second example shows, even in his final libretto Mendelssohn continued to use Marx's original text as much as possible, probably out of concern for offending his friend by overcorrecting his work.

In addition to not acknowledging that Mendelssohn had followed his example in assembling a *Moses* libretto, and despite his complaints about Mendelssohn's final product, in the end Marx did not, as he claimed, "let the text fall." Indeed, a comparison between Mendelssohn's *Moses* text and the one Marx eventually set in his oratorio *Mose* demonstrates that Marx continued to incorporate a considerable amount of Mendelssohn's libretto, especially those passages in which Mendelssohn used text from outside the Exodus narrative. To cite a single example for the moment, a comparison of the Egyptian persecution-song (*Spottlied*) in *Mose* with the passage Mendelssohn took from Lamentations 2:16 for the same episode in his libretto clearly indicates that Marx did not find this passage on his own.

Mendelssohn, *Moses* Text IV, p. 2

Knabenchor	*Boys Chorus*
Hah! Wir haben sie vertilgt! Das ist der Tag, deß wir haben begehrt. Wir haben es erlangt, wir haben es erlebt.	Hah! We have destroyed them! This is the day we have longed for. We have reached it, we have lived it!

Marx, *Mose*, no. 4

Ein Aegypter	*An Egyptian*
Das ist der Tag, deß wir haben begehret!	This is the day we have longed for!
Wir haben es erlangt, wir haben es erlebt:	We have reached it, we have lived it:
sie sind niedergestürzt und gefallen!	they have been cast down and have fallen!
wir aber stehen aufgerichtet!	but we remain upright!

(This fact in itself could explain Mendelssohn's reaction to *Mose* when Marx requested a performance: there before him was much of the text Marx had supposedly rejected, now being appropriated without permission or credit!) Even Marx's stated excuse for abandoning Mendelssohn's libretto raises doubts, since transforming a responsorial narrative into a dramatic one would not have been excessively difficult—certainly not difficult enough to warrant starting from scratch. Therefore, something else about the libretto must have bothered Marx.

CHRISTOLOGY, ANTI-SEMITISM, AND *MOSES*

In his biography, Eric Werner proposed one possible explanation to the question of why Marx objected to Mendelssohn's libretto: that Marx, an "eager convert" to Lutheranism, felt *Moses* had "a strictly Old Testament flavor, with which Marx did not wish to identify himself as he desired a more christological interpretation" (i.e., one that revealed Moses' relevance to Christianity).[12] But as even a quick perusal of the text reveals, *Moses* clearly is Christological—indeed, a great deal more so than Marx's *Mose* or the numerous other oratorios written around this time on this most important and symbolic of prophets.[13] One of the most obvious examples of this appears in the transition between the first two scenes of Part I. Here, just before God calls Moses to service, two angels announce the people's coming *redemption* (*Erlösung*)—not just physical salvation—in a manner clearly reminiscent of, and using text similar to, the angel's annunciation to the shepherds of Christ's birth.

Moses Text IV, p. 3–4

Zwei Engel	*Two Angels*
Fürchte dich nicht! Denn ich habe dich	Fear not! For I have redeemed you,
erlöset, ich habe dich bei deinem Namen	I have called you by name;
gerufen; du bist mein!	you are mine!

Luke 2:10–11

Fürchtet euch nicht; . . . Denn euch ist	Fear not; . . . For today is born to you the
heute der Heiland geboren, welcher ist	savior, who is Christ the Lord, in the city
Christus der Herr, in der Stadt Davids.	of David.

Mendelssohn continues to strengthen this image of Moses as a kind of Old Testament Christ in Part III by having him experience and perform various Christlike acts, building mostly on text taken from outside the Exodus narrative. Among the many examples are an attempted stoning (in which the crowd cries out an obvious adaptation of Jn. 19:15); the betrayal of Moses by his closest "disciples," Aaron and Miriam; and Moses' attempt to take the sins of the people upon himself at the close of the work.

Moses Text IV, p. 12, adapted from Nu. 14:5,9; Jn. 19:15

Mose aber und Aaron fielen auf ihr Angesicht vor der ganzen Versammlung und sprachen: Fallet nicht ab vom Herrn, der Herr ist mit uns. Fürchtet Euch nicht.	But Moses and Aaron fell on their faces before the entire assembly and said: Do not abandon the Lord, the Lord is with us. Fear not.
Chor. Weg, weg mit denen. Steinigt sie! [*cf.* Jn. 19:15–Weg, weg mit dem! Kreuzige ihn!]	*Chorus.* Away, away with them. Stone them! [*cf.* Jn. 19:15–Away, away with him! Crucify him!]

Moses Text IV, p. 12, adapted from Nu. 12:1–3

Und Mirjam und Aaron redeten wider Mose und sprachen: Redet denn der Herr allein durch Mosen? Redet er nicht auch durch uns?	And Miriam and Aaron spoke against Moses and said: Does the Lord only speak through Moses? Does He not also speak through us?

Moses Text IV, p. 15, adapted from Ex. 32:31–33, 34:6; Dt. 9:18; Nu. 14:20

Da wandte sich Mose und fiel nieder vor dem Herrn und sprach:	Then Moses turned and fell before the Lord and said:
[*Mose:*] Ach das Volk hat eine große Sünde gethan, und haben sich goldne Götter gemacht. Nun vergieb ihnen ihre Sünde, wo nicht so tilge mich auch aus deinem Buche, das du geschrieben hast.	[*Moses:*] Oh, this people have sinned a great sin, and have made for themselves gods of gold. Now forgive their sin—if not, blot me out of your book that you have written.
Der Herr aber sprach zu Mose: Was? Ich will den tilgen aus meinem Buch, der an mir sündigt.	But the Lord said to Moses: What? I will blot out of my book those who have sinned against me.
Mose: Ach vergieb ihnen ihre Sünde, Herr, Herr Gott, barmherzig und gnädig und geduldig und von großer Gnade und Treue. Und fiel vor dem Herrn nieder vierzig Tage und vierzig Nächte.	*Moses:* Oh, forgive their sin, Lord, Lord God, compassionate and merciful and patient and filled with mercy and faithfulness. And he fell before the Lord for forty days and forty nights.
Und der Herr sprach: Ich habe vergeben, wie du gesagt hast.	And the Lord said: I have forgiven, as you have said.

Significantly, Mendelssohn's design of *Moses* as an intensely Christological work, while allowing him to portray his protagonist in a manner reminiscent of Christ, simultaneously necessitated that the Jews be portrayed as they are in the New Testament—in a predominantly negative light.[14] Moreover, Mendelssohn's depiction of the Jews tied into several common nineteenth-century anti-Semitic stereotypes, including representations of them as greedy, slothful, and dependent on other peoples; as adhering to a religion based on sometimes barbaric ritual; and as a people incapable of true faith.[15]

The image of the Jews as lazy, parasitic, and obsessed with wealth might seem anachronistic in an era of emancipation, but the lifting of the laws and trade monopolies that restricted Jews to certain occupations (such as the handling of money and the trade and sale of goods) could hardly have been expected to cause an instantaneous transformation in the concentration of Jews in those occupations. Nevertheless, in the first half of the nineteenth century, numerous authors used the concentration of Jews in certain trades to substantiate their anti-Semitic rhetoric, which often accused the Jews of being too lazy to take on strenuous work, such as agriculture. As a result, these writers claimed, the Jews functioned as parasites, living off the hard work of the citizens of the lands in which they took up residence. As Christoph Heinrich Pfaff wrote in his 1819 essay, *On the Relationship between Christian Governments and States and the Jews at the Present Time* (*Über das Verhältnis christlicher Regierungen und Staaten gegen die Juden in dem gegenwärtigen Zeitpuncte*), the Jews were "a caste of tradesmen and hawkers who shun every serious and strenuous work, agriculture and handicraft." This commonly held belief—combined with the prevailing view of the Jews as existing as a separate state within their adopted homeland—led Pfaff and his contemporaries to liken the Jews to "a rapidly growing parasitic plant that winds round the still healthy tree to suck up the life juice until the trunk, emaciated and eaten up from within, falls moldering into decay."[16]

Moses' mention of animal sacrifices and burnt offerings would have resonated especially strongly with nineteenth-century anti-Semitic stereotypes, considering the long-held belief by many Christians that Judaism was a religion based on empty ceremony[17] and that Jews themselves engaged in a secret ritual that involved the sacrifice of a Christian child and the drinking of his or her blood. Belief in this ritual (known as the "blood libel") was particularly prevalent during the Middle Ages, but was hardly confined to it. Accusations of ritual murder resurfaced throughout Germany in the early nineteenth century and were particularly numerous in the predominantly Catholic Rhineland, with a total of eleven cases being reported there before the century's end. In truth, the "sacrifices" were usually children who died as a result of sexual abuse at the hands of non-Jews; in order to cover their tracks, those responsible would claim to have found the body, a victim of ritual murder. Such accusations often had disastrous consequences for the Jewish community. In several cases during the first half of the century, purported child killings were followed by violent pogroms, including those in the Rhineland in 1819 (shortly after the Hep-Hep riots in other parts of Germany) and 1834, and that in Höchberg bei Würzburg in the 1830s.[18]

The ideology that the Jews were not merely a faithless people, but, in fact, the enemies of God—because of their suspected association with magic, the devil, and especially the Antichrist—was another widely held belief from the Middle Ages that found new life in the nineteenth century, especially during the Napoleonic wars. As Napoleon's forces swept through Europe, depictions of him as the Antichrist (who since the folk legends of the Middle Ages was believed would come from Jewish lineage) became more and more commonplace. This association, and the connection of contemporary Jews to it, solidified further in 1806, when Napoleon assembled the "Great Sanhedrin," a council based on the ancient Israeli high court, to govern Jewish affairs in newly emancipated France.[19]

While Mendelssohn may not have consciously intended to invoke the full depth of these stereotypes, their appearance throughout the *Moses* libretto demonstrates a distinct lack of concern on his part for the safety of the Jewish image, something also visible (as shall be seen in the next chapter) in his oratorio *Paulus*, on which he had begun work a few months before composing the *Moses* libretto. Granted, the image of the Jews presented in the Exodus story is not exactly flattering; but as was the case with most of the elements he used to make *Moses* Christological, Mendelssohn also imported negative imagery from outside the Exodus narrative, an act that demonstrates definite intent. Furthermore, a comparison of these narrative segments in Mendelssohn's text to those same segments as finally set in Marx's *Mose*—where the Jews are treated more sympathetically—helps to place these images in sharp relief.[20] As I shall argue, in fact, Marx's disappointment with Mendelssohn's text was rooted precisely in *Moses'* unflattering portrayal of the Jews and stemmed from the very different relationship the two composers had with their shared Jewish heritage.

As he did with the Christological content of *Moses*, Mendelssohn concentrated negative imagery regarding the Jews in Part III, but elements of it appear as early as the second scene of Part I. Here, during the conversation between God and Moses, Moses comments on the doubting quality of his people: "Moses answered [God] and said: See, they will not believe me, but instead will say: the Lord has not appeared to you" (*Mose antwortete und sprach: Siehe, sie werden mir nicht glauben, sondern werden sagen: der Herr ist dir nicht erschienen* [Ex. 4:1]). At this point, rather than follow the Exodus narrative and have God empower Moses' staff to become a symbol of proof (Ex. 4:2–3, where the staff becomes a snake), Mendelssohn instead depicts God as confirming Moses' statement by incorporating text from Isaiah 43:8–9, "The Lord said: Let this blind people come forth, so that they may hear and say: it is the truth" (*Der Herr sprach: Laß hervortreten das blinde Volk, so wird man es hören und sagen: es ist die Wahrheit*).

Marx himself wrote Moses' statement "See, they will not believe me . . ." into his original libretto draft (Text II), but was apparently uncertain about it from the very beginning. At the time he gave his draft to Mendelssohn, he did not know how God should respond (and may even have been questioning whether to keep the statement at all), since after Moses speaks, Marx left a blank space—the only one on the page—between it and Moses' next complaint about his "heavy speech." When Mendelssohn completed the draft, he filled the space with God's call for "this blind people" to come forth. Marx, however, eventually decided against the entire passage. In no. 9 of *Mose*, the scene progresses from Moses asking for God's name, to his abdication ("My Lord, send whom You will"), skipping this segment and the slur against the Jews that accompanies it.

Near the opening of Part II of his libretto, Mendelssohn confirms Moses' doubts in the Israelites' faith. After Pharaoh throws Moses out of his chambers, he burdens the Israelites further, causing them to rise up against Moses and Aaron, almost exactly as occurs in the Exodus narrative (Ex. 5:19, 21).

Moses Text IV, p. 6–7

Und da die Kinder Israel sahen, daß es ärger ward, sprachen sie zu Mose und Aaron[:]	And when the children of Israel saw that they were in evil plight, they said to Moses and Aaron:
Chor. Der Herr sehe auf Euch und richte es; Ihr habt unsern Feinden das Schwert in die Hand gegeben, daß sie uns tödten.	*Chorus.* The Lord look upon you and judge; you have put a sword in the hand of our enemies, that they may kill us.

Marx's original draft contains this first encounter with Pharaoh, up to the instant in which Pharaoh orders more labor for the Israelites, at which point the draft ends. That Marx stopped at precisely this moment suggests that he was again unsure about how to proceed, since the next step should have been simple: the very next sentence, Exodus 5:21, contains the Israelites' reaction to this encounter, exactly as Mendelssohn wrote it when he completed the libretto. But Marx likely questioned the suitability of this text or he would have added it when he wrote the remainder of the scene. As before, then, Marx seems to have hesitated when on the brink of having to portray the Jews in a negative light. This hypothesis is borne out in *Mose* (nos. 13–14), where Marx carefully avoids this negative portrayal: he sends Moses and Aaron to Pharaoh accompanied by numerous representatives of the people, so as to prevent blame being placed solely on the prophet and his brother. Once Pharaoh throws them out, a chorus of Egyptians announces that their "days of celebration will be turned into days of mourning!" The people respond, "You [plural] have brought misfortune to us! Horror has befallen me!" The placement of the people's complaint immediately after the chorus of Egyptians (with no intervening statement from Moses) makes the subject of the complaint vague—it could be directed against either the Egyptians or the *group* who visited Pharaoh. If the latter, the attitude of the people is one of unhappiness and disappointment, but not rebellion.

As in this first encounter, Mendelssohn set the subsequent meetings between Moses and Pharaoh as they appear in Exodus, again presenting the Jews in a negative light. In these later encounters, the image changes from unbelieving to greedy and, occasionally, cultish. After the plagues commence, Pharaoh begins to make concessions, but Moses continues to ask for more. During the hailstorm, Pharaoh agrees to allow the Jews to make their offering to God "in the land," but Moses insists that they must offer to God in the desert. After the plague of darkness, Pharaoh agrees to let them leave, on the condition that they leave their sheep and cattle behind. Moses replies, "You must also give us sacrifices and burnt-offerings, so that we may sacrifice to our God the Lord" (*Du mußt uns auch Opfer und Brandopfer geben, das wir unserm Gott dem Herrn thun mögen;* Text IV, p. 8; Ex. 10:25). Here, the demand for offerings from Pharaoh not only portrays the Jews as dependent, but also invokes images of barbaric ritual.

Since Mendelssohn set the actual Exodus text here, he cannot be placed entirely at fault, but a comparison to Marx's setting demonstrates one possible alternative and suggests the very different concept Marx had of the prophet and his people, as well as the care he took to protect the Jewish image. Rather than set the Exodus text of Moses' final two meetings with Pharaoh verbatim, Marx chose not to include the first meeting (thus eliminating the repeated requests for assistance), and for the second (no. 20), he modified Moses' words both to create a more heroic character and to eliminate any of the anti-Semitic stereotypes reflected in the Exodus text.

Marx, Mose, no. 20

Pharao
Ziehet hin, ziehet hin! Vergebt mir meine
Sünde und dienet dem Herrn! Ziehet hin!

Pharaoh
Depart, depart! Forgive my
sin and serve the Lord! Depart!

Mose
Rüstet euch! Hebet euch auf, von
dannen!

Moses
Make ready! Rise up from
there!

Pharao
Allein—eure Heerden und Güter lasset
hier!

Pharaoh
Alone—leave your herds and goods
here!

Mose
Was unser ist, soll mit uns gehn; denn
von dem Unsern werden wir nehmen
zum Dienst unsers Gottes.

Moses
What is ours shall go with us; for
from what is ours shall we take
for the service of our God.

Here, rather than asking for (or even mentioning) offerings, Moses, in response to Pharaoh's demand that they leave their goods behind, instead forcefully announces that he and his people will take what is theirs—"What is ours shall go with us." Indeed, Marx's text even promotes an air of religious maturity and sophistication, with its allusion to the term *Gottesdienst* (the modern German word for a religious service) in Moses' declaration that the Israelites will use their possessions "for the service of our God" (*zum Dienst unsers Gottes*).[21]

The image of the Israelites as, if not cult-like, at least primitive reappears in Mendelssohn's libretto in the final chorus of Part II, with their polytheistically flavored question, "Lord, who is Your equal among the gods?"[22] By omitting the mention of other gods ("Who is Your equal, O Lord?"), Marx again eliminated such pagan overtones in his version of the final Part II chorus (no. 21), which otherwise uses most of Mendelssohn's text.

Mendelssohn, *Moses* Text IV, p. 10–11, emphasis added

Ich will dem Herrn singen, denn er hat eine herrliche That gethan. Roß und Wagen hat er ins Meer gestürzt. *Herr, wer ist dir gleich unter den Göttern?* Wer ist dir gleich, der so mächtig heilig, schrecklich, loblich und wunderthätig sei? Der Herr wird König sein immer und ewig.	I will sing to the Lord, for He has done a magnificent deed. Horse and wagon He has cast into the sea. *Lord, who is Your equal among the gods?* Who is Your equal, so mighty in holiness, terrible, glorious, and capable of wonders? The Lord shall be king for ever and ever.

Marx, *Mose*, no. 21, emphasis added

Sie sind niedergestürzt und gefallen! Wir aber stehen aufgerichtet!—*Wer ist dir gleich, O Herr?* so mächtig, so schrecklich, so wunderthätig, so heilig! —Ich will dem Herrn laut und fröhlich singen! Er hat fürwahr eine herrliche That gethan: Roß und Mann hat er ins Meer gestürzt! Herr ist sein Name.	They have been cast down and have fallen! But we remain upright!—*Who is Your equal, O Lord?* so mighty, so terrible, so capable of wonders, so holy! —I will sing loud and joyfully to the Lord! He has truly done a magnificent deed: Horse and man He has cast into the sea! Lord is his name.

Over the course of Mendelssohn's libretto, the image of the Jews steadily deteriorates to the point that Part III focuses entirely on their negative qualities. Marx, telling basically the same story, presents an image which, while not depicting the Jews as blameless, is far more positive and attempts to avoid common stereotypes, often by incorporating a modified version of Mendelssohn's text. For instance, Part III of *Moses* opens with an image of dependence and lack of faith, with the Israelites demanding water from Moses after three days in the wilderness ("Give us water so we may drink") and questioning the Lord's presence ("Is the Lord among us or not?"). Marx, on the other hand, opens Part III of *Mose* with two choruses of Israelites marching forth with confidence, one singing of their recognition of God's mercy to the righteous, and the other singing Psalm 114, "When Israel went out of Egypt."

Mendelssohn, *Moses* Text IV, p. 11–12

Da murrete das Volk wider Mose und sprach:	Then the people grumbled against Moses and said:
Chor. Was sollen wir trinken?	*Chorus.* What shall we drink?

Mose. Was zanket ihr mir? Warum versuchet ihr den Herrn?	*Moses.* Why do you scold me? Why do you test the Lord?
Chor. Gebt uns Wasser, daß wir trinken.	*Chorus.* Give us water so we may drink.
Und murreten noch lauter und sprachen:	And they grumbled still louder and said:
Chor. Warum hast du uns lassen aus Aegypten ziehn, daß du uns alle Durstes sterben ließest? Ist der Herr unter uns, oder nicht?	*Chorus.* Why have you allowed us to leave Egypt, only to allow us all to die of thirst? Is the Lord among us or not?
Mose schrie zum Herrn und sprach: Was soll ich mit dem Volke thun? Es fehlt nicht weit, sie werden mich noch steinigen.	Moses cried to the Lord and said: What shall I do with this people? They are almost ready to stone me.
Und Mirjam und Aaron redeten wider Mose und sprachen: Redet denn der Herr allein durch Mosen? Redet er nicht auch durch uns?	And Miriam and Aaron spoke against Moses and said: Does the Lord only speak through Moses? Does He not also speak through us?

Marx, *Mose,* no. 22

Die eine Schaar Nun merk' ich, daß der Herr dem Gerechten hilft und erhöret ihn in seinem heiligen Himmel. Seine Hand hilft gewaltig.	*First Group* Now I know that the Lord helps the righteous one and hears him in His holy heaven. His hand helps mightily.
Die andre Schaar Da Israel aus Aegypten zog, das Volk aus fremdem Volk: da ward Juda sein Heiligthum, Israel seine Herrschaft.	*Second Group* When Israel went out of Egypt, the people from a foreign people, Judah became His sanctuary, Israel his dominion.

As in Mendelssohn's libretto, the Israelites' dissatisfaction with their situation gradually begins to emerge in *Mose* as well, but at no time does Marx's text resonate with stereotypes of dependence or faithlessness. When the Jews complain of their thirst, Marx chooses the first of the two complaints used by Mendelssohn ("I am thirsty! what shall we drink?"), an expression of distress, but not a demand that someone obtain water for them. This same contrast between Mendelssohn's and Marx's text continues in the Israelites' complaint of hunger later in Part III: whereas Mendelssohn has them cry, "Give us meat, so we may eat," Marx simply has them shout, "Shall we all die of hunger?"

Marx continues to emphasize the Israelites' steadfast faith throughout Part III, even in the rebellion scene (nos. 24–26). After the complaint of thirst, tension eventually builds to the point that one of the Israelites, Korah, leads an uprising. But unlike Aaron and Miriam's rebellion in *Moses,* Korah's is against the authority Moses and

Aaron have assumed, not against God. In fact, when Moses accuses the people of "testing" and "murmuring against" God, Korah protests, "You have gone too far; for the entire congregation is holy." Marx then takes great care to retain this image of the Israelites' unyielding faith throughout the remainder of this segment of Part III by interspersing the episodes of discontent with arias from the faithful, such as the young boy's aria, "God the Lord is sun and shield," which appears immediately after the thirst complaint. Similarly, after an old man loses his strength, his daughter reassures him: "Be patient! be comforted, wait on the Lord and do not despair! He gives power to the faint, and ample strength to the powerless." When the old man succumbs to his fears once again, the young boy responds, "He has given His angels charge over you, that they may protect you on all your paths," before reprising his previous aria.

In *Moses*, on the other hand, when the prophet and Aaron appeal to the people not to fall away from God, they reply, "Away, away with them. Stone them!" Even the appearance of God's glory, which interrupts the attempted stoning, fails to make an impression. After the ground appears "like a beautiful sapphire and as the body of heaven, when it is clear," and Moses and Joshua depart to receive the commandments, in addition to failing to react to the event or to the falling of bread from heaven that follows, the people turn almost immediately to Aaron and instruct him to make them a new god.

Moses Text IV, p. 12–13, cross-outs original

Chor. Weg, weg mit denen. Steinigt sie!   *Chorus.* Away, away with them. Stone them!

Da erschien die Herrlichkeit des Herrn allen Kindern Israels; unter seinen Füßen war es wie ein schöner Saphir und wie die Gestalt des Himmels, wenn es klar ist. Und das Ansehn der Herrlichkeit des Herrn war wie ein verzehrend Feuer auf der Spitze des Berges. Und der Herr sprach zu Mose:	Then the glory of the Lord appeared to all the children of Israel; [the ground] under their feet was like a beautiful sapphire and as the body of heaven, when it is clear. And the appearance of the glory of the Lord was like a consuming fire on the peak of the mountain. And the Lord said to Moses:
Wie lange lästert mich das Volk? Und wie lange wollen sie nicht an mich glauben? Siehe, ich will euch Brod vom Himmel regnen lassen, und ihr sollt inne werden, daß ich der Herr, euer Gott bin.—Du Mose komm herauf zu mir auf den Berg, daß ich dir gebe meine Gebote, die du sie lehren sollst.	How long will the people blaspheme against me? And how long will they not believe in me? Behold, I will allow bread to rain from heaven for you, and they shall know that I am the Lord, your God.—You, Moses, come up to me on the mountain, so that I may give you my commandments, which you shall teach to them.
Da aber das Volk sahe, daß Mose und sein Diener Josua ~~vierzig Tage und~~	But when the people saw that Moses and his servant Joshua failed to return from the

~~vierzig Nächte~~ verzogen von dem Berg wieder zu kommen, sammelte es sich wider Aaron und sprach zu ihm:	mountain ~~for forty days and forty nights~~, they gathered together before Aaron and said to him:
Chor. Auf mache uns Götter, die vor uns hergehen. Denn wir wissen nicht, was diesem Mann Mose widerfahren ist, der uns aus Aegyptenland geführet hat.	*Chorus.* Arise, make us gods who shall go before us. For we do not know what has happened to this man Moses, who led us out of Egypt.
Und er machte ein gegossen Kalb.	And he made a molten calf.

As the editorial markings in the libretto demonstrate, the immediacy of the Israel-ites' fall is the result of a last minute deletion on Mendelssohn's part. Originally, Mendelssohn specified that Moses and Joshua did not return from the mountain for forty days and nights, after which the Israelites turned to Aaron for new leader-ship. Mendelssohn then intensified the sense of unfaithfulness by deleting this ref-erence before sending the final copy to Marx.

The episode of the golden calf represents the epitome of the negative treatment of the Jews in Mendelssohn's libretto, as well as the completion of Aaron and Miriam's Christologically charged betrayal of not just Moses, but also God. Mendelssohn took the calf scene from Exodus verbatim with two exceptions: the chorus of praise to the calf (which does not exist in the biblical account), and a fiery aria (below) for Moses following his destruction of the covenant tablets, a text Mendelssohn as-sembled from passages of Deuteronomy and Hosea (Dt. 32:6, 32:16–17; Hos. 8:7, 9:7; Dt. 9:24; Hos. 7:13).

Moses Text IV, p. 14, emphasis added

Dankest du also dem Herrn, deinen Gott, du toll und thörigt Volk? Durch Greu[e]l erzürnst du ihn? Den Feldteufeln opferst du und nicht deinem Gott? Ihr säet Wind und werdet Ungewitter einerndten, die Zeit der Heimsuchung ist gekommen, die Zeit der Vergeltung. *Denn ihr seid ungehorsam dem Herrn gewesen solange ich euch gekannt habe.* Wehe euch, ihr seid von ihm gewichen.	Do you thus thank the Lord, your God, you foolish and senseless people? With abominations do you provoke him to anger? You sacrifice to demons and not to your God? You sow wind, and shall reap the whirlwind, the time of punishment has come, the time of recompense. *For you have been rebellious against the Lord for as long as I have known you.* Woe to you, for you have strayed from him.

While the entire aria focuses on the faults of the Israelites, of particular interest is the inclusion of Deuteronomy 9:24, "For you have been rebellious against the Lord for as long as I have known you," the statement that, more than any other in the libretto, resonates with the stereotype of the Jews being incapable of true faith, and, even worse, declares that this has always been the case. Its presence here seems inevitable, however, since it summarizes the image of the Jews Mendelssohn has cultivated throughout the course of the oratorio. In fact, despite its harshness, Moses' accusation does little to change the Israelites' attitude. For even when Moses destroys the calf and God announces his "day of vengeance," the Israelites do not repent. Instead, Moses pleads for forgiveness *for them*—a symbol of both his Christlike demeanor and the people's continuing dependence. Only once God grants His forgiveness do the people then thank Him for His kindness.

That Marx chose not to include the golden calf episode (which, according to his outline, had been his original intention) and that Mendelssohn did is significant, since both choices further demonstrate the composers' concern, or lack thereof, for the Jewish image. For *Mose*, Marx instead imported Korah's rebellion, the largest in the Pentateuch, from Numbers 16 and 26:9–11, where the uprising occurs in response to the restrictions Moses placed on the sons of Levi, which prohibited them from the office of the priesthood. But both the original biblical account and, as noted earlier, Marx's setting of the rebellion leave God out of the equation entirely: the revolt is solely against Moses.

MENDELSSOHN, MARX, AND THE NINETEENTH-CENTURY ANTI-SEMITIC TRADITION

Mendelssohn's negative depiction of the Jews in the *Moses* libretto stems, I believe, from a desire to demonstrate his detachment from his Jewish heritage at this time in his life. Given his father's encouragement that he separate himself from Judaism (as noted in chapter 1), Mendelssohn may have believed that a noticeably positive representation of Jews (such as that found in Handel's oratorios and, to a somewhat lesser extent, in *Mose*) would have led to doubts concerning the sincerity of his Christian faith. Even worse, it might have been construed as a particularly obvious declaration of a philo-Semitic agenda, especially since negative depictions of Jews were fairly standard in the oratorios of the early nineteenth century. For example, Carl Loewe's 1830 *The Destruction of Jerusalem* (*Die Zerstörung von Jerusalem*)—a copy of which Mendelssohn would later own[23]—begins by portraying the Jews as a people of strength, rising up against their Roman oppressors; but this depiction changes radically once infighting among the Jews begins and especially once the Christians, who assume the moral high-ground, are introduced. The oratorio's climax comes after negotiations between Titus (the Roman governor) and the Jews fail and the Romans begin their attack. As the Jews fight back, they cry with an almost animal-like fury, "I will rage! I will kill; I laugh; I laugh; Revenge." Meanwhile, the Christians at Golgotha pray for the Jews, asking God to grant them the courage to bear their impending suffering. Once the Romans begin to gain the upper hand, Titus pronounces death for the Jews, but promises mercy for the Christians. As the defeat of the Jews nears, a high priest cries out, "What sin, O Lord, has your poor people committed?" to which "spirit-voices" respond, "His blood be upon us and our children!" (Mt. 27:25). Their battle lost, the Jews cry out "Jehovah! Jehovah!" which, as a note in the score explains, indicates that they were convinced of their imminent destruction, since the sin of uttering the name of God was punishable by death.[24] The oratorio then closes with the chorus of prophets and Christians declaring that "those are the days of revenge, so that what was foretold would be fulfilled!" Thus, Loewe characterized the destruction of Jerusalem as the direct result of the Jews' rejection of Christ. (Loewe's own setting from the Pentateuch, his 1834 *The Brazen Serpent* [*Die eherne Schlange*], is also a punishment narrative, one in which the entire plot revolves around God's chastisement of the Jews for the failure of their faith in the wilderness.)

Equally negative is another oratorio that Mendelssohn would later own and know well, Louis Spohr's 1835 *The Savior's Last Hour* (*Des Heilands letzte Stunde*).[25] Based on a libretto by Friedrich Rochlitz (a mutual acquaintance of the two composers),[26] the text is a loose adaptation of the passion narrative, which enables it to be considerably more anti-Semitic than the gospels themselves. Of particular interest is the work's alignment with what Schleiermacher (speaking in general terms, not of Spohr's oratorio) called Judaism's "limitation of the love of Jehovah to the race of Abraham," by which it "betrays a lingering affinity with Fetichism [*sic*]."[27] This ideology is evident in the numerous segments of the work in which the Jews not only claim to be the chosen people (a posture that would have seemed offensive to a Christian audience), but also maintain that God led them in their decision to crucify Christ.

While Mendelssohn's portrayal of the Jews in *Moses* may have stemmed from a fear that a positive depiction would have been poorly received, and led to questioning of his Christian credentials, it remains uncertain whether this would in fact have occurred. Handel's oratorios, for instance, enjoyed tremendous popularity in Germany in the first half of the nineteenth century despite their heroic portrayal of the Jews.[28] Likewise, there were at least two contemporaries of Mendelssohn—one Protestant born (Friedrich Schneider) and one converted Jewish (Marx himself)—who were able to include positive images of the Jews in their works with no evidence that it adversely affected their careers. Schneider's setting of the Exodus story in *Pharao* (1828), for example, portrays the Jews as nothing less than steadfast in their faith, and as a people who praise God at every opportunity. This heroic portrayal of the Jews, however, did not prevent the work from becoming one of Schneider's most oft-performed oratorios, as well as the most popular of the century's settings involving Moses.[29] The oratorio begins just after the last of the ten plagues, with Israel celebrating while Egypt mourns and calls for revenge. Out of fear, however, Pharaoh allows the Jews to leave. In the second part, the Israelites continue to celebrate freedom and the promise of a "Fatherland," all granted by the grace of God. The Egyptians pursue, however, and for one brief instant, with their backs up against the Red Sea, the Jews' faith waivers. But with the parting of the sea, their faith returns, and after crossing, they shout out, "Hosanna in the highest!"

Marx's highly positive depiction of the Jews in *Mose* likewise had little impact on the work's overall reception. As noted earlier, Gebhard von Alvensleben, a reviewer of the 1841 premiere in Breslau, heralded the highly dramatic work as a "new star" in the history of oratorio, a sentiment that was echoed in numerous other publications in the years that followed. In 1843, for example, Gustav Adolph Keferstein published a lecture he had delivered at the Academy of Sciences in Erfurt, in which he advocated "the idea of oratorio as a true, pure music drama," a concept he found well executed in *Mose*. A year later, Gustav Heuser made a similar demand on the genre, and likewise lauded *Mose* as the perfect embodiment of this ideal. And in 1853, after Franz Liszt conducted the work in Weimar, reviewer Joachim Raff aptly summarized prevailing opinion by describing it as "a music drama in evening dress," and even questioned Marx's use of the label "oratorio," rather than "musical-dramatic poem."[30]

Given the public tolerance of other philo-Semitic oratorios of the day, that Mendelssohn could have provided a more benevolent depiction of the Jews in *Moses* but did not not only suggests his apparent desire to separate himself from his heritage, but also strikes at the heart of why Marx chose to reject the libretto. Marx commented in his memoirs that the libretto left him feeling "cold" because of its responsorial format. As Marx's initial prose draft (Text II) demonstrates, however, Mendelssohn's choice of this format derived not only from his own personal leanings but also from the model Marx provided in his draft. Marx may have realized this when he placed the blame for the libretto's inadequacies on himself, writing in his memoirs, "Why had I neglected or been unable to clearly show him the new form that was so important to me?"[31] But the responsorial format was something Marx could have corrected for (and often did when he adapted segments of Mendelssohn's text). Moreover, the comparison between *Moses* and *Mose* conducted here demonstrates that this was hardly the sole difference between the two libretti. Indeed, the most palpable difference between the works bears on the portrayal of the Jews, with that in *Mose* being notably more positive than that in *Moses*. While Marx did not state outright that Mendelssohn's negative depiction was a factor in his rejection of the libretto, the likelihood that he found it offensive is great, given his upbringing and attitude toward his Jewish heritage.

Like Mendelssohn, Marx was born into a Jewish family and converted during his youth. But unlike Mendelssohn, who had Christianity chosen for him by his father, Marx found Christianity on his own, much to his father's dismay. Not that Marx's father, Moses, was a devout member of what Marx consistently referred to as the "old church" (*alte Kirche*)—quite the contrary, in fact.[32] He was a textbook Rationalist, who adhered firmly to the teachings of Voltaire and who, despite being the son and grandson of rabbis, considered Judaism and Christianity to be faiths of superstition and ridiculed them both.[33] But, as Marx recalled, his father held it a point of honor to remain a Jew (and even occasionally attended synagogue), despite the restrictions society placed upon him as a result. He was also dead set against his son's conversion, likely believing it to represent a rejection of the family's cultural and religious heritage. Once Marx had set his baptismal date, his father threatened that the bed from which he spoke would be his deathbed should the conversion take place. Marx, however, was resolved and followed through with his plan. (His father survived.)[34]

Knowing his father considered the choice between religions meaningless (in his eyes, they were all equally absurd), Marx was perplexed by his father's strong opposition to his conversion. But when considered in light of his father's other comments on the subject (which attack Judaism as a religion but never the Jews themselves) and his occasional visits to the synagogue despite his rationalist leanings, one gets the sense that, despite his abandonment of Judaism, his father retained a strong sense of Jewish cultural identity, one that he did not want to see his son forsake. Having raised his son as a nonobservant Jew, Marx's father probably doubted the authenticity of his son's new-found Christian faith and believed the motivating force behind his conversion to be the improvement of his social status. Since Moses Marx had been willing to forgo the social advantages baptism would have provided—likely for the sake of preserving his cultural identity—such a superficial baptism would, in his mind, have been a cynical betrayal of that identity. But as Adolf's frank discussion of the events of his youth reveal, not only was his conversion genuine, it never led him to deny his Jewish heritage.

What truly spurred Marx toward Christianity was Christian music: pieces such as Handel's *Messiah* and Mozart's *Requiem* led him to a passionate, zealous interest in the Bible. "Particularly inspiring to me were most parts of the Old Testament and from the New, the Gospels of Matthew and Luke," he wrote, adding that he found these particular writings more revealing of the true meaning of both Judaism and Christianity than the Epistles or any other theological writings known to him. Of the Gospels he noted that he was especially impressed by the Sermon on the Mount, by Christ's arguments with the Pharisees, and by what they each revealed of Christ's character and the meaning of his coming.[35] Marx would later find that this new passion for Bible study would, "quite unexpectedly, turn out to have a great influence . . . on me as a composer and author."[36] This influence is particularly apparent in *Mose*, whose subject matter seems to have been central to his interest in the Bible. His mention of the Gospel of Matthew in the same breath as the Old Testament is particularly revealing, as the Gospel presents an image of Christ as the "New Moses" throughout.[37] That Marx was aware of this image of Christ is undeniable, given *Mose*'s prophetic penultimate chorus with its adaptation of Deuteronomy 18:18—"Behold, I will send them a prophet, who shall speak to them all that I command him"—a text that contemporary Bibles connected with numerous points in the New Testament.[38] Marx's specific mention of his affection for the Sermon on the Mount further reveals the importance Moses held for him, given his general attraction to the Old Testament and the strong connections between the sermon (Mt. 5:17–48) and Moses' reception of the law on Mount Horeb (Ex. 31:18).

Despite the fervor of Marx's Christian faith, which perhaps surpassed even Mendelssohn's, Marx never attempted to disassociate himself from his Jewish heritage. Indeed, Marx spent the entire first chapter of his memoirs discussing his father's convictions, his own early experiences in the synagogue, and finally, the impetus for his conversion. Moreover, Marx's use of the term "old church" when referring to Judaism suggests that like many Jewish converts, he saw Protestantism as the natural successor to Judaism.[39] And like many of those other converts, Marx did not view the crossover into Christianity as a declaration that his former faith or its members were somehow inferior; Judaism may have been the "old church," but that made it and its adherents no less a part of the nation. Nor did he ever find it necessary to deny his heritage or attack the "old church" in order to proclaim either his patriotism or his faith.[40]

As we have already seen, Mendelssohn was not only led to the church by his father but was actively encouraged by him to disassociate himself from his Jewish heritage. As *Moses* helps to demonstrate, Mendelssohn equated disassociation with disparagement. It was not enough to prove the strength of his faith by filling his libretto with Christian symbolism. *Moses* would need to attest to Mendelssohn's complete separation from Judaism by embracing contemporary anti-Semitic standards, which had been largely defined for him by the two oratorio composers (aside from Marx) he knew best: Carl Loewe and Louis Spohr.[41] Granted, there were other composers who successfully managed to portray the Jews favorably without reprisal, but—and this is a crucial distinction—these men did not bear the burden of being the grandson of Moses Mendelssohn, a name that was still of "great import" (to quote Abraham) to German Jews[42] and was well known to most Gentiles. Indeed, Felix heard his name uttered in the same breath as his grandfather's in biographies, publicity articles, and elsewhere throughout his life, a situation which may very well have led him to believe (and not unjustly) that he and his music were continually under the closest scrutiny by those who, as his father had warned him, felt that a Christian Mendelssohn was an impossibility.[43]

Mendelssohn's tendency to attack the Jewish image and Marx's to protect it would continue in their collaboration on Mendelssohn's *Paulus*, which was completed before the total collapse of their relationship. In composing his first oratorio, Mendelssohn would again find himself influenced by his family, friends, and professional associates, all of whom would, by word and example, encourage him to leave his heritage behind.

Paulus

You stiff-necked ones! You always resist the Holy Spirit.

—Acts 7:51, as quoted in Mendelssohn's Paulus

IN JULY 1831, Mendelssohn left Italy to begin the final segment of his extensive European tour, a trip that would include prolonged stays in both Paris and London. En route to the former, he stopped in Frankfurt for a few days in mid-November, lodging with longtime friend and fellow Bach enthusiast Johann Nepomuk Schelble, the director of the Frankfurt Cecilia Society (*Cäcilienverein*).[1] During Mendelssohn's stay, Schelble doted on him, both at home and through hastily arranged performances by the society of several of Mendelssohn's new choral works. Perhaps the greatest honor came in the form of a commission for an oratorio, a project whose scale inspired both excitement and apprehension.[2] When writing his father from Frankfurt with the news, Mendelssohn did not specify a subject for the oratorio;[3] indeed, the first hint of one would not come until a month later, when he asked Karl Klingemann to pass along a message to his brother Paul: "Tell him that I have a contract for an oratorio, whose title will be that of his namesake, the apostle."[4] That Mendelssohn failed to mention the subject of his oratorio in his letter to his father supports a long-held assumption that the composer himself—not the Cecilia Society—decided upon Paul, a possibility that has led to a great deal of speculation concerning the motivation for the choice. Eric Werner's hypothesis is typical: "[t]he figure of the Apostle, who was born a Jew and, after his conversion, always remained a friend of his people, must have struck a deep chord in Felix."[5]

But the key to understanding Mendelssohn's *Paulus* and the motivations behind its composition does not lie with Paul as he is depicted in the Bible; rather, we need to focus on Mendelssohn's unique interpretation of the apostle. Mendelssohn's Paul—even as he appears in the published version of the oratorio—is not Werner's Paul, who, not surprisingly, blends seamlessly with Werner's overall understanding of Mendelssohn as a man with strong pride in his Jewish heritage. Indeed, Mendelssohn's Paul is anything but "a friend of his people." Rather, *Paulus*—Mendelssohn's most popular work during his lifetime—has always been problematic for the post-war Mendelssohn interpretation, forcing critics to gloss over or creatively explain its anti-Semitic content. Even the more recent attempts to view *Paulus* as a symbolic bridge between Judaism and Christianity are unconvincing,[6] as they fail to account for the fact that Mendelssohn's protagonists, Stephen and Paul, reject and ridicule the Jews throughout the work. (Stephen, for example, calls them "stiff-necked" and "resist[ing of] the Holy Spirit," and Paul accuses them of rejecting the word of God.) Moreover, Mendelssohn's Jews provide Stephen and Paul with little reason to feel otherwise, given their continuous persecution of the two, all while dogmatically reciting the law.

While *Paulus*'s anti-Semitic bent is clearly present in its published version, it is even more apparent in Mendelssohn's libretto drafts, which reveal that *Paulus*'s bias was neither accidental nor merely a result of following the original biblical story. For although the image of the Jews throughout the book of Acts (from which the *Paulus* story originates) is hardly positive, that image deteriorated rapidly as work on the *Paulus* libretto progressed, quickly conforming to the depictions of Jews found in other contemporary oratorios. As a result, *Paulus* fits remarkably well into the nineteenth-century anti-Semitic oratorio tradition. Simultaneously, the work recapitulates—as we shall see—a related focus of contemporary theology and oratorio, the celebration of German Christian heritage and the great missionaries (particularly St. Paul and St. Boniface). Viewed together, *Paulus*'s ideological alignments suggest that Mendelssohn, in this, his first oratorio, tried to assuage real or imagined public doubts about his Christian faith by writing a work that conformed to popular expectations, both through its call for the conversion of nonbelievers and its depiction of the narrow-mindedness of those who refuse to see the light (namely, the Jews). *Paulus* also demonstrates, however, the mental anguish that such a depiction caused Mendelssohn, anguish that led to his eventual reevaluation of this approach.

Before we look directly at the Jewish image in *Paulus*, it is important to understand the three major influences on the oratorio—the compositional process and role of Mendelssohn's libretto contributors; Mendelssohn's father and his fellow composers; and the tendency of German Christians to glorify their Gentile heritage and celebrate the means by which Christianity came to their land.

A Textual History of *Paulus*

In the months that followed his announcement that the subject of his first oratorio would be the apostle Paul, Mendelssohn began to piece together the various sections of the work in his mind, establishing an overall plan. He first described his intentions in his letter of March 10, 1832, to Eduard Devrient, of whom he also made a substantial request:

> I also have something to ask you, Eduard; answer me right away about it. I am to compose an oratorio for the Cecilia Society, . . . for which I have already many designs in my head. The subject is to be the Apostle Paul; in the

first part: the stoning of Stephen and the persecution; in the second part: the conversion; in the third, the Christian life and preaching, and either his martyrdom or his farewell to the congregation. I would like the words to be chiefly from the Bible and hymnal, and a few free passages (the little Christian flock would sing, for instance, the chorales in the first part; I would take the principal features of Stephen's defense from the Bible). But I cannot put these texts together myself. Will you do it? You are better acquainted with the Bible than I, and know exactly what I want; it would give you little trouble.[7]

Devrient, however, "did not feel equal to this trust," believing himself insufficiently versed in the Bible. He instead recommended Mendelssohn contact one of their "theological friends," a suggestion Mendelssohn would act on that summer.[8] In the meantime, however, Mendelssohn decided to assemble his own outline of the work, something to serve as a guide for whomever he would eventually choose as his librettist. The draft (Text I in table 4.1) consists primarily of biblical citations, along with an occasional textual fragment and some designations of sections for which Mendelssohn had not yet chosen text (e.g., "chorus of disciples," "final chorus"). As will be noted from the table, the version of the outline that survives was not written until the following winter; it is, however, most likely a copy of one that Mendelssohn sent that same spring—shortly after hearing back from Devrient—to a practically unknown contributor: the Jewish Hebraist and Orientalist Julius Fürst.[9]

The quantity and impact of Fürst's contributions to the *Paulus* libretto have been greatly underappreciated, in part because his drafts remained partially unrecognized and completely untranscribed until quite recently,[10] and also because Mendelssohn kept fairly quiet about Fürst's participation.[11] Even Fanny was surprised to hear of Fürst's involvement. After waiting over a year to thank him for his efforts, Mendelssohn finally sent Fürst a package—via Fanny—that included an apologetic letter of appreciation and a copy of the then current version of the libretto (probably Text VIII).[12] Fanny, noticing the address on the package, wrote to her brother, "Aren't you amazed at my self-control that prevented me from opening up the package of *St. Paul* addressed to Fürst in order to read it first? How did Fürst get to move among the prophets?"[13]

Exactly how Fürst came to "move among the prophets" remains unclear. He and Mendelssohn likely became acquainted when the two were students at the University of Berlin. (They may even have attended Hegel's lectures on aesthetics together.) Fürst eventually went on to teach a variety of subjects—including Hebrew and Aramaic grammar and literature, Syriac, and biblical exegesis—at the university in Leipzig, to publish several books, and to become the founder and editor of the weekly magazine *Der Orient*.[14] At the time Mendelssohn requested the libretto, however, Fürst was just completing his studies.[15]

Between the time Mendelssohn asked Fürst to construct a libretto (ca. late spring 1832) and the time of its arrival that winter, two more friends were invited to con-

TABLE 4.1. The *Paulus* Texts

Text	Library Sigla	Author	Date	Comments
I	GB-Ob MS. M. Deneke Mendelssohn c. 42, p. 6–7	Mendelssohn	Dec. 22, 1832	An outline of the work. Mailed to J. Schubring on Dec. 22, but was probably originally written in the late spring of 1832 and sent to J. Fürst.
II	GB-Ob MS. M. Deneke Mendelssohn d. 30, no. 214	Schubring	Jan. 23, 1833	Partial draft of the beginning through Stephen's death. Shows influence of I.
IIIa	GB-Ob MS. M. Deneke Mendelssohn d. 53, no. 87	Fürst	[ca. Jan. 1833]	Complete prose draft. Fürst was probably asked to write it in the spring of 1832. Mendelssohn sent it back to him for improvements. Shows influence of I.
IIIb	GB-Ob MS. M. Deneke Mendelssohn d. 30, no. 215	Fürst	[ca. May 1833]	Arias to supplement IIIa. The package in which this was sent also included the revised IIIa.
IV	GB-Ob MS. M. Deneke Mendelssohn d. 53, no. 88	Marx	Mar. 15, 1833	Complete prose draft. Shows influence of I, II, and IIIa.
V	GB-Ob MS. M. Deneke Mendelssohn d. 30, no. 211	Mendelssohn	Sept. 6, 1833	Complete prose draft. Shows influence of I–IV. Mendelssohn mailed it to Schubring, who sent it back with annotations and extensive comments on Oct. 5, 1833.
VI	GB-Ob MS. M. Deneke Mendelssohn d. 30, no. 212	Schubring	Oct. 5, 1833	Commentary on V; Completion of II (Saul's persecution of the Christians through the end).
VII	GB-Ob MS. M. Deneke Mendelssohn c. 27, fol. 28r–30v	Mendelssohn	[late Oct. 1833]	Complete prose draft. Shows influence of VI.
VIII	GB-Ob MS. M. Deneke Mendelssohn c. 27, fol. 31r–32r	Mendelssohn	[late Oct. 1833]	Complete prose draft. Builds directly on VII; has shorthand references to VII.
IX	D-Bsb MN MS 19, p. 1–14	Mendelssohn	[Apr. 1834– Apr. 1836]	Musical sketches and drafts of X and XIII.
X	D-Bsb MN MS 28, p. 169–260	Mendelssohn	[Apr. 1834– Apr. 1836]	Musical drafts and discarded pieces from XIII.
XI	PL-Kj MN Bd. 55	Mendelssohn	[Apr. 1834– Apr. 1836]	Compositional piano-vocal score for both XIII and the published score.*
XII	US-NYp Drexel 4779	Mendelssohn, Rietz	[before Apr. 18, 1836]	Piano-vocal score copy by Julius Rietz; includes minor corrections in Mendelssohn's hand. The score represents a "snapshot" of the work, shortly before the completion of XIII.
XIII	PL-Kj MN Bd. 53–54	Mendelssohn	Apr. 18, 1836	"Düsseldorf full score." Score lacks last minute changes that were integrated into a now lost copy. Score is in two volumes, with the first dated April 8.
XIV	GB-Ob MS. M. Deneke Mendelssohn d. 30, no. 216b, 217	Mendelssohn	[late Apr. 1836]	Draft of the textbook for the Düsseldorf premiere. Text postdates XIII. Written in Mendelssohn's and an unknown hand.

(continued)

TABLE 4.1. (continued)

Text	Library Sigla	Author	Date	Comments
XV			[early May 1836]	Printed textbook for the Düsseldorf premiere.
XVI	PL-Kj MN Bd. 55	Mendelssohn	[May–Sept. 1836]	Compositional piano-vocal score for both XIII and the published score.
GA			[before Oct. 7, 1836]	Published final text, as appears in 1836 and 1837 scores and complete edition (*Gesamtausgabe*). Final version premiered on Oct. 7, 1836. (MS scores of final version lost.)

*Complete transcriptions of all of these texts (except XII) are available in Sposato, "The Price," 2: 49–231 (NB. the numbering of the texts listed here does not consistently match those in that volume). This list does not include some minor sources of individual arias and the like (see Reichwald, *Musical Genesis*, 25–27 for a list of some of these). A comprehensive list of all the *Paulus* sources—including libretti, scores, sketches, fragments, and copies—has yet to be published.

tribute to *Paulus*: Adolf Bernhard Marx and Pastor Julius Schubring (one of the "theological friends" Devrient had suggested). Marx's involvement came just after Mendelssohn's return from his European tour in late June 1832, whereupon Marx proposed the *Moses-Paulus* libretto exchange discussed in the previous chapter. Anxious to begin work on his new project and having received nothing from Fürst at this point, Mendelssohn agreed, and fulfilled his end of the bargain with dispatch, completing the *Moses* text on August 21. Marx, on the other hand, failed to produce a libretto until the following spring. That the exchange would be problematic was evident from the beginning: even in the initial discussion of their respective projects, Marx was critical of Mendelssohn's vision for *Paulus* and voiced strong misgivings regarding the subject. (He suggested St. Peter might make a better choice.[16]) Shortly thereafter, Mendelssohn requested that Marx include chorales in the libretto, to which Marx replied, "What? Chorales in Paul's time? And in the events that make up his life?" and flatly refused.[17]

At this point, Mendelssohn realized he would need to recruit additional help if he hoped to create the work he envisioned, and started testing the waters with Schubring. He began quite subtly, casually mentioning in his August 25, 1832, letter that he was "thinking of composing an oratorio" on St. Paul that winter; no details were provided, no requests were made, nor did Mendelssohn reveal that he had already been working on the project for several months.[18] Schubring took the bait; although Schubring's reply is lost, Mendelssohn's next letter suggests that the theologian expressed a passionate interest in the project and volunteered to assist in assembling the libretto.[19] Mendelssohn responded by sending Schubring his outline for the work (Text I); the request that accompanied it, however, was not for a complete prose libretto, as that was something he still hoped to receive from Marx (and possibly Fürst). Mendelssohn's vision of Schubring's role was less grand but appropriate to the theologian's talents: "I believe you could best serve the cause if you would recommend chorales from the hymnal, along with the places where they should go; no one could do that better than you, since you also have the melodies in your head."[20]

Within a month, Schubring's first effort (Text II) was on its way to Berlin. But despite the specificity of his request, Mendelssohn received more—and less—than he had expected. Instead of a list of chorales for the entire oratorio, Schubring sent him a complete prose libretto for the first scene, Stephen's martyrdom. While this was probably not what he had hoped for, Mendelssohn may have unwittingly encouraged Schubring to make a broader contribution by asking the theologian (in a short note at the top of his outline) to provide both his opinion of the plan as a whole and biblical passages for those sections without appropriate texts. Further encouragement may have come from Mendelssohn's letter itself, in which he seemed anxious to begin composing and eager for a complete libretto: "I want to concern myself first with the text once it lies finished, so that I can approach the music completely fresh and with all my strength."[21] Schubring clearly misinterpreted Mendelssohn, however, as Mendelssohn was referring here to his agreement with Marx, and even borrowed from Marx's own words about the benefits of having someone else assemble the libretto.[22] Mendelssohn tried to clarify his needs in his next letter to Schubring: "I await the arrival of a complete textual draft in the next few weeks, and when I have it, then I will be able to say more exactly what I need to supplement it."[23] (Marx, whom Mendelssohn would later reveal to Schubring as the author of the awaited draft,[24] finished a few days later.) Eventually, Schubring came to understand his desired role in the project, describing it in his reminiscences of the composer as being of "a subordinate kind."[25]

Shortly after its arrival in late January 1833, Mendelssohn sent Schubring's draft (or a copy) off to Marx.[26] It was also around this time that Mendelssohn finally received Fürst's libretto (Text IIIa), and passed a copy of it along to Marx as well.[27] (The original, however, went back to Fürst, marked with changes and requests for additional material.[28]) Building from Mendelssohn's outline and these sources, Marx completed his greatly anticipated libretto (Text IV) on March 15, 1833.[29] But despite the fact that the libretto was a complete, highly detailed text, Mendelssohn's reaction, like Marx's response to Moses, was lackluster. To Schubring, Mendelssohn commented matter-of-factly that "Marx has now completed his work and the text is assembled; only in the details does it still seem to lack much; he accepted and used almost all of your recommendations, by the way."[30] Of course, what Marx did not take from Schubring's draft were the chorales, a decision that may have insulted Mendelssohn, who had made his wish for their inclusion plain. It is also quite possible that Mendelssohn was aware of Marx's rejection of his Moses libretto at this point, and that the disintegration of their friendship was already underway.

In late May 1833, Mendelssohn traveled to Düsseldorf to direct the Lower Rhine Music Festival. In his most recent correspondence with Fürst, Mendelssohn instructed him to send the corrections to his draft there.[31] Fürst complied, sending

Mendelssohn both his corrected draft (Text IIIa) and a set of supplemental pages (Text IIIb) with eight additional arias, each marked with a roman numeral that corresponds with one written on the corrected draft. But while Mendelssohn appreciated Fürst's contributions—his last to the project, as it would turn out—he once again discovered that this was not to be the libretto he envisioned for *Paulus*. By the following summer, Mendelssohn had abandoned entirely the idea of having a single outside librettist for his oratorio[32] and began to assemble the text on his own.

In constructing his own libretto, Mendelssohn incorporated elements from all the drafts in his possession, the evidence of which still survives in the published score. In the first scene of the oratorio, for example, Fürst deserves credit for most of the opening chorus, as well as for one of the work's most popular arias, *Jerusalem* (GA 6). Schubring suggested the placement of the chorales (after the opening chorus and Stephen's stoning, respectively), as well as the text and melody for the second chorale (GA 8, *Dir, Herr, dir will ich mich ergeben,* set to the tune of *Wer nur den lieben Gott läßt walten*). (Mendelssohn himself chose the text and melody of the first chorale [GA 2], *Allein Gott in der Höh' sei Ehr.*) Even Marx's work finds a place in the soprano recitative preceding Stephen's defense (GA 5, *Und sie sahen auf ihn*).

Naturally, the influence of these contributors appears more prominently in Mendelssohn's libretto drafts; indeed, in the process of revising, he often switched sources upon the receipt of new material or spliced it together with the older text. In his first prose libretto attempt (Text V), for example, Mendelssohn based the text of Stephen's defense on Marx's draft; soon afterward, Schubring sent Mendelssohn a new version (Text VI), which Mendelssohn used to replace Marx's in his next draft (Text VII). Later, Mendelssohn reincorporated some of Marx's text, as well as added biblical passages he found on his own.

Another practice Mendelssohn observed while composing his libretto drafts was to return to the original Bible passages from which his contributors' texts derived, a process he described in the acknowledgment letter he sent Fürst:

> When composing, I usually look up the Bible passages myself, and so you'll find that much is simpler, shorter, and more concise than in your text; whereas before, I couldn't get enough text and was always longing for more. Since working this way, I feel completely different, and now I can make a selection.[33]

Once Mendelssohn began returning to the Bible text, he made it a habit, even giving scripture priority, as he noted in letters to both Schubring and his friend and fellow librettist Friedrich Rochlitz:[34]

> Your notes for *St. Paul* were splendid, and I have used all of them without exception; it is strange (and good) that while composing, at all of the places where for some reason or other I had previously wanted to rearrange a phrase or change it, little by little things came back to the way in which I find them in the Bible; that remains, after all, the best way.[35]

[*Paulus*] is compiled throughout entirely from the Bible words, and whilst writing it I have felt with fresh pleasure how forcible, exhaustive, and harmonious the Scripture language is for music to me. There is an inimitable force in it, and the rhythm which has often seemed of itself to suggest the music to me.[36]

These letters show that while he greatly appreciated his friends' contributions, Mendelssohn remained staunchly independent while composing the actual *Paulus* libretto, never hesitating to revise their work or to introduce material he discovered himself. As Schubring later commented:

[T]he very best touches in his oratorios result from his delicate tact—for instance, the words for the air of Paul during the three days of his blindness, when he had just been converted before Damascus, for which Mendelssohn, dissatisfied with everything proposed to him, himself hit upon the 51st Psalm, that seems as though it had been written on purpose. . . .

He rejected, also, much that was suggested, being so well acquainted with his Bible, that he obtained a great deal of valuable materials himself: for any assistance, he was, however, extremely grateful.[37]

Mendelssohn probably assembled his own first textual draft (Text V) sometime during the summer of 1833, and mailed it to Schubring in early September for his comments.[38] Schubring's first reaction to the draft was to ask Mendelssohn to come to his home in Dessau to discuss it,[39] but Mendelssohn was apparently unable to find time to make the trip. Instead, Schubring sent the heavily annotated text back on October 5, along with the second and final installment of his own draft (Text VI). Mendelssohn described these contributions as "the best suggestions I had yet received" and began working with them the very morning they arrived.[40] Such eagerness suggests that Mendelssohn's next, undated draft (Text VII) came rapidly and was likely complete by mid-October. This draft included, among other things, texts for numerous items that had been marked with placeholders in Text V (e.g., *Chor* followed by a blank space). Mendelssohn then began his last libretto draft (Text VIII, also undated), which he likely completed soon thereafter, judging from its use of the same paper type as Text VII and his shorthand references to this earlier text.

Outside input into the *Paulus* libretto continued even after Mendelssohn began composing the music in April 1834.[41] At this point, however, Mendelssohn seems to have been set squarely on his own course, as he chose not to integrate any of the changes suggested to him, including those that arrived in December from his father.[42] Abraham, who took great interest in the work (and whom Felix had apparently been supplying with textual drafts), had suggested that Paul appear at Stephen's stoning, an idea his son agreed with in principle, but which he could find no means of carrying out. Also of concern to Abraham was the length of Stephen's defense, but Felix assured him that, owing to the rapid pace of his musical setting, the entire speech would last only two or three minutes.[43] Schubring also made some eleventh-hour libretto suggestions, including a new prayer for Paul's first attempt at preaching and a reworked version of the scene in which Paul heals a lame man.[44] As Siegwart Reichwald's study of paper types in the *Paulus* manuscripts reveals, at this point—early October 1835—Mendelssohn had already composed a substantial amount of music[45] and no doubt felt Schubring's suggestions too comprehensive to consider; moreover, many of the texts Schubring recommended were already in use elsewhere in the oratorio. In his reply, Mendelssohn never mentioned that he would be unable to set the theologian's text, but rather expressed great excitement at his suggestions and—perhaps out of politeness—requested still more:

> One passage [you sent] for *St. Paul* was excellent, "you, who are the righteous father" ["der du der rechte Vater bist," Eph. 3:15]. I have a chorus in my head for it, which I will write down shortly. . . . If any good passages occur to you, continue to send them to me, for you know the plan of the whole.[46]

But Mendelssohn never followed through with his plan to set the passage, nor did he respond to Schubring's request for a copy of the current version of the libretto so that he could make additional suggestions. Without it, Schubring wrote, he would be unable to offer any further advice on the work.[47]

Although Mendelssohn had originally estimated that *Paulus* would take six months to complete (text and all),[48] by this point, work had already dragged on for almost four years. Mendelssohn repeatedly underestimated the oratorio's complexity and his ability to commit to it, given his many other responsibilities and projects. Year after year, self-imposed deadlines passed as each episode of renewed zeal fizzled before he could finish, and plans to premiere the work with, among others, Schelble and the Frankfurt Cecilia Society (the oratorio's sponsors) had to be abandoned.[49] In July 1834, for example, Mendelssohn's excitement and energy was readily apparent in his report to Schubring: "I have finished more than half of the first part, and am thinking that it will be completed by the fall, and then perhaps the whole thing in February."[50] But doubt and uncertainty quickly set in; writing Schubring again three weeks later, Mendelssohn noted that "the first part of *St. Paul* is now nearly completed, and I stand before it like a cow that is unable to go through a new door, and cannot seem to finish it."[51] Indeed, even this assessment had some sugar-coating. In a letter he wrote two weeks later to English composer and organist William Horsley, Mendelssohn's description of Part I is more pessimistic: "My Oratorio is not yet so advanced as you think it, for I have not quite finished the first part."[52]

This pattern seemed ready to repeat itself in the summer of 1835, during which Mendelssohn wrote several more letters showing his frustration with *Paulus*.[53] This time, however, his feelings were accompanied by a determination to finally finish the work. To pianist Ignaz Moscheles, Mendelssohn wrote:

> I do feel sometimes as if I should never succeed; and to-day I am quite dissatisfied with my work, and should just like to write my Oratorio over again from

beginning to end. But I am quite decided to bring it out at Frankfurt next winter, and at the Düsseldorf Musical Festival at Whitsuntide; so I must finish it now. Besides, I think I have worked too long at it; at least, I am quite impatient to get to other things, so it is evidently high time to end.[54]

The premiere in Frankfurt—tentatively planned for October or November 1835—fell through. Although Schelble's illness was officially the cause this time around, the state of the still very incomplete score would have forced Mendelssohn to cancel again in any event.[55] Perhaps hearing of the cancellation and worried that his son might again be losing momentum, Abraham nudged Felix for an update on the project in his letter of November 11.[56] Felix wrote back a few days later, reassuring his father with news of two planned performances for the spring, the first in March with Schelble in Frankfurt, followed by one in May at the Lower Rhine Music Festival in Düsseldorf.[57] Before he could send the letter, however, his father died on November 19.

Abraham's death was a defining event in Felix's life, one (as we shall see) that would have a substantial impact on the character of the *Paulus* libretto. One immediate consequence, however, was Mendelssohn's renewed focus on the work and an acceleration in the composition of the score, a result of his reconceptualization of the oratorio as a final tribute to his father.[58] With this notion driving him, Mendelssohn now banished any thought of allowing composition to continue past the planned spring performances.

As it turned out, Schelble's illness dragged on into the new year, causing another Frankfurt cancellation and granting Mendelssohn a temporary reprieve until the Düsseldorf performance.[59] Despite this final extension, Mendelssohn had to work franticly to finish *Paulus* in time. Writing to his sister Rebecka on April 10, 1836—two days after completing the first volume of the two-volume score—he described the final dash: "Except for meals, I sit all day long at my desk and work on *St. Paul,* which will now be completely finished in 5–6 days."[60] Mendelssohn was not far off the mark; he completed and dated the second volume on April 18. It was on May 22 that *Paulus* was—at long last—premiered at the Lower Rhine Music Festival.

When it came to composing the music, Mendelssohn worked on what will be referred to here as the "Düsseldorf full score" (Text XIII), while simultaneously writing ideas into both a sketchbook (Text IX) and a compositional piano-vocal score (Texts XI and XVI).[61] He also occasionally rewrote some sections and removed others, many of which still survive (Text X).[62] Despite the finished quality of the Düsseldorf score, Mendelssohn continued to make minor revisions until shortly before the performance, as demonstrated by the printed textbook for the premiere (Text XV) and its draft (Text XIV), both of which contain minor textual changes. Mendelssohn likely entered these revisions into a now lost score that he sent ahead to the festival organizers for the preparation of parts.[63]

Shortly after the festival, Mendelssohn began to evaluate *Paulus*'s weaknesses and to assemble a final version in preparation for publication. No manuscript of this final version survives, although Mendelssohn may have returned to his compositional piano-vocal score (which contains some post-Düsseldorf versions of individual pieces [Text XVI]) to work out some of his new ideas. Otherwise, the planning for the revisions appears to have been minimal and the changes themselves made rapidly, with Mendelssohn making no requests for suggestions from his former libretto contributors—or anyone else, for that matter. (This is not to say, however, that letters with suggestions were not forthcoming—particularly from Fanny.[64]) The revised version was performed in Liverpool on October 7, 1836, in an English translation by William Ball. That same year, *Paulus* appeared in print in the form of piano-vocal scores published simultaneously by Simrock in Bonn (with the original German text) and Novello in London (with Ball's English text). The full score—with both German and English texts—appeared the following year from Simrock. The Simrock score later served as the source for the *Paulus* volume of the complete Mendelssohn edition (*Gesamtausgabe*) that appeared in the mid-1870s, and which will serve here as a reference for the final text.[65]

While detailed and complex, the history of the *Paulus* libretto is strongly intertwined with the emergence of the predominantly negative Jewish image in the work. Of particular significance is the extent to which Mendelssohn was involved in the libretto's composition, given that, to date, Mendelssohn's role has been almost completely unacknowledged, the text being generally attributed to Schubring instead (with an occasional nod to Marx and Fürst).[66] As my discussion here has shown, however, Mendelssohn's was the dominant voice in the libretto's composition, and, as a result, any blame for the oratorio's anti-Semitic tone cannot reside elsewhere. Indeed, had Mendelssohn followed the advice of his contributors more closely, the level of *Paulus*'s anti-Jewish invective would likely have been considerably less than what we find in the published score.

Paulus and the Influences of Carl Loewe, Louis Spohr, and Abraham Mendelssohn

The second major influence on *Paulus*'s depiction of the Jews was the models afforded by Mendelssohn's fellow composers, which combined forcefully with Abraham Mendelssohn's own advice to his son. For as with his edition of the *St. Matthew Passion* and his *Moses* libretto, Mendelssohn's tendency to depict the Jews negatively in *Paulus* derived from an overwhelming personal desire to assimilate into German Christian culture. Since Mendelssohn's surname—as his father reminded him—made him "*eo ipso* a Jew,"[67] the fact that he had been baptized would never sufficiently prove to his audience that his works were genuinely Christian. Mendelssohn therefore overcompensated, especially in the formative years of his career and while he was under his father's watchful eye. For the *St. Matthew Passion*, that meant editing the work as he perceived other Christian conductors would, thereby keeping the anti-Semitic segments of it intact. In Mendelssohn's own works, this meant portraying the Jews in a manner that conformed to popular stereotypes. This depiction has already been observed in *Moses*, in which the Jews are depicted as parasitic, as adherents to a barbaric religion based on empty ritual, and as a people incapable of true faith. In *Paulus*, the last two of these images predominate, as the Jews are portrayed throughout the work as ritual-bound and obsessed with the letter of the law, while ignoring its spirit. More significant, the stereotypes take on an exceptional virulence here—far beyond that in *Moses*—as they are invoked every time the Jews appear. This increase in the level of invective was most likely the result of additional influences by people whom Mendelssohn knew personally.

One circumstance that may have pushed Mendelssohn to depict the Jews more negatively in *Paulus* than in *Moses* was the appearance in print of similarly hostile works by two of the three prominent oratorio composers of the era: Carl Loewe, whose *The Destruction of Jerusalem* (*Die Zerstörung von Jerusalem*) was published in 1833, and Louis Spohr, whose *The Savior's Last Hour* (*Des Heilands letzte Stunde*) was published in 1835.[68] As noted in the last chapter, Mendelssohn owned the scores of both these works;[69] more significant, however, he maintained strong personal relationships with both composers. (The era's other prolific oratorio composer, Friedrich Schneider, was generally positive in his treatment of the Jews, but his relationship with Mendelssohn—especially in the 1830s—was minimal and quite formal.[70])

Mendelssohn and Carl Loewe were first introduced by their mutual friend Adolf Bernhard Marx during Loewe's July 1826 visit to Berlin. Shortly afterward, Loewe heard Mendelssohn perform several of his own piano works (including two of his newly composed Capriccios), and was greatly struck by the young man's endearing personality and remarkable performing skill.[71] The encounter led Loewe to invite Mendelssohn to visit him a few months later in Stettin (Szczecin), where, during a February 20 concert, Loewe premiered Mendelssohn's *Midsummer Night's Dream* Overture and Concerto for Two Pianos and Orchestra in Ab Major, with both composers serving as soloists. (Mendelssohn also performed in several private venues during the course of the visit.[72]) Mendelssohn remained in Loewe's company for several days,[73] during which time he may well have heard segments of *Zerstörung*, which Loewe was then actively composing.[74] After Mendelssohn returned to Berlin, he stayed in contact with Loewe and was presumably responsible for Loewe's attendance at the first of the 1829 *St. Matthew Passion* performances (an event that inspired Loewe to lead a performance of the work in Stettin in 1831).[75] The two composers remained friendly in the years that followed, with Loewe visiting Mendelssohn again (this time in Leipzig) in 1835.[76] Although Mendelssohn seems to have been critical of Loewe's music (in 1834 he wrote his sister Rebecka, "[I]t always strikes me how you and Fanny like Loewe's music, and that [it] pulls me away and nothing comes of it"[77]), he did obtain a copy of the *Zerstörung* score upon its publication, suggesting that he may have held this particular work in esteem or, at the very least, was curious about contemporary oratorio trends.

Mendelssohn's relationship with Louis Spohr began in 1822, when, at the age of thirteen, he arrived at Spohr's home in Cassel with a letter of introduction from Carl Friedrich Zelter. Spohr welcomed him and graciously asked the string quartet performing at his home that evening to play one of Mendelssohn's pieces (possibly the Piano Quartet in D Minor).[78] Spohr and Mendelssohn met again when the former came to Berlin in late 1824 to supervise a production of his opera *Jessonda*. As Sebastian Hensel noted, "Spohr's presence at Berlin had . . . a great influence on Felix," whom Spohr visited frequently.[79] As with Loewe, Mendelssohn was little impressed with Spohr's work at one point, calling one of his choral works "simply disgraceful" in an 1829 letter.[80] Nevertheless, Mendelssohn visited Spohr again in October 1834, at which time the two played through half of *Des Heilands letzte Stunde*,[81] a work Mendelssohn must have been sufficiently impressed with to warrant adding it to his library when it was published the following year. The visit also marked a reversal in Mendelssohn's attitude toward Spohr and his music, both of which he treated with the utmost respect from that moment on.[82] Indeed, their relationship strengthened to the point that in 1836, Mendelssohn offered to program at the Gewandhaus any new work Spohr cared to submit,[83] and during the 1840s, the two dedicated pieces to one another.[84]

At the time Mendelssohn first heard Spohr's oratorio fragment, he had nearly finished the first part of *Paulus*,[85] and had most likely heard or read through the published score of Loewe's *Zerstörung*. Given that these two works were the only contemporary oratorios Mendelssohn kept in his library,[86] and that both were written by close personal associates and highly respected practitioners of the genre, it seems likely that Mendelssohn would have gleaned from them some sense of current oratorio trends, including a tendency to recapitulate cultural perceptions and stereotypes in their portrayals of Jews.

In considering the impact of such musical trends, it is important to bear in mind that although *Paulus* has often been criticized as old fashioned—based more in traditions of the baroque than the early romantic—Mendelssohn considered the work to be thoroughly modern. As his father noted, with *Paulus* Mendelssohn attempted something quite new: to "solve the problem of combining ancient conceptions with modern means."[87] Felix was not blind to the similarities that existed between *Paulus* and older oratorios, however. As a result, when arrangements were underway to premiere the work at the Düsseldorf Lower Rhine Music Festival, he requested that *Paulus* not appear on the same concert program with works of the "great musicians" (i.e., baroque and classical masters), but rather with those of other contemporary composers,[88] so that the audience would hear the work as either contemporary in style or as a stylistic fusion, rather than as a baroque re-creation.

By far the strongest influence on *Paulus*'s treatment of the Jews was Mendelssohn's father. As discussed in chapter 1, during Felix's youth, Abraham Mendelssohn continually encouraged his son to separate himself from his Jewish roots, both through instruction and by example. Also during those early years, Abraham took an interest in his son's talent and in the emergence of his career; he seldom concerned himself, however, with the compositional details of specific works. But *Paulus* would prove a notable exception. As noted earlier, Felix kept his father well informed during the compositional stages of his first oratorio, and his father, in turn, was not shy about offering his opinions on various elements of the work's structure, demonstrating both Abraham's interest and Felix's unshakable devotion.[89] For instance, when Abraham raised concerns about the length of Stephen's defense and Paul's absence at his stoning, Felix replied with a touching petition: "[D]ear Father, I would entreat of you not to withhold from me your valuable advice, for it is always clear gain to me; and if I cannot rectify the old faults, I can at least avoid committing new ones."[90] Felix's devotion to his father continued after the latter's death on November 19, 1835. In his letter to Schubring written a few weeks later, Mendelssohn described his feelings toward Abraham, as well as Abraham's keen interest in *Paulus*:

> I do not know if you knew how, for some years past, my father was so good to me, so much like a friend, that I was devoted to him with my whole soul, and during my long absence I scarcely lived an hour without thinking of him; but as you knew him in his own home with all of us, in all his kindliness, you can well realize my state of mind.—The only thing that remains is to do one's duty, and this I strive to accomplish with all my strength: for he would wish it were he still here, and, as before, I shall not stop seeking to gain his approval, even though I can no longer enjoy it. . . . I shall now work with double zeal on the completion of *St. Paul*, for my father urged me to it in the last letter he wrote to me, and in recent times he had impatiently awaited the completion of this work. I feel as if I must exert all my energies to finish *St. Paul* in as good a manner as possible, and then think that he takes part in it.[91]

Fanny was also quick to comment on her father's satisfaction with the work-in-progress:

> We have returned to music again by taking up "St. Paul," of which Felix left some pieces here at Christmas, which we sang yesterday with a few friends, in honour of his birthday. We are much delighted with it, and like to think of father's enjoyment of this music, for which he was indebted to the Woringen party, who sang most excellently several of the pieces, after we unfortunately had left Düsseldorf. Father took immense pleasure in it, and especially thought the sermon of St. Stephen and the following pieces perfectly original. It was remarkable, and often struck Felix as well as myself, that a person's judgment on a subject of which he had, strictly speaking, no technical knowledge could have been so acute, and even at times so indisputably correct, as father's was in music.[92]

Abraham's warnings to Felix about calling attention to his Jewish heritage, Felix's devotion to his father, and Abraham's own interest in *Paulus* all had an impact on the *Paulus* libretto. While it would certainly be an overstatement to claim that

Abraham actively encouraged his son to attack Judaism in the work, I would maintain that knowing of his father's interest in *Paulus,* Felix wrote it in a manner he thought his father would approve of. Felix, therefore, may have feared that the inclusion of philo-Semitic (or even neutral) material in *Paulus* could lead not only to a negative reaction from his predominantly Christian audience but also to disapproval from his father. With such a compelling personal reason to make the oratorio anti-Semitic, and the almost simultaneous appearance of anti-Semitic oratorios by other composers, the reasons for *Paulus*'s harsh treatment of the Jews begin to take shape.

As will soon become clear, Mendelssohn frequently felt conflicted when handling anti-Semitic imagery. In most cases, the combined strength of the influences around him carried the day—but not always. Most notably, Abraham Mendelssohn's death enabled a definite change in the depiction of Jews in his son's works. At the time, Felix was hard at work on Part II of *Paulus* and was rushing to finish the score by Christmas.[93] Upon recovering from the news of his father's death, there was little time to do anything but finish the work as originally planned if he hoped to have it ready for the premiere that spring.[94] But once that deadline had passed, Mendelssohn took the opportunity to revise the score before publishing it, at which point he softened the anti-Semitic bent of certain scenes. While this melioration would not be sufficient to change *Paulus*'s overall anti-Semitic character, it represented the first step toward the more tolerant image of the Jews that he would present in his future oratorios.

Paulus and Philo-Heathenism

Yet a third set of influences would have a major impact on Mendelssohn's depiction of the Jews in *Paulus*—the tendency of his fellow countrymen to glorify their Gentile heritage. As we saw in chapter 3, Mendelssohn's theological choices regarding his *Moses* protagonist had a direct bearing on that work's representation of the Jewish people. Specifically, Mendelssohn's portrayal of Moses as a kind of Old Testament Christ—a depiction in line with the contemporary Christological view of the Old Testament—caused him to endow the Jews in that work with the character traits of their oppressive *New* Testament counterparts. Although Old Testament Christology has no bearing on *Paulus,* given its New Testament subject matter, the basic pattern observed in *Moses* still holds. Like his Moses, Mendelssohn's Paul is a suffering servant of God, while the Jews are portrayed as entirely responsible for his suffering—far more than in the original biblical story.

Mendelssohn built the suffering-servant motif in *Paulus* out of Paul's encounters with resistance and rebellion at every turn—on Paul's missionary failures, as Martin Meiser puts it.[95] Significantly, however, Mendelssohn's Paul is not a total failure. In fact, the only people with whom he has no success are the Jews. By contrast, in most versions of the libretto (including that used for the published score),

Paul achieves marked success in converting the Gentiles. By distinguishing Paul's experiences with the Jews and Gentiles, Mendelssohn molded his oratorio to fit contemporary ideologies—as well as some basic Lutheran tenets—that glorified the Germanic Gentile heritage at the expense of the Jews.

As far back as the Reformation itself, German Protestants had emphasized the fact that Christianity in their land could be traced not to Judaism but to Paul's mission to "bring light to the Gentiles" (or "heathen," as the more literal translation from the German *Heiden* would suggest).[96] This enabled Protestant theologians, from Luther (who repeatedly referred to himself and his fellow Christians as "us Gentiles" [*uns Heiden*]) to Mendelssohn's friend Friedrich Schleiermacher (the century's most prominent theologian), to minimize the historical connections between Christianity and Judaism. Luther made clear his view on this subject in his essay on how Christians should regard Moses:

> That Moses does not bind the Gentiles can be proved from Exodus 20, where God himself speaks, "I am the Lord your God, who brought you out of the land of Egypt, out of the house of bondage." This text makes it clear that even the Ten Commandments do not pertain to us. For God never led us out of Egypt, but only the Jews. . . . We will regard Moses as a teacher, but we will not regard him as our lawgiver—unless he agrees with both the New Testament and the natural law.[97]

This "natural law," Luther noted, has much in common with the Ten Commandments ("there is one God, no one is to do wrong to another, no one is to commit murder or steal"), but was "written by nature into their [the Gentiles'] hearts; they did not hear it straight from heaven as the Jews did."[98] Luther here implies that since this law was written by nature, most of it (except, perhaps, "there is one God") was also written into the hearts of Gentiles before their conversion, thereby inviting Germans to view their ancestors not just as pre-Christian, but as proto-Christian, and therefore a people they could look back on with pride and respect.

Three hundred years later, this pride in a Germanic pre-Christian heritage—what I will term "philo-Heathenism"—underwent a significant revival, no doubt in part because of the growing anti-Semitic movement and the resulting desire to understand Christianity as historically independent from Judaism. Friedrich Schleiermacher codified this position in the 1820s in the era's most prominent theological treatise, *The Christian Faith* (*Der christliche Glaube*):

> Christianity does indeed stand in a special historical connexion [*sic*] with Judaism; *but as far as concerns its historical existence and its aim, its relations to Judaism and Heathenism are the same.* . . .
>
> [They] are the same, inasmuch as the transition from either of these to Christianity is a transition to another religion. The leap certainly seems greater in the case of Heathenism, since it had first to become monotheistic in order

to become Christian. At the same time, the two processes were not separated, but Monotheism was given to the heathen directly in the form of Christianity, as it had been previously in the form of Judaism. And the demand made upon the Jews, to give up their reliance upon the law, and to put a different interpretation upon the Abrahamitic promises, was just as large a demand. Accordingly we must assume that Christian piety, in its original form, cannot be explained by means of the Jewish piety of that or of an earlier time, and so *Christianity cannot in any wise* [*sic*] *be regarded as a remodeling or a renewal and continuation of Judaism.*[99] (emphasis added)

Schleiermacher, like Luther, then used this argument to discount the importance of those elements of the Old Testament that do not directly relate to the New (i.e., those lacking Messianic prophecy). In the process, however, he upset the equivalence he had established between Judaism and Heathenism in the previous passage and betrayed his distinct preference for the latter:

[Except for prophecy,] almost everything else in the Old Testament is, for our Christian usage, but the husk or wrapping of its prophecy, and that whatever is most definitely Jewish has least value. So that we can find rendered with some exactness in Old Testament passages only those of our religious emotions which are of a somewhat general nature without anything very distinctively Christian. For those which are distinctively Christian, Old Testament sayings will not provide a suitable expression, unless we think certain elements away from them and read other things into them. And that being the case, we shall certainly find quite as near and accordant echoes in the utterances of *the nobler and purer Heathenism*; as indeed the older Apologists were no less glad to appeal to what they held to be heathen Messianic prophecies, and thus recognized there a striving of human nature towards Christianity.[100] (emphasis added)

Such a notion of Christianity's independence from Judaism was not limited to theological discussion. In music it most often took the form of oratorios about the evangelization of the heathen Germanic tribes by St. Boniface (*Bonifacius* or *Bonifazius*). Boniface (ca. 675–754), the so-called German Apostle, was the Anglo-Saxon missionary responsible for bringing Christianity to most of central Germany and for organizing churches there. Before his work, only the Rhineland and Bavaria had converted, leaving the vast central regions of the country dominated by Heathenism.[101] Among the oratorio subjects set by German composers in the first half of the nineteenth century, St. Boniface was the most popular after Christ and Moses. Karl Ludwig Drobish wrote the first of the century's Boniface oratorios (*Boniface, the Apostle of the Germans* [*Bonifazius, der Apostel der Deutschen*]) in 1826. A surge of interest in the subject—in the form of four additional settings—came in the late 1830s: August Wilhelm Bach's *Boniface, the German Apostle* (*Bonifacius der deutsche Apostel,*

1837),[102] August Mühling's *Bonifazius* (1839), F. Keller's *Bonifacius* (ca. 1840), and Friedrich Schneider's unfinished *Bonifacius* (1837–39, 1848), for which Schubring served as the librettist.[103]

Paul—the missionary archetype—was the fourth most popular German oratorio subject in the first half of the nineteenth century; as was the case with Boniface, most of the settings were composed in the 1830s.[104] Only one of these predates Mendelssohn's *Paulus* concept: that of Eduard Grell, another student of Zelter's, who completed his *Paulus* in 1824.[105] Two other Paul oratorios appeared in 1835 while Mendelssohn was composing *Paulus*—Heinrich Elkamp's *Paulus* and Carl Loewe's *The Apostles from Philippi* (*Die Apostel von Philippi*)[106]—and at least one more appeared after *Paulus*'s completion, Christian Gottlob August Bergt's *Paul's Conversion* (*Pauli Bekehrung*, 1841). These settings suggest that, as with Boniface, there was significant interest in the apostle and his missionary work at that time. This was certainly the case among theologians, for whom Paul became a topic of renewed discussion around the same time the composition of these oratorios was under way.

As Albert Schweitzer wrote in his 1911 survey of Pauline scholarship, "The Reformation fought and conquered in the name of Paul" and "[c]onsequently the teaching of the Apostle of the Gentiles took a prominent place in Protestant study."[107] This connection between Paul and German Protestantism was undoubtedly obvious to the members of Mendelssohn's circle, as Marx's description of the apostle as "Paul, the teacher, the wise man—I might almost have said the Protestant, the rationalist," attests.[108] Mendelssohn too acknowledged this connection in his draft ending for *Paulus*, in which the apostle leads the people in singing the flagship of Protestant chorales, Luther's *A Mighty Fortress Is Our God* (*Ein feste Burg ist unser Gott*) (ex. 4.1).

Although the Protestant focus on Paul had been continuous since Luther, a burst of activity occurred around 1830 with the publication of several groundbreaking works. Among the earliest was the first purely historical study of Paulinism, Leonhard Usteri's *The Development of the Paulinian System* (*Die Entwicklung des paulischen Lehrbegriffs*) of 1824, which spawned several other significant historical studies, including Karl Schrader's five-volume *Der Apostel Paulus* (1830–1836) and August Ferdinand Dähne's *Entwicklung des paulinischen Lehrbegriffs* (1835).[109] Similar to the interest in Boniface, this heightened attention to Paul was likely grounded in a desire among Germans to locate the origins of their Christian faith in the missions to the Gentiles, as well as to define that origin as wholly separate from Judaism. This distinction had a direct bearing on their view of Paul, whom they viewed not as a converted Jew, but rather as a formerly Jewish Gentile, despite Paul's own clear testimony of his Jewish lineage (through the tribe of Benjamin) in Philippians 3:5. The comments of G. W. Fink in his review of Mendelssohn's *Paulus*, for instance, suggest that while Germans acknowledged Paul's Jewish faith, they put more emphasis on his birth as a Roman citizen in the Greek city of Tarsus. "He was born Greek, was Jewish educated and from a persecutor became, through the light of the vision and

EXAMPLE 4.1. *D-Bsb MN 28 (Text X), no. 28, mm. 37–53, vocal parts only.*

through the voice of the word, a preacher of the victory," Fink exclaimed.[110] Contemporary theologians such as Karl Schrader and Johannes Hemsen also commonly labeled Paul a "Hellenistic Jew"—a title that in itself implies a dual identity as both Jew and Gentile—and were quick to point out Paul's ability to function in both Jewish and Greek society.[111] Both Schrader and Hemsen strengthen this image of dual heritage with their claim that the apostle was given both a Gentile name (Paul) and a Hebrew name (Saul) at the time of his birth.[112]

The Evolution of the Anti-Semitic Image in *Paulus*

Not surprisingly, nineteenth-century German ideologies that glorified the German people's Gentile heritage and delineated their Christianity from the Jewish past had a profound effect on *Paulus*'s depiction of Paul's successful mission to the Gentiles and his unsuccessful attempts to convert the Jews. With their obsession with the letter of the law and their inability to grasp its spirit, *Paulus*'s Jews function as the sole persecutors of the great missionary and the source of his Christlike suffering. Significantly, however, the piece did not start out that way. Although the work had a strong anti-Semitic bent even in its earliest incarnation (Text I), it still contained scenes in which Paul met resistance from both Jews *and* Gentiles. But even at this point, Mendelssohn showed no inclination to avoid depicting the Jews as oppressors and nonbelievers. This anti-Semitic bent is most apparent in the outline for Part III (what would eventually become Part II), in which Mendelssohn labeled one set of biblical citations as "Paul's sadness over the faithlessness of the Jews" (*Pauli Trauer um die Ungläubigkeit der Juden*). As Mendelssohn's work on the libretto progressed, the Jewish image worsened. And while numerous opportunities arose—usually in the form of suggestions from Fürst, Marx, or Schubring—for Mendelssohn to depict the Jews more favorably, he did not avail himself of them. Consequently, most of *Paulus*'s scenes exhibit a pattern of intensification in their anti-Semitic content—at Mendelssohn's hand—over the course of the work's development. Only in the last set of revisions of the piece—those made after his father's death—did Mendelssohn make a genuine, comprehensive attempt to temper the attacks on the Jews, albeit one not sufficient to prevent the oratorio from continuing to glorify the Gentiles at their expense.

While Mendelssohn's tendencies to glorify the Germanic Gentile ancestry and to intensify the work's anti-Semitic content are evident in the development of nearly all of *Paulus*'s scenes,[113] the most vivid display emerges in the scene following the Gentiles' worship of Paul and Barnabas as the gods Mercury and Jupiter (GA 35–37). In the published score, Mendelssohn demonstrates Paul's missionary success by having the now former pagans celebrate their new faith by joining the apostle in singing "But our God is in heaven" (*Aber unser Gott ist im Himmel*), along with most of the first sentence of the Nicene Creed (through the embedded Luther chorale "We all believe in one God" [*Wir glauben all' an einen Gott*]) (ex. 4.2).

EXAMPLE 4.2. Paulus, *GA 35, mm. 106–49, with the chorale* Wir glauben all' an einen Gott *in the second soprano voice.*

EXAMPLE 4.2. *(continued)*

EXAMPLE 4.2. (*continued*)

Mendelssohn immediately follows this, however, with one of several depictions of Paul's failures with the Jews, who declare "Here is the Lord's temple" and seek to . stone him for speaking out "against the law and against this holy place" (GA 37). What makes this scene of particular importance when considering the emergence of anti-Semitism in *Paulus* is that in its early incarnations, it was the Greeks, not the Jews, who were cast in the role of the persecutors.

In his outline (Text I, p. 7), Mendelssohn noted that he would base the uprising scene predominantly upon Acts 19:26–28, which takes place among the Greeks in Ephesus. (Significantly, the biblical passage makes no mention of Jews being present.) In this biblical passage, Paul declares that "gods made with hands are not gods" (Acts 19:26), after which the goldsmiths, seeing their trade in idols threatened, speak out:

> And you see and hear that . . . throughout almost all Asia this Paul has turned away and persuaded many people, saying that gods made with hands are not

gods. And there is danger not only that this trade of ours may come into disrepute but also that the temple of the great goddess Diana may count for nothing, and that she may even be deposed from her magnificence, she whom all Asia and the world worship. (Acts 19:26–27)[114]

Soon they succeed in sparking an uprising, crying out, as Mendelssohn wrote in his outline, "Great is Diana of the Ephesians" (*Groß ist die Diana der Epheser*). Paul responds:

All men are fools with their art, and all goldsmiths are put to shame by their images; for their idols are false, and have no life in them. They are worthless, and works of delusion; they shall perish at the time of their punishment. (Jer. 51:17–18)

Paul and his disciple Silas are then thrown into prison.

Since Mendelssohn's outline was little more than a list of biblical citations, the bulk of Fürst's work when he composed his draft (IIIa) involved turning the passages Mendelssohn specified into coherent prose and assigning characters; he also occasionally added supplemental text and/or characters so as to make the work more dramatically interesting and improve the flow of the story. One particularly interesting embellishment of this scene (fol. 4v) was Fürst's addition of a "maidservant with the spirit of prophesy" (*Magd mit dem Wahrsagergeist*). The woman describes Paul and his unnamed disciple(s) as "servants of God the almighty, who will preach the way of blessedness to you" (*Knechte Gottes des Allerhöchsten, die euch den Weg der Seligkeit verkündigen*). The "masters of the maidservant" (*Herren der Magd*) protest, however, that "[t]hese men are causing confusion in our city and are Jews, and advocate customs which are not proper for us to accept or practice" (*Diese Menschen machen unsere Stadt irre und sind Juden, und verkündigen eine W[ei]se welche uns nicht ziemet anzunehmen noch zu thun*). By clearly identifying the "masters" as non-Jews, Fürst restricts this minor uprising to the Gentiles (in accordance with Mendelssohn's outline). (Indeed, Fürst—a Jew himself—seems to be making a strong statement about anti-Semitism here, suggesting that the reason the Ephesians refuse to listen to Paul is as much due to the fact that he is a Jew as anything else.)

Marx, in his draft of this scene (Text IV, fol. 7v), was equally clear that those involved in the uprising were non-Jews: their recurrent cry of "Great is Diana of the Ephesians," followed by "The gods have descended!" plainly identify them as Gentiles. Unlike their depiction in other drafts, however, the Gentiles appear conflicted here: some wish to stone Paul, others want to praise him as a god. Eventually, those wishing to stone him prevail.

Chor	*Chorus*
Groß ist die Diana der Epheser!—	Great is Diana of the Ephesians!—
Die Götter sind hernieder kommen!—	The gods have descended!—
Rein ab mit diesen Spöttern!—	Away with these mockers!—

Rec.	Recit.
Und steinigten Paulum und schleiften ihn zur Stadt hinaus, meineten, er wäre gestorben.	And [they] stoned Paul and dragged him out of the city, thinking he was dead.

Significantly, although Marx took the stoning text (*Und steinigten Paulum*) from Acts 14:19 (during Paul's visit to Iconium, not Ephesus), he deliberately ignored that same biblical passage's description of the role of the Jews in the uprising: "But Jews came there from Antioch and Iconium; and having persuaded the people, they stoned Paul and dragged him out of the city, thinking he was dead."

Mendelssohn's own first prose draft of the *Paulus* libretto (Text V), which he sent to Schubring, consolidated the contributions of Marx and Fürst into a much shorter scene (fol. 401v), consisting of two narrative recitatives and two presentations of the "Great is Diana of the Ephesians" chorus, with, again, no mention of Jews.

[Recit.:] Es erhub sich aber zugleich nicht eine kleine Bewegung; denn da die Goldschmiede hören, wie Paulus sprach, wurden sie voll Zorns und sprachen:	[Recit.:] About that time there arose no little stir: for when the goldsmiths heard what Paul said, they were enraged and said:
<u>Chor</u> Groß ist die Diana der Epheser.	<u>Chorus</u> Great is Diana of the Ephesians.
[Recit:] Und die ganze Stadt ward voll Getümmels. Sie stürmeten einmüthiglich zum Schauplatz und ergriffen Pauli Gefährten, und es erhob sich eine Stimme von allem Volk und schrieen:	[Recit:] And the entire city was filled with commotion. They rushed together to the theater and took hold of Paul's travel companions, and there arose a single voice of all the people and they cried out:
<u>Chor</u> Groß ist die Diana der Epheser.	<u>Chorus</u> Great is Diana of the Ephesians.

Schubring apparently approved, writing only "See the original text.—(Your manuscript)" at this point in his draft (Text VI, fol. 406v). Mendelssohn's next draft (Text VII, fol. 29v) expanded the scene slightly by introducing in the opening recitative the impetus for the uprising (Paul's statement that there are no gods made by human hands) and by adding Paul's response to the choruses, the passage from Jeremiah he had noted in his original outline ("All men are fools with their art").

In his next draft of the scene, written a month or so later (Text VIII, fol. 31v), Mendelssohn opened with Paul's "All men are fools with their art" monologue, but otherwise rewrote the entire scene from scratch. The new material began with a chorus based on a text he had never used before, "Arise, O God, and plead thy cause" (*Mache dich auf, Gott, und führe deine Sache*), which he adapted from Psalms 74:22 and 82:6–7.

Text VIII, fol. 31v, left column

Mache dich auf, Gott, und führe deine Sache. Gedenke an die Schmach, die dir	Arise, O God, and plead thy cause. Remember how the impious

täglich von den Thoren widerfähret. Wir
haben wohl gesagt[:] Ihr seid Götter, und
allzumal Kinder des Höchsten, aber ihr
werdet umkommen, wie Menschen.

daily scoff at thee. Truly we
have said: You are gods, and
also sons of the Most High, all of you; but
you will die like men.

Mendelssohn eventually decided against this chorus (it appears crossed-out in the draft). Nevertheless, it represents the first step in a new direction for this scene—away from both the previous versions and the biblical narrative of Paul in Ephesus itself—in that it changes the identity of the accusers from Gentiles to Jews, as the chorus's mention of God (in the singular) reveals. Indeed, Mendelssohn made this connection even more concrete in his corrections to the draft by replacing the first sentence of the *Mache dich auf, Gott* chorus with the words "Here is the Lord's temple, here is the Lord's temple" (*Hier ist des Herrn Tempel, hier ist des Herrn Tempel*) and by adding the exclamation "Stone him" (*Steinige ihn*) to the end.

Text VIII, fol. 31v, right column

Hier ist des Herrn Tempel, hier ist des
H[err]n Tempel. Wir haben wohl
gesagt[:] Ihr seid Götter, aber ihr werdet
umkommen, wie Menschen. Steinige
ihn.

Here is the Lord's temple, here is the
Lord's temple. Truly we have
said: you are gods, but you will
die like men. Stone
him.

Clearly, with its reference to both God and gods and its use of the second person plural and the third person singular, this is a text in transition. Still, there remains little doubt that despite the lack of any explicit identification, this chorus is comprised primarily of Jews.

In the next stage in the evolution of the work, as represented by Mendelssohn's compositional piano-vocal score (Text XI, no. 39), the text takes on its nearly final form, and a description of the crowd as being partially composed of Jews has now been added to the preceding recitative (ex. 4.3).

While the mention of both Jews and Gentiles here would seem to make the attack on Paul universal, in composing the Düsseldorf full score (Text XIII, no. 39) Mendelssohn changed the music of the recitative slightly, and in so doing placed a definite accent on the first syllable of *Juden* (in the example above, both syllables are set on g^1, while in the Düsseldorf score, the first syllable leaps up to e^2, the highest note in the entire recitative). This emphasis remains in the published score (GA 36) (ex. 4.4).[115] More significant, in the chorus that follows (Texts XI–XIII, no. 40; GA 37), all mention of pagan gods has been removed and the stereotype of Jews as unable to see beyond the law has been inserted in its stead.[116] Thus, despite the mention of the Gentiles' presence in the recitative, the chorus—which depicts the uprising itself—now contains nothing that even hints at their participation.

EXAMPLE 4.3. *PL-Kj MN Bd. 55 (Text XI), no. 39. The text translates: "But the people were stirred up against them, and there arose a storm of Jews and Gentiles, and they were enraged and cried aloud: [Here is the Lord's temple . . .]"*

| Hier ist des Herren Tempel! Hier ist des Herren Tempel! Ihr Männer von Israel helfet! Dies ist der Mensch, der alle Menschen an allen Enden lehret wider dies Volk, wider das Gesetz und wider diese heil'ge Stätte. Steiniget ihn! Steiniget ihn er lästert Gott. Steiniget ihn! | Here is the Lord's temple! Here is the Lord's temple! You men of Israel, help! This is the man who is teaching men everywhere against this people, against the law and against this holy place. Stone him! Stone him, he blasphemes God. Stone him! |

Further establishing the identity of this group are textual, rhythmic, and melodic connections between this chorus and those in the oratorio's first scene, in which Stephen is accused, tried, convicted, and stoned by a group easily recognizable as Jews. The plainness of the Jews' identity in the first scene comes from their charge that Stephen has spoken "blasphemous words against Moses and against God" in GA 4 (*Dieser Mensch hört nicht auf*), a chorus whose principal motive is melodically and rhythmically similar to that in *Hier ist des Herren Tempel* (ex. 4.5). Additionally, the two choruses share textual themes, as both complain of teachings against the law, God, and "this (holy) place," using analogous phrasing and key words (e.g., *wider Mosen und wider Gott* in GA 4, vs. *wider dies Volk, wider das Gesetz* in GA 37; *Jesus von Nazareth wird diese Stätte zerstören* in GA 4, vs. *wider diese heil'ge Stätte* in GA 37). Phrases similar to these from *Hier ist des Herren Tempel* also appear in the testimony of the false witnesses against Stephen (GA 3), where he is likewise accused of speaking out against "this holy place" and against the law (*wider diese heil'ge Stätte*

EXAMPLE 4.4. Paulus, *GA 36, mm. 3–4.*

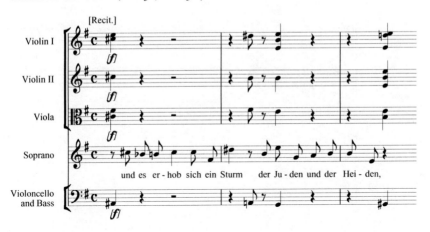

EXAMPLE 4.5. Paulus, *GA 37 (mm. 1–2) and 4 (mm. 1–2) principal motives and GA 4 text with translation.*

Dieser Mensch hört nicht auf zu reden Lästerworte wider Mosen und wider Gott. Haben wir euch nicht mit Ernst geboten, dass ihr nicht solltet lehren in diesem Namen? Und sehet, ihr habt Jerusalem erfüllt mit eurer Lehre. Denn wir haben ihn hören sagen: Jesus von Nazareth wird diese Stätte zerstören und ändern die Sitten, die uns Mose gegeben hat.	This man never ceases to speak blasphemous words against Moses and against God. Have we not strictly ordered that you should not to teach in this name? And see, you have filled Jerusalem with your teachings. For we have heard him say: Jesus of Nazareth will destroy this place and change the customs that Moses gave us.

und das Gesetz). More significant, however, is the musical borrowing that takes place between the *Hier ist des Herren Tempel* stoning chorus and Stephen's stoning chorus (GA 7); although they are in different keys, the music is otherwise nearly identical (ex. 4.6).[117]

EXAMPLE 4.6a. Paulus, *GA 7, mm. 6–8 (chorus and strings only).*

EXAMPLE 4.6b. Paulus, *GA 37, mm. 35–37 (chorus and strings only).*

In addition to confirming the identity of those singing the *Hier ist des Herren Tempel* chorus as Jews, these parallels further establish them as being both unable to see beyond the law and—like those who stoned Stephen—"stiff-necked" and resistant of the Holy Spirit.

As this evolution from initial outline to final version demonstrates, Mendelssohn rejected the options provided by the actual biblical story in Acts 19:26–28 and by his contributors to position the Gentile Greeks at the heart of the uprising against Paul, choosing instead to place the Jews in that role. Moreover, although Mendelssohn may have felt a need to protect the image of the Greeks because of the pride Germans felt in their own Gentile heritage, he made no similar effort to protect the Jews, despite the options explored in his earlier prose drafts, which kept their identity vague. Instead, Mendelssohn included additional text with each successive draft that identified the Jews with greater and greater clarity, until finally declaring their presence and role outright.

A second short but highly dramatic example of Mendelssohn's repudiation of Judaism appears in the Düsseldorf score (no. 24). After the soprano recitative announcing Paul's recovery of sight and his preaching of Christ, Paul recites a compilation of passages taken from Romans 7:25 and 8:2 that had not been suggested by any of Mendelssohn's contributors: "I thank God through Jesus Christ our Lord, for the law of the Spirit, which gives life through Jesus Christ, has set me free from the law of sin and of death" (*Ich danke Gott durch Jesum Christ unsern Herrn, denn das Gesetz des Geistes, der da lebendig macht in Christo Jesu, hat mich frei gemacht von dem Gesetz der Sünde und des Todes*). That Mendelssohn himself found and included this condemnation of the old law "of sin and death" (a typical New Testament reference to the law of Moses) represents perhaps his most zealous attempt throughout the entire genesis of the oratorio to emphasize the protagonist's (and, by extension, his own) separation from Judaism.

But just as significant as its inclusion in the Düsseldorf score is the fact that Mendelssohn chose to omit this passage from the published edition. Indeed, this deletion is but one of several instances in which the composer softened the anti-Semitic intensity of certain scenes during the final revision process. Although none of the changes would significantly alter the anti-Semitic tenor of the work, they do represent Mendelssohn's first step away from the fear of his heritage instilled by his father and the resulting compulsion to repudiate it so vehemently. Both attitudes began to fade after he had recovered from his father's death and *Paulus* had been successfully premiered.

Lessons from *Paulus*: A Reevaluation of *Die erste Walpurgisnacht*

My observations in this and the preceding chapter regarding Mendelssohn's sacred libretti of the early 1830s raise interesting questions for another work that has often been discussed in relation to the composer's Jewish heritage: the secular cantata *The First Walpurgis-Night* (*Die erste Walpurgisnacht*). Mendelssohn began setting Johann

Wolfgang von Goethe's 1799 ballad of the same name shortly after visiting the poet for two weeks in Weimar in May 1830. From there, Mendelssohn continued his journey toward Italy, making an extended stop in Munich, and another in Vienna, where his friend, the opera singer Franz Hauser, gave him two Goethe volumes: *Faust* (part one, which Mendelssohn already knew well) and a collection of poetry that likely included *Die erste Walpurgisnacht.*[118] Hauser also probably gave Mendelssohn the book of Luther chorale texts he received shortly before leaving Vienna. (Mendelssohn, however, only identifies the giver as "an acquaintance."[119]) Lacking much in the way of German literature during his travels, Mendelssohn made extensive use of these volumes for both leisure reading[120] and as textual sources for many of the vocal works he composed along the way.[121] The Goethe volume proved useful almost immediately, as Mendelssohn began composing the *Walpurgisnacht* while still in Hauser's company.[122]

The majority of the *Walpurgisnacht* score was composed in Italy, with Mendelssohn completing the first version of the vocal movements in Milan on July 15, 1831. (The overture would not be completed until February 13, 1832, while he was in Paris.[123]) On October 11, a few months after his return home to Berlin, Mendelssohn premiered the work before a small private audience at one of Fanny's "Sunday Music" (*Sontagsmusik*) programs in the Mendelssohn home. On January 10, 1833, it received its public premiere—on the last of three charity subscription concerts at the Singakademie—to mixed reviews. (The long overture was viewed as particularly problematic.[124]) No doubt disappointed, Mendelssohn set the piece aside until December 1842, when, perhaps inspired by the more successful and similarly structured *Lobgesang* (1840), he began revising it in preparation for a performance before Saxon king Friedrich August II in Leipzig on December 21. The death of his mother on December 12 forced Mendelssohn to cancel, but by mid-January work on the score had resumed and a revised version of the cantata was performed at the Gewandhaus on February 2, 1843, this time to much greater acclaim. In the months that followed, Mendelssohn continued to revise the work for submission to Leipzig publisher Friedrich Kistner; it was not until July 15 that Mendelssohn finally declared it finished.[125]

In addition to the score itself, Kistner's edition included a segment of a letter Goethe sent the composer on September 9, 1831:

> In a true sense the poem is highly symbolic in intention. For in world-history it must continually be repeated that something old, established, proven, re-assuring is pressed, shifted, displaced by emerging innovations, and, where not wiped out, none the less penned up in the narrowest space. The medieval era, where hatred still can and may produce countereffects, is here impressively enough represented, and a joyous indestructible enthusiasm blazes up once more in radiance and clarity.[126]

This quotation—especially Goethe's statement that the work is "highly symbolic in intention"—has led to a number of interpretations not only of Goethe's poem, but also of Mendelssohn's score, and to theories as to what inspired the composer to set

the ballad. The poem itself tells the story of the medieval Druids, who, while traveling up the Brocken (also known as the Blocksberg, the highest peak in the Harz
mountains) to sacrifice to the "Father of the Universe" (*Allvater*), reflect on their
increasing marginalization and the persecution they will face at the hands of Christians if discovered.[127] But rather than abandon their ritual, they instead take the pre-
caution of posting guards dressed as devils and other hellish creatures, in hopes that
the guards and the spectacle of the rite itself will scare off the superstitious
"dimwitted, gullible Christians" (*dumpfen Pfaffenchristen*). Indeed, when the Christians arrive, they see the "wolf-men and dragon-women" (*Menschen-Wölf' und
Drachen-Weiber*) and flee in terror, leaving the Druids to complete their rite in peace.

Goethe's declaration that the events depicted in the poem are not just symbolic,
but historical—an example of a recurring phenomenon—does seem to invite comparison to the situation of another historically oppressed and persecuted group: the
Jews. Given Mendelssohn's background and the postwar assumption that his connection to his heritage remained strong throughout his life, this interpretation has been
offered repeatedly by scholars, despite the lack of any documentary support.[128] The
most emphatic statement came from Heinz-Klaus Metzger, who declared that despite
"whatever Goethe meant in his ballad and Mendelssohn may have said or withheld
in connection with his composition," he saw the piece "as a Jewish protest against
the domination of Christendom. Goethe's 'Druids' are none other than the Jews in
Mendelssohn's composition."[129] More recently, Julie Prandi has argued that Enlightenment ideology stands behind the dignified manner in which the Druids and their
rite are depicted in both Goethe's poem and Mendelssohn's score, as in the closing
hymn-like praise of the fire that symbolizes the light of the Druids' faith.[130] Crucial to
both of these interpretations is Goethe's letter declaring the poem's symbolic intent, a
fact that raises a problem of chronology, since Mendelssohn received the letter only
after completing everything but the overture (to which none of these arguments refers).

The lateness of Goethe's letter in the compositional history of *Die erste Walpurgisnacht*, combined with my arguments regarding the works that Mendelssohn composed at roughly the same time, call for a reassessment of the cantata. Given
Mendelssohn's conservative editing of the Bach *St. Matthew Passion* score, and, more
significant, the unflattering manner in which he portrayed the Jews in the *Moses* and
Paulus libretti, the idea that the Druids represent the Jews becomes untenable. What,
then, led Mendelssohn to set the ballad?

Mendelssohn's earliest exposure to Goethe's *Walpurgisnacht* may have come not
through Hauser, but through Zelter, who thrice tried unsuccessfully to set it and for
whom Goethe likely wrote the ballad. (Goethe sent the text—which includes segments intended to be sung by choirs—to Zelter less than a month after completing
it.[131]) While, on the one hand, it seems unlikely Zelter would have pointed out his
compositional failures to his young student, the tone of Felix's letter to Fanny in-
forming her of his work on the poem suggests that both siblings were familiar with
the text, as well as, perhaps, with the difficulties in setting it. "Hear and be amazed[!],"

Felix wrote. "Since Vienna I have partially composed Goethe's *Die erste Walpurgis-nacht* and yet have lacked the courage to write it down."[132] No doubt his visit to Goethe helped to (re-)kindle Mendelssohn's desire to set one of the eminent poet's works, but Mendelssohn does not appear to have specifically discussed *Die erste Walpurgisnacht* while in Weimar, as his first letter to Goethe on the subject demonstrates. "[W]hat occupies me almost exclusively for some weeks is the music to the poem of Your Honorable Excellency that is called The First Walpurgis Night," Mendelssohn wrote.[133] Mendelssohn's access to the text itself through Hauser's gift (which also reacquainted him with the *Walpurgisnacht* in *Faust*) was certainly instrumental in making the setting possible, but what made this story stand out among the dozens in the volume was its potential for inclusion of music written in Mendelssohn's unique "fairy" or "elfin" style (a sample of which appears in ex. 4.7).

Mendelssohn's "fairy" scherzo style is most strongly associated with—and receives its moniker from—his 1826 *Midsummer Night's Dream* concert overture. (The style is first heard in the incessant, oscillating, staccato eighth-note sequences that appear in the violins just after the distinctive opening woodwind chords, as in ex. 4.8.) But as Catharine Melhorn has pointed out, Mendelssohn made extensive use of the style in the years before and after the composition of the *Midsummer Night's Dream* Overture, including in several works that were inspired by the subject of the Walpurgis night.[134] The most noted of these was the scherzo of the acclaimed 1825 Octet (op. 20), in which, as Fanny revealed, Mendelssohn attempted to capture the spirit of the last stanza from the Walpurgis-night dream in *Faust*: "The flight of the clouds and the veil of mist I Are lighted from above. I A breeze in the leaves, a wind in the reeds, I And all has vanished." Fanny also clearly believed her brother succeeded in conveying this program in the Octet, writing that "one feels so near the world of spirits, carried away in the air, half inclined to snatch up a broomstick and follow the aërial procession."[135]

Another elfin work from 1825 is the scherzo of the Piano Quartet in B Minor (op. 3). Here again, Mendelssohn's intention to evoke the supernatural was not lost on his audience, which in this case included Goethe—the work's dedicatee—for whom its

EXAMPLE 4.7. Die erste Walpurgisnacht, *no. 7, mm. 13–19.*

EXAMPLE 4.8. Midsummer Night's Dream *Overture, mm. 8–15.*

"endless whirling and turning brought the witches' dances of the Blocksberg before my eyes."[136] In the years that followed, Mendelssohn's fascination with the supernatural—and witches in particular—remained strong, leading him in 1829 to set for voice and piano poet Ludwig Hölty's "Another May-Song" (*And'res Maienlied*), also known as "Witches' Song" (*Hexenlied*, op. 8, no. 8), a Walpurgis-night scene set on the Brocken.

As Mendelssohn's numerous letters on the project reveal, the same fascination that led him to these earlier works sparked his interest in *Die erste Walpurgisnacht*. Particularly significant is the letter in which he announced the project to Fanny, where he confesses his "particular weakness" (*besonderes faible*) for the "witches' spook":

> The thing [*Die erste Walpurgisnacht*] . . . can really be fun; for at the beginning there are plenty of spring songs and such; then, when the watchmen raise a ruckus with their pitchforks and spikes and owls, the witches' spook is added, and you know I have a particular weakness for that. Then the druids, ready to sacrifice, come out in C major with trombones, then again the watchmen . . . and finally at the end the complete sacrificial song.[137]

Conspicuously absent from the letters, however, is any reference to any symbolic meaning within Goethe's text. It would seem, therefore, that for the twenty-one-year-old Mendelssohn, the decision to set *Die erste Walpurgisnacht* had little to do with any desire to champion Enlightenment sensibilities or to construct an allegory of the history of Jews in Christendom. Mendelssohn's motives, rather, found their origin in much less lofty concerns: here was a text which blended well with his current interest in the supernatural and lent itself to numerous musical possibilities.

Given Mendelssohn's understanding of his precarious standing in the Christian community, one question regarding *Walpurgisnacht* remains: How did he reconcile himself to the pro-pagan bent of the text? The findings of the preceding pages suggest two explanations. The composer hints at the first of these in his correspondence and through his use of "elfin" music in the piece, both of which imply that he saw the story not as symbolic—as Goethe later described it—but simply as a legend or fairytale, similar to *Midsummer Night's Dream* or the more closely related *Hexenlied*. The legend of the Brocken was quite well known, with many of the numerous tourists to the region (including, in 1827, Mendelssohn himself) commenting on it in their journals.[138] Indeed, Goethe himself likely contributed to the legend's notoriety, having made the Brocken the setting for the Walpurgis-night scene in *Faust*.

A second reason is suggested by the dignity that both Goethe and Mendelssohn accorded the Druids and their rite. This noble treatment was recognized by Mendelssohn's contemporaries, including Marx, who noted that the Druids' "striving for eternal light" in Goethe's text was "actually characteristic of Christendom," and that the depiction of witchcraft in Mendelssohn's score "never becomes real witchcraft, with its cruel power, but rather hovers between prank and reality."[139] While Marx saw the latter as a defect in the work, his observation illustrates the sympathies both Goethe and Mendelssohn displayed for the Druids in this conflict. While some have attributed this to the Enlightenment views both men shared,[140] such interpretations fail to appreciate the thirty-one years that passed between the creation of the poem and the music. While Enlightenment ideologies may shed light on Goethe's intent, Mendelssohn's motivations can be better explained by the prevalence of philo-Heathenism in the 1820s and 1830s, a possibility that seems even more likely, given the impact philo-Heathenism had on *Paulus*, the other work in which Mendelssohn depicted pagans positively. Indeed, the impact of philo-Heathenism is even more pronounced in *Die erste Walpurgisnacht*, since the Druids in that work are not just any pagans but are Germans—or, more specifically, Saxons—a fact that Mendelssohn was not only keenly aware of, but that he also shared with others, including Fanny, to whom he described the overture as "the Saxon A minor."[141]

As the *St. Matthew Passion* edition and the *Moses* and *Paulus* libretti demonstrate, Mendelssohn carefully avoided setting or editing works in a manner that might have led to doubts as to the sincerity of his Christian faith or to accusations that he harbored a philo-Semitic agenda. The likelihood, therefore, that he would have deliberately composed a work which would have led to such an accusation seems small. To Mendelssohn, Goethe's *Die erste Walpurgisnacht* posed no such risk, while demonstrating simultaneously the potential for a variety of compositional possibilities, including the use of "fairy" music. Meanwhile, recent claims that the work is "anti-Christian" ignore the fact that the Christians in the poem were medieval Catholics, the group that Luther would later fight against and whom Mendelssohn could easily place in an adversarial role and mock as "dimwitted" without risk of reprisal. (Indeed, Marx's comments suggest Protestants identified strongly with the Druids, given both groups' struggle to overcome Catholic oppression.) Even more important, in siding with and dignifying the Druids, Mendelssohn managed to glorify the Germanic Gentile ancestry—an ancestry that, given his German pride, he most certainly viewed as his own.[142]

5

Elias

[A]t a performance of *Elias,* one is a guest of the Jewish faith.
—*Paul-Gerhard Nohl*

T HE COMMON INTERPRETATION of Mendelssohn's second oratorio, *Elias,* as a purely Old Testament work and the belief that Mendelssohn himself retained a strong sense of pride in his Jewish heritage have long been mutually self-supporting views. Downplaying *Elias's* Messianic ending,[1] critics and audiences alike have seen Mendelssohn's composition of a work based on the life of a central Old Testament prophet as evidence of his Jewish identification. Meanwhile, this assumption that Mendelssohn retained a lingering attachment to Judaism has led critics to interpret *Elias* as a wholly Jewish work.[2] What such circuitous logic ignores, however, is that *Elias,* like Mendelssohn's *Moses,* is, in fact, a New Testament–oriented work, and that—as the libretto drafts reveal—it was intended as such from the outset.

As we have seen with *Moses,* the custom of orienting Old Testament works toward the New Covenant found a theological basis in the writings of thinkers such as Mendelssohn's own spiritual mentor, Friedrich Schleiermacher, who argued that "[except for prophecy,] almost everything else in the Old Testament is, for our Christian usage, but the husk or wrapping of its prophecy."[3] Elijah was one of the most significant prophetic figures, as he—like Moses—plays an extremely important role throughout the New Testament. Mendelssohn recognized this role and designed not only the character of Elijah—whom he depicts as an Old Testament Christ—but also the entire plan for *Elias* so as to remind the listener of the gospel story. While this Christological program is still quite discernable in the published score, it is more clearly evident in the drafts of the libretto, which often included more obvious Elijah-Christ parallels.

Although not a Jewish work per se, as many have argued, *Elias* does represent a sharp improvement in Mendelssohn's relationship to his Jewish heritage, given the sympathetic manner in which he depicts the Jews throughout the work, despite its Christological program. For although Mendelssohn continued in *Elias* the pattern he established in both *Moses* and *Paulus* of depicting his protagonist as a Christlike figure, he succeeded here in avoiding representing the Jews as they appear in the New Testament—as a law-obsessed people incapable of true faith. As the drafts of the libretto reveal, however, this sympathetic depiction came about slowly and was the product of intense experimentation on Mendelssohn's part.

A Textual History of *Elias*

No doubt inspired by *Paulus*'s enthusiastic reception, Mendelssohn had already started thinking about composing a second oratorio, and had even begun to search for a librettist, before completing the final revisions to his first. Having experienced so many problems with his *Paulus* contributors, Mendelssohn approached a proven collaborator this time around: his long-time friend Karl Klingemann, who was now working in London as secretary to the Hanoverian legation. Klingemann had already provided Mendelssohn with a libretto for his 1829 *Liederspiel, The Return from Abroad* (*Die Heimkehr aus der Fremde*), as well as with the texts for several songs. In his initial request, written on August 12, 1836, Mendelssohn showed no particular partiality toward any specific subject for his new oratorio, only a determination to build on the momentum established by *Paulus*, whose Liverpool performance Klingemann had helped to bring about:

> [I]f you only knew what an incomparably greater favor [than your assistance with the Liverpool performance] you would do me if, instead of doing so much for my old oratorio, you would make me a new one! and, in this way, would stir me up to fresh activity, instead of my having to do this myself. When I have finished a piece, I am actually pleased only by the progress I see in it and what it leads me to next; therefore I always long to be rid of all care for the finished work; and I feel as if I could only really thank you, from my heart, if you showed me that you like my piece sufficiently to encourage me to write a new one, and if you would give all the thought you bestowed on the old one preferably to an Elijah, or [St.] Peter, or, as far as I am concerned, Og of Bashan.[4]

Mendelssohn did not receive a response from Klingemann for several months. During that time, his ideas about the subject matter of his future oratorio became more specific, settling on St. Peter and Elijah, with a distinct preference for the latter. Nonetheless, the subject remained less important to him than the speedy commencement of a new work, as demonstrated by his second request to Klingemann, written six months later:

> Now comes my request. Write for me within the next few weeks a text for a biblical oratorio, that I can set over the course of the summer. I told you already of two subjects that I like equally well—St. Peter and Elijah. What I would like best would be for you to take Elijah; divide the story into two or three parts, and write it out in choruses and arias, either in prose or verse of your own, or compile it from the Psalms and Prophets, but with thick,

powerful, full choruses. The translations of Handel's oratorios you made gave you so little trouble that I think you will only require a few evenings, and the will to give them up to it, and it will be done. You may arrange it dramatically, like [Judas] Maccabaeus, or epically, or both combined—it would all be fine with me; you need not ask my advice, but just write out what you think best. Then I can compose it at once. If both subjects no longer please you, then I am willing to take any other you choose—[King] Saul, for instance. But I think Elijah, and his ascent to heaven in the end, would be the most beautiful. And if you wish to use biblical passages, read Isaiah chap. 60, and 63 to the end of the prophet, and Isaiah chap. 40, and the Lamentations of Jeremiah and the Psalms. This will most certainly provide you with the language and everything else. Just think what sort of an oratorio you think I should write, and such a one send me. It ought to be my wedding present; it would be the best thing you could give me; please don't refuse it to me!5

Klingemann endorsed Mendelssohn's preferred subject, replying, "If you will still trust me, then I am your man for Elias, and therefore I am not sending the plan immediately. . . . You shall have the first part in four weeks, and the rest later."6 Six weeks later, Mendelssohn's wedding came and went with no sign of the libretto. A month after that, while still on his honeymoon, Mendelssohn wrote again to Klingemann, asking, "[W]ill you soon fulfill your promise to me about Elias?" but heard nothing.7 With Klingemann's silence lasting into July, Mendelssohn began to consider other options.

With no libretto for *Elias* forthcoming and anxious to compose a piece in "church music style,"8 Mendelssohn poured his compositional energy into a setting of Psalm 42 (op. 42). He also began reconsidering the idea of an oratorio based on St. Peter, about which he contacted Julius Schubring—who had proven so willing to help with the *Paulus* libretto—on July 14, 1837:

I wish to ask your advice in a matter of importance to me. . . . It concerns the selection of a subject of an oratorio, which I intend to begin next winter. . . .

Several external reasons argue in favor of choosing St. Peter as the subject—namely, that it is intended for the Düsseldorf Music Festival at Pentecost, and the prominent position the feast of Pentecost would occupy in this subject. In addition to these external reasons, I may add my wish (in connection with a greater plan for a later oratorio) to bring the two chief confessors and pillars of the Christian Church side by side in oratorios, that is, to have a St. Peter to go with my St. Paul. I need not tell you that there are sufficient internal reasons that make the subject matter worthy, and of these internal ones, far above all is the outpouring of the Holy Ghost, which must form the central or main point. But the question is (and this you can decide far better than I can, because you possess the knowledge in which I am deficient, to guide you) whether the position that Peter occupies *in the Bible*, apart from the prestige he enjoys in the Catholic or Protestant Churches, as a martyr, or as the first Pope, etc.—whether what is said of him *in the Bible* in and of itself is sufficiently important to form the basis of a *symbolic* oratorio. . . .

My question therefore is, . . . if you believe that, even if [such a work is] actually feasible, it can be done entirely with biblical passages, and what particular parts of the Bible you would especially emphasize.[9]

As Arno Forchert has argued, Mendelssohn's initial decision to direct his *Elias* inquiries to Klingemann and his *Petrus* inquiries to Schubring was likely based on his assessment of the particular abilities of both men. Since Mendelssohn intended *Elias* to have a strong dramatic element, Klingemann, who had searched for and assembled opera libretti for him in the past, would be the most appropriate choice for librettist. In the case of a *Petrus* oratorio, the apostle's "theological weight"—to quote Forchert—was paramount, lending itself more to Schubring's talents and training.[10]

Schubring responded to Mendelssohn's request sometime before the composer's departure for England on August 24. The letter itself is lost, but the one that followed (November 29) demonstrates that Schubring had enthusiastically agreed to serve as Mendelssohn's librettist for *Petrus*. However, Schubring's comments also indicate that Mendelssohn had not written him again about the subject since his initial inquiry, a silence that led the theologian to suspect that Mendelssohn had found someone to replace him.[11] The truth was that while in London, Mendelssohn spent two weeks (August 27–September 13) at Klingemann's home, where, on the mornings of August 30 and 31, they sketched out a few ideas and a basic list of scenes for *Elias* (Text I in table 5.1).[12] Mendelssohn informed Schubring, however, that he had merely decided to put *Petrus* aside;[13] he did not cite *Elias* as an explanation, perhaps believing, as Forchert proposed, the project to be unsuitable for him.

Mendelssohn left the *Elias* plan in London upon his departure, with the understanding that Klingemann would use it to construct a prose libretto, but the project turned out to be far more demanding than Klingemann had anticipated. In January 1838, as Mendelssohn waited patiently for Klingemann's draft, he received (postage due) an English "Elijah" libretto by the Reverend James Barry that had been forwarded by Charles Greville (both men were unknown to Mendelssohn), in hopes that the composer would consider setting it to music. Whether he felt committed to working with Klingemann or just found Barry's text unsatisfactory, Mendelssohn declined the invitation.[14] However, the text's arrival gave renewed urgency to the *Elias* project. "[T]hey have already dedicated the aforementioned *Elias* to the Duchess of Kent," Mendelssohn wrote Klingemann of the Barry text, "and no doubt will make much ado about the aforementioned *Elias*, if I do not take it on; and then [Sigismund] Neukomm, or someone else may quickly compose it and make it known. . . ." "[T]herefore," he continued, "I ask you for two things: 1. make our sketch into verse and send it to me while it's still hot (*brühwarm*) . . . so that I may compose it while it's still hot; 2. send me, in any case—whether you fulfill my request

Table 5.1. The *Elias* Texts

Text	Library Sigla	Author	Date	Comments
I	GB-Ob MS. M. Deneke Mendelssohn c. 27, fol. 42r–44v	Klingemann, Mendelssohn	[Aug. 30–31, 1837]	Loose ideas and a rough outline of the work, written while Klingemann and Mendelssohn visited in London. Also contains notes and corrections in Schubring's hand.
II	GB-Ob MS. M. Deneke Mendelssohn c. 27, fol. 33r–41v	Klingemann	[before late May 1838]	A nearly complete prose draft. Shows the influence of I. Also has cuts marked in Mendelssohn's and Schubring's hands.
III	GB-Ob MS. M. Deneke Mendelssohn d. 53, no. 92a	Schubring	Oct. 28, 1838	Prose draft of the first five numbers, outline of the rest of Part I through the challenge. Shows influence of II.
IV	GB-Ob MS. M. Deneke Mendelssohn d. 53, no. 92	Schubring	Oct. 31, 1838	Prose draft of the beginning through the challenge. Shows influence of II and III.
V	GB-Ob MS. M. Deneke Mendelssohn d. 53, no. 93	Schubring	Nov. 17, 1838	Nearly complete prose draft of Part II. Shows influence of II. Includes some notes in Mendelssohn's hand.
VI	GB-Ob MS. M. Deneke Mendelssohn c. 27, fol. 1r–4r	Mendelssohn	[Summer 1845]	Prose draft of Part I and most of Part II. Shows influence of II–V. Written on same paper as X; likely written shortly before or after accepting the Birmingham commission (July 24, 1845).
VII	GB-Ob MS. M. Deneke Mendelssohn c. 27, fol. 7r–7v	Mendelssohn	[after VI]	Two drafts of Obadiah's call. Shows influence of VI. Written on same paper as X.
VIII	GB-Ob MS. M. Deneke Mendelssohn c. 27, fol. 5r–6v	Mendelssohn	[after VII]	Prose draft of Part I. Shows influence of VI and VII. Written on same paper as X.
IX	GB-Ob MS. M. Deneke Mendelssohn c. 27, fol. 15r–16r	Mendelssohn	[after VI]	Prose draft of Part II. Shows influence of VI. Written on same paper as X.
X	GB-Ob MS. M. Deneke Mendelssohn d. 53, no. 94	Mendelssohn	Dec. 16, 1845	Nearly complete prose draft that was mailed to Schubring. Returned to Mendelssohn with extensive corrections on Jan. 9, 1846. Shows influence of VIII and IX.
XI	GB-Ob MS. M. Deneke Mendelssohn c. 27, fol. 11r–12v	Mendelssohn	[after Jan. 9, 1846]	Prose draft of Part II. Shows influence of X.

	Source	Author/Copyist	Date	Description
XII	GB-Ob MS. M. Deneke Mendelssohn c. 27, fol. 8r, 10r	Mendelssohn	[after XI]	Prose drafts of the ending.
XIII	GB-Ob MS. M. Deneke Mendelssohn c. 27, fol. 13r–14v	Mendelssohn	[after May 23, 1846]	Prose draft of Part II. Shows influence of XI and XII.
XIV	GB-Ob MS. M. Deneke Mendelssohn c. 27, fol. 7r–10r	Mendelssohn	[ca. Apr., June 1846]	Rough ordering outline for XVIII. Each part's outline was likely written just before the part was composed.
XV	GB-Ob MS. M. Deneke Mendelssohn d. 49, no. 320	Schubring	June 15, 1846	Prose suggestions for Part II. Does not appear to reflect XIII.
XVI	D-Bsb MN MS 22, p. 1–12, 17–28, 37–117	Mendelssohn	[ca. Aug. 1845–July 27, 1846]	Musical sketches and drafts for XVIII.
XVII	PL-Kj MN Bd. 41	Mendelssohn	[ca. mid May–early Aug. 1846]	Drafts of two pieces for XVIII, one of which was cut ca. early Aug. 1846.
XVIII	GB-Bp MS 1721	Copyists Eduard Henschke* and William Bartholomew	[Original score: early Apr.–Aug. 11, 1846; copy: early May–July 28, 1846]	Copy of first version ("Birmingham") full score, in German, with English incipits. The original score was cannibalized to create the final version score (XXVII).
XIX	GB-Ob Deneke 265	Bartholomew	[first week of Aug. 1846]	Printed chorus parts for the premiere, in English.
XX	GB-Ob MS. M. Deneke Mendelssohn c. 51/1, fol. 51–61	Bartholomew	[ca. Aug. 19, 1846]	Printed textbook for the premiere, in English. *Elias* premiered in Birmingham on Aug. 26, 1846.
XXI	GB-Ob MS. M. Deneke Mendelssohn c. 27, fol. 16v	Mendelssohn	[after Aug. 26, 1846]	Prose drafts for Obadiah's plea for rain, and queen's and widow's scenes.
XXII	GB-Ob MS. M. Deneke Mendelssohn c. 27, fol. 16r	Mendelssohn	[after Aug. 26, 1846]	Prose drafts for Obadiah's farewell and queen's scene.
XXIII	GB-Ob MS. M. Deneke Mendelssohn c. 27, fol. 4v	Mendelssohn	[after XXII]	Prose drafts of Obadiah's farewell, queen's scene, and introduction for GA 37.

(continued)

TABLE 5.1. (continued)

Text	Library Sigla	Author	Date	Comments
XXIV	D-Bsb MN MS 22, p. 13–16, 29–36	Mendelssohn	[ca. Sept. 1846–late Feb. 1847]	Musical sketches and drafts for XXVII.†
XXV	D-Bsb N. Mus. 653, 654	Mendelssohn	[before Mar. 3, 1847]	Musical draft of the revised widow's scene.
XXVI	GB-Ob MS. M. Deneke Mendelssohn c. 39	Mendelssohn	[ca. Dec. 1846–late Feb. 1847]	Final version piano-vocal score.
XXVII	PL-Kj MN Bd. 51	Mendelssohn	[before Mar. 16, 1847]	Final version full score.‡
GA				Published final text, as appears in 1847 score and complete edition (Gesamtausgabe). Final version premiered on March 16, 1847.

Complete transcriptions of all these texts are available in Sposato, "The Price," 2:235–467. This list does not include some minor sources of individual arias and the like (see Mendelssohn, ed. Todd, Elias, 458–61 for a list of these). A comprehensive list of all of the Elias sources—including libretti, scores, sketches, fragments, and copies—has yet to be published.

*Henschke is the copyist for the entire score with the exception of no. 30 (the tenor recitative "Under a juniper tree" and the soprano/alto duet "Lift thine eyes"), which William Bartholomew added in 1852. My thanks to Peter Ward Jones for his insights on the history of the Birmingham score. See also Mendelssohn, ed. Todd, Elias, 459.

†Although I have drawn on Donald Mintz's extensive analysis of this sketchbook volume (p. 40–105), at the time of his writing (1960), he was unable to view the Birmingham score and was therefore not able to distinguish between drafts for it and for the published version. I have therefore recategorized the drafts into two groups: those for the Birmingham score (XVI) and those for the final score (XXIV).

‡The full score manuscript is dated 11 August 1846, a date that, as Peter Ward Jones has suggested to me, Mendelssohn likely wrote on the score in the winter of 1846/47 and which represented to him the day he considered the Birmingham version of the score finished. The composer's correspondence, however, shows that he completed the revised version and sent it off for publication shortly before its premiere on 16 March 1847. See Sposato, "The Price," 1:348–51.

for no. 1 or not—a copy of our plan or sketch, as we made earlier (with all remarks), and write to me as well."[15]

Mendelssohn's letter had the intended effect on Klingemann, who on February 2, 1838, replied:

> The devil take the clowns who would steal *Elias* from us! But what should we do? I would not gladly give it up. Write these people that you don't need an *Elias*, since you already have one and have yourself written a plan with M[r.] Kl[ingemann] in London.[16]

Klingemann also noted his intention to begin work immediately on a prose draft of the oratorio, but seemed uncertain about how rapidly he could complete the project—if, in fact, he could complete it at all.[17] These contradictory statements understandably made Mendelssohn uneasy, leading him to prod Klingemann for updates repeatedly in the months that followed. (None were forthcoming, however.[18]) Then, a couple of weeks after Mendelssohn's May 19 request to have at least the outline returned to him, Klingemann sent Mendelssohn a package containing it and a very extensive, but still incomplete, prose draft (Text II); no cover letter was included. A month later, Klingemann finally confessed his inability to help Mendelssohn further with the *Elias* libretto:

> In accordance with your desire, I wanted to serve you at once, and yet didn't do it, because I always thought the right moment was yet to come, and I could send you a few verses or a finished act. But, as always, nothing came of it; I came up with nothing except my anger at the miserable word "at once" (*umgehend*)—which I unfortunately always use like a celestial spirit in its other, dilatory, sense ["eventual"]—and you received nothing from it except, presumably, annoyance.
>
> Then I collected the papers, and, in continual melancholy longing for the aforementioned "right moment," could not part from them [and return them to you] without retaining a copy.—Hours and minutes went by so completely that I was too pressed for time to write even two miserable accompanying words and the package reached your eyes not only late, but also in annoying silence.
>
> It is sad that I have made you give up on me this way, but what is one to do when one is lazy and has his stupid job. If I didn't have it, however, I surely would have done nothing.[19]

Despite the fact that Klingemann had indeed provided Mendelssohn with a nearly complete prose draft (it lacked only the ascension and closing scenes), Mendelssohn soon realized he would need to turn elsewhere for additional help. Klingemann's libretto was far too long and detailed, and even after marking extensive cuts, Mendelssohn was unable to instill in it any kind of dramatic coherence or sense of direction. Thus, when Schubring visited Mendelssohn in Leipzig during the early fall of 1838, Mendelssohn finally told him of his work on *Elias* and asked if he would be willing to take over the role of librettist. Schubring agreed and returned to Dessau with the Klingemann drafts in hand.[20] After having an opportunity to study the prose draft, Schubring wrote Mendelssohn saying that he too found the libretto highly problematic, noting, among other things, that it was too long, a problem he felt caused all the life to be drained out of the various stories. Schubring therefore thought it best to start fresh and borrow passages from Klingemann's draft when appropriate,[21] which was, in fact, precisely how Mendelssohn had hoped he would proceed.[22] Schubring also discussed how he planned to begin the oratorio and included highly detailed descriptions of the first five numbers, followed by a looser outline that went up to the offerings to Baal and Jehovah (Text III). He followed this a few days later with a complete prose version of that same segment (Text IV).

After receiving Mendelssohn's enthusiastic approval of his work to date ("How can you even ask whether I wish you to proceed in the same way? When everything comes together like this, I have almost nothing to do but to add the music"),[23] Schubring began composing the remainder of the libretto, starting with the end of Part I (the offering through the rain miracle). This particular segment, which Schubring assembled during the first two weeks of November 1838, has since been lost. Schubring's final installment, sent on November 17, does survive, however, and contains a nearly complete prose draft of the second half of the oratorio (Text V).

Despite Mendelssohn's praise for Schubring's work, a difference in their respective conceptions for *Elias* soon became evident. Mendelssohn apparently told Schubring that he wanted *Elias* to be both religiously edifying and dramatic, emphasizing that the latter should take precedence. Schubring attempted to comply but found himself continually dissatisfied with the result. In the letter that accompanied the first major installment of his prose libretto (Text IV), he attempted to persuade Mendelssohn to reverse his priorities and emphasize the sacred over the dramatic:

> [W]hat I hoped to avoid and wrote to you about has in fact come to pass; that the thing is becoming too objective—an interesting, even thrilling picture, but far from edifying the heart of the listener. All the curses, the scenes of the sacrifice and the rain, Jezebel, etc., in all this there is nothing which now-a-days would come from the heart, and therefore nothing which would go to the heart. Pieces in *Paulus*, like Paul's first aria in B minor ["Vertilge sie"], or choruses, "Ihr Männer von Israel helfet," etc., are certainly beautiful and characteristic—but they are interesting rather than edifying. You will probably never hear people singing that aria at the piano for their pleasure. But Paul's second and third arias, or the tenor aria towards the close ["Sei getreu bis in den Tod"] and others like it, they are for everybody. *Paulus*, however, has many more passages of general interest than there are in this text at present. Therefore you must carefully consider whether this time you prefer

to turn away from *church* music (i.e., that which refreshes [the soul]) and create a tone-picture—after the manner of the *Blocksberg-Cantata* [i.e., *Die erste Walpurgisnacht*]. Otherwise we must work with renewed effort to keep down the dramatic, and raise the sacred.[24]

Mendelssohn likewise sensed that he and Schubring were not on the same page and wrote Schubring asking *him* to reverse *his* priorities (the letters crossed in the mail):

In my opinion, it is best to do full justice to the *dramatic* element, and, as you say, there must be no epic narration. I am also glad that you are search- ing out the basic, emotionally touching meaning of the scriptural words; but if I might make one observation, it would be that I would like to see the dra- matic element emerge more succinctly and clearly here and there. Statement and response, question and answer, sudden interruptions, etc., etc.—not that it disturbs me that, for example, Elijah first speaks of assembling the people, then forthwith addresses the assembled people—such liberties are the natu- ral privileges of such a representation in an oratorio; but I would like such a representation itself to be as lively as possible. . . .

But we are no doubt likely to agree about this; I would only entreat you, when you resume your work, to think of this wish of mine.[25]

But Schubring was not as agreeable as Mendelssohn had hoped. In the letter ac- companying the final installment of his libretto draft (Text V), Schubring followed his remarks and questions about further revisions with the testy comment, "For the rest, I am more and more convinced that you will have to supply the principal part of the text yourself. How is one to know what is running through your mind on this or that occasion? Therefore the words are only set down as hints, suggesting what might be written."[26]

Tension between the two intensified into December, when Mendelssohn not only firmly restated his position, but also harshly decried the lack of drama in a libretto Schubring was writing for Friedrich Schneider on St. Boniface (*Bonifacius*).[27] Schubring, no doubt upset by Mendelssohn's comments, refrained from replying for nearly two months. When he finally did—on the occasion of Mendelssohn's birthday—he began in a conciliatory tone, as if to repair the breach that had developed between them, and then added, "I always thought that the *Elias* would turn out all right, but it will not, and you must seek help elsewhere."[28] (Despite this break in their collaboration, Schubring would later claim to have been continually involved in the process: "We arranged *Elijah* together from beginning to end."[29])

Schubring's withdrawal from the project depressed Mendelssohn greatly, caus- ing him to lose interest both in his upcoming conducting engagement at the Lower Rhine Music Festival in Düsseldorf and in *Elias* itself.[30] For several years, Mendelssohn gave up all hope of completing the work, although he was not deterred from com- posing a new oratorio altogether. Almost immediately after Schubring's withdrawal,

Mendelssohn began to explore the possibilities of an oratorio based on the subjects of "Earth, Hell, and Heaven" (what would eventually become known as *Christus*), as well as one based on the life of John the Baptist (*Johannes*). As will be seen in the next chapter, Mendelssohn had made little progress on these two works before *Elias* again occupied his thoughts. In a report written at the end of August 1844 to Klingemann of his recent activities and upcoming plans, Mendelssohn remarked, "I have . . . begun to think anew very seriously about *Elias*. I will, after all, take it on soon."[31]

Mendelssohn had likely just resumed work on *Elias*[32] when a commission arrived from the Birmingham Festival Committee in mid-July 1845.[33] In addition to asking Mendelssohn to conduct during the next year's festival, the committee requested that he compose "a new oratorio, or other music, for the occasion."[34] Mendelssohn accepted, writing in his letter to the festival's manager, composer Joseph Moore, that "[s]ince some time I have begun an oratorio, and hope I shall be able to bring it out for the first time at your Festival." Having learned his lesson with *Paulus*, whose completion took far longer than he anticipated and forced him to back out of several planned premieres, Mendelssohn was unwilling to guarantee the new oratorio's completion in time for the festival, however.[35] This caution continued in his correspondence with Moore over the course of the next year, with Mendelssohn repeatedly expressing doubt that he would finish in time. It was only when he wrote Moore on May 8, 1846, (just two-and-a-half months before the festival) to inform him that he was sending the whole first part of the oratorio to William Bartholomew for translation (via Ignaz Moscheles, the festival's chief conductor and Mendelssohn's personal friend), that the matter was fully settled.[36]

Mendelssohn's first assignment upon resuming work on *Elias* was to complete the libretto, a project he now decided to undertake himself. In the years since his aborted collaboration with Schubring, Mendelssohn had apparently thought a great deal about *Elias*, since his first prose draft (Text VI) demonstrates a remarkable similarity to the published text, while resembling Schubring's drafts from the 1830s only superficially.[37] Since Mendelssohn wanted to begin composing music as soon as possible, he decided that instead of finalizing the libretto for the entire work at once, he would write and polish one part at a time. As a result, this first libretto draft includes detailed prose for Part I of the oratorio, but only a loose collection of textual fragments for Part II. Apparently, the most significant challenge Mendelssohn faced in constructing Part I was finding an appropriate text for Obadiah's call for repentance (GA 3–5), so much so that he wrote two drafts and a musical sketch of this scene alone (Text VII; Text XVI, p. 79–84) before redrafting the entire part (Text VIII; see fig. 5.1 later in this chapter). This he followed in short order with a more mature, albeit still rough draft of Part II (Text IX).

At some point shortly after Mendelssohn resumed work on *Elias*, he once again requested Schubring's assistance. This time, however, Schubring's role would involve correcting and evaluating Mendelssohn's text, not providing a libretto of his own.[38] Schubring agreed, and on December 16, 1845, Mendelssohn sent him a new, highly detailed libretto draft (Text X), in which Part I was nearly finalized, while Part II remained "in a very unfinished condition."[39] This latest text attempted to incorporate some of Schubring's vision for a religiously edifying work, while still retaining a clear dramatic focus, something Mendelssohn asked Schubring to bear in mind when making his comments.[40] Two weeks later, just after the new year, Mendelssohn visited Schubring in Dessau, where they undoubtedly discussed the oratorio at length.[41] On January 9, 1846, shortly after Mendelssohn returned to Leipzig, Schubring returned Mendelssohn's draft along with two sets of corrections, the first in ink and the second in pencil (likely made before and after Mendelssohn's visit, respectively).[42] With Mendelssohn now more open to Schubring's suggestions, the theologian displayed renewed enthusiasm for the project, and their working relationship was quickly restored.[43] As was the case with *Paulus*, however, now that Mendelssohn had taken control of assembling the text, he would never relinquish it; although Schubring would continue to make suggestions over the next several months, at no time did he ever become Mendelssohn's librettist, as has been so often assumed.

One of the primary thrusts of Schubring's commentary on Mendelssohn's latest effort (Text X) was his conviction that *Elias* had to end with a more obvious reference toward the New Testament. (Text X ends like its predecessors, with Elijah bestowing a "double portion" of his spirit on his servant Elisha.) While Mendelssohn's subsequent Part II draft (Text XI) reveals that he agreed with only a few of Schubring's specific suggestions (such as including the summary of Elijah's deeds from Sirach [Ecclesiasticus] 48), he did take Schubring's overall concern to heart and began to plot out a new, more overtly Messianic ending, two drafts of which appear in Text XII. Mendelssohn incorporated most of the material from the second of these drafts into his last complete Part II draft (XIII), which was close enough to being finished for him to write numbers in pencil over the various recitatives, arias, and choruses. On its last page, however, the draft contains an alternative closing chorus, as well as an entire second version of Jezebel's scene, indications that these segments were not yet fully settled in his mind.

Mendelssohn's work on the full score for the Birmingham Festival (referred to henceforth in this chapter as the "Birmingham score," a copy of which survives as Text XVIII) began no later than early April 1846, while he was still hard at work on the libretto of Part II.[44] By May 15 or 16, Mendelssohn had finished the score for Part I as well as several numbers in Part II,[45] which still did not have a completed libretto. He therefore contacted Schubring again on May 23, asking for one final "rich harvest of fine Bible texts" with which he might finish the second half. Mendelssohn stressed to Schubring that he would require the texts in three weeks, at which time he would return from directing the Lower Rhine Music Festival in Aachen and would need to finish the Birmingham score with dispatch.[46] But despite Schubring's punctual offering (Text XV, dated June 15), Mendelssohn either made more progress on the libretto during his trip than he had anticipated or found Schubring's suggestions unsuitable. In either case, Schubring's final submission went completely unused.[47]

As a result, all that can be said with reasonable certainty about the timing of Mendelssohn's completion of the Part II libretto (Text XIII) is that it postdates his May 23 request, since the draft does not include the character of Elisha, about whom Mendelssohn had asked Schubring's advice in his letter.[48]

With Part I of the Birmingham score completed and work progressing on Part II, and with little time remaining before the scheduled August 26 premiere, Mendelssohn began sending sections of the oratorio as they were finalized to his copyist in Leipzig, Eduard Henschke, and then passed the copied section on to his translator in England, William Bartholomew.[49] By July 18, Mendelssohn had completed and sent the entire oratorio to Bartholomew, with the exception of nos. 36 (*O Herr ich habe dich gehört*, an earlier incarnation of *Ich gehe hinab in der Kraft des Herrn*) through 39 (*Dann werden die Gerechten leuchten*), three of which (36, 38, and 39) followed ten days later.[50] In addition to no. 37 (*Ja, es sollen wohl Berge weichen*), still missing was an overture, which Mendelssohn had initially decided not to compose. While both Klingemann and Schubring began their drafts with an overture depicting the famine (*Hungarsnoth*), Mendelssohn thought it would lessen the dramatic impact of Elijah's curse ("there shall not be dew nor rain these years"), with which he wanted to open the work. Bartholomew, however, made the innovative suggestion to have the overture follow the curse, so as to symbolize the three years of famine. Indeed, without it, Bartholomew wrote, "the chorus [*Hilf, Herr!*] . . . comes so very quickly and suddenly after the curse, that there seems to elapse no time to produce its results."[51] On July 3, Mendelssohn replied that he would consider Bartholomew's idea, and on August 9 wrote that he had in fact written an overture—"and a long one"—which he would bring with him to London, along with no. 37.[52]

The overture was not the only item Mendelssohn reconsidered between the time he mailed the final major installment of *Elias* to Bartholomew on July 28 and his departure for London on or around August 13. Shortly before leaving Leipzig, he opted to delete the chorus *Er wird öffnen die Augen der Blinden*, which had appeared immediately before the no. 42 quartet, *Wohlan, Alle die ihr durstig seid*.[53] He also had second thoughts about the alto aria, *Sei stille dem Herrn* (no. 32), which he planned to rewrite before traveling to London, but which he instructed Bartholomew to delete from the manuscript for the printed textbook that was to be sold at the premiere, should it need to go to press immediately.[54] Fortunately, publication of the textbook was able to wait until Mendelssohn arrived with a new version of the aria in hand.

Meanwhile, Bartholomew was busy making preparations for Mendelssohn's arrival in London. In addition to assembling the textbook manuscript, Bartholomew was occupied with completing the translated chorus parts (Text XIX), which he sent off to the publisher (Ewer & Co.) during the first week of August.[55] Upon Mendelssohn's arrival on August 17 or 18, the two men immediately set to work polishing the English text and integrating last-minute changes and the new music Mendelssohn had brought with him into the textbook manuscript and (at the eleventh hour) the printed chorus parts.[56] As with *Paulus*, then, the printed textbook (Text XX)—rather than the Birmingham score copy—most clearly represents the actual text sung at the premiere.[57]

Elias was premiered to critical acclaim at the Town Hall in Birmingham on the morning of August 26, 1846.[58] Mendelssohn himself was also very pleased with the performance, as he noted in a letter to Jenny Lind: "The performance of my *Elijah* was the best first performance that I have ever heard of any one of my compositions. There was so much go, and swing, in the way in which the people played, and sang, and listened. I wish you had been there."[59] As for the piece itself, Mendelssohn still believed it to be in need of work, and he began revising it for publication almost immediately. His first mention of this revision appears in his September 26, 1846, letter to Bartholomew, in which he discussed Bartholomew's recent alterations to the translation (requested, perhaps, before Mendelssohn left England) and his plan to send Bartholomew a new version of Jezebel's scene.[60] It was also around this time that a friend of Mendelssohn's, the painter Eduard Bendemann, sent him a copy of the Birmingham textbook with some suggestions for changes written in the margins.[61] Although this source is lost, Bendemann's ideas can be discerned from Mendelssohn's reply, in which he noted that he incorporated several of the suggestions, including a reworking of the widow's scene (Bendemann had suggested it be deleted) and the following of the *Heilig* chorus (GA 35) by God's command to Elijah to resume his mission.[62]

Mendelssohn made rapid progress on the revised version of *Elias*. As he reported in a letter to Klingemann, by the first week of December he had completed the text of the new widow's scene,[63] as well as that for Obadiah's plea for rain (GA 8 and 19; Text XXI).[64] This was soon followed by texts (XXI–XXIII) for a new version of Jezebel's scene (GA 23–24), Obadiah's farewell to Elijah (GA 25), and Bendemann's suggestion of God's command to Elijah to resume his mission (GA 36). (As always, Mendelssohn continued to revise these texts—especially the widow's scene—as he composed the new music.)

At the same time that he began composing new texts for the final score, Mendelssohn began sketching musical drafts (Texts XXIV and XXV), a process that continued until the final score was finished. Once the text and music had been drafted, Mendelssohn composed each revised section first in the form of a piano-vocal score (XXVI). Starting with Part I on December 30, 1846, this piano-vocal score was then sent piecemeal to Bartholomew for translation of the new and revised texts, and then forwarded to Edward Buxton of Ewer & Co. for engraving.[65] Part II followed on February 2, 1847, at which time Mendelssohn sent a note to Buxton indicating that the version of the widow's scene in the Part I piano-vocal score was not to be engraved, as he had chosen to rework it yet again.[66] By February 17, however, the piano-vocal score of this new scene—as well as the rest of the oratorio—was in Bartholomew's hands.[67] Mendelssohn's work on *Elias*'s final score (Text XXVII) overlapped his work on the piano-vocal score and was sent in two installments to his German publisher (Simrock), with the last being mailed on March 12.[68] (As was the case with *Paulus*, the Simrock score served as the template for the *Elias* volume of the complete edition [*Gesamtausgabe*], which is used here as the source of the published text.) Mendelssohn premiered the revised version of *Elias* at Exeter Hall in London on March 16, 1847, and conducted three additional performances there on the 23rd, 28th and 30th.

CHRISTOLOGY IN *ELIAS*

That the last few numbers of *Elias* revolve around Messianic prophecy is undeniable. But to date, only Martin Staehelin has found any Messianic import elsewhere in the oratorio (namely, in the aria *Es ist genug* [GA 26], in which he sees connections to *Es ist vollbracht* from Bach's *St. John Passion*).[69] On the whole, reviewers since Otto Jahn have instead chosen to interpret the work as fundamentally historical, rather than allegorical. But as Jahn's 1848 article shows, interpreting *Elias* in such a manner invariably points to problems.

> What we find in *Elijah* is not true action, which develops steadily, but rather a series of situations in which Elijah is the focus, and which show his originality from various points of view. This is the source of the work's unity. But these individual scenes must also be externally connected; since the simplest means for this—namely narrative—has been discarded, the result is a certain disjointedness, sometimes even indistinctness, as one is introduced unexpectedly into the midst of a situation that only gradually becomes comprehensible, as it develops.[70]

This "disjointedness," he continues, has a particularly devastating effect on the secondary characters (the widow, Jezebel, Obadiah, Ahab, and the boy), whom Mendelssohn never develops to any recognizable depth. Also particularly problematic in Jahn's view are those episodes that do not drive the basic story forward, such as the widow's scene, which itself "is weakened by Elijah's threefold repetition of his prayer before it is answered."[71] Much more recently, Charles Rosen has interpreted Mendelssohn's oratorio in a similar historical vein, noting that all of the composer's oratorios—*Elias* included—were nothing more than "religious kitsch" that "neither expressed nor represented anything."[72] But as Rüdiger Bartelmus has pointed out, Mendelssohn's teacher, Carl Friedrich Zelter, made similar critiques about Handel's *Messiah* to Goethe, calling it "a more or less random collection of individual pieces."[73] Of course, Handel and his librettist, Charles Jennens, did not expect *Messiah* to be interpreted historically (i.e., as the stories of Isaiah, Malachi, and other Old Testament figures). They instead intended the work to serve as a kind of theological proof that Jesus was the Christ by telling the story of his life through the Old Testament prophecies, thereby sparking recollections in the listener's mind of how those prophecies were fulfilled.[74] Viewing *Elias* from a similar—that is, Christological—perspective causes the problems raised by Jahn, Rosen, and others to fall away, and affords the work a new coherence, one more concerned with the New Testament implication of events than with their faithfulness to the Old Testament narrative.

Mendelssohn was certainly open to the possibility of making his second oratorio a symbolic work, as his concept for the *Petrus* oratorio he explored with Schubring indicates:

> [A]s I see it, the subject [of St. Peter] absolutely must not be treated histori-cally. . . . In a historical treatment, Christ would have to appear in the earlier part of St. Peter's career, and where He appears, St. Peter could not lay claim to the chief interest. I think, therefore, it must be symbolic—though all the historical points should probably be included, the betrayal and repentance, the keys of heaven given him by Christ, his sermon at the feast of Pentecost—but all of that not historical, but prophetic.[75]

Mendelssohn's description to Schubring of the character of Elijah, in which he stresses making the prophet significant to contemporary audiences, likewise indicates his intention to create a work that was more symbolic than historical: "I conceived Elijah as a genuine prophet through and through, such as we could use again in our own day—strong, zealous, but also indeed stern, and wrathful, and gloomy; in contrast to the court rabble and popular rabble, and in contrast to almost the entire world, and yet carried as though on angels' wings."[76]

Mendelssohn's decision to make *Elias* not merely symbolic, but also Christological, was no doubt determined by his continued adherence to contemporary oratorio practices. These conventions, as noted in relation to *Moses*, demanded that Old Testament works orient themselves in some way toward the New. Indeed, Schubring would later remind the composer of this convention, stressing that Mendelssohn, of all people, could not afford to ignore it:

> I recognize now with perfect clarity that the oratorio can have no other than a New Testament ending; the Old Testament (Malachi) and also the New Testament definitely demand it. Elijah must help to transform the old cov-enant into the new, that is his great historical importance. Let Handel in his Old Testament oratorios move within this narrow circle—people like Saul, etc., are just themselves, nothing more—but with Elijah, and with you, in our day, it must be otherwise.[77]

As noted with *Moses*, the practice of including Christological material in Old Testa-ment oratorios stemmed from a theology codified by (among others) Friedrich Schleiermacher, who asserted that the value of the Old Testament was restricted to what it could teach Christians about the New. In fact, despite his overall interpreta-tion of the oratorio as a historical work and his complaints about its dramatic flow, even Jahn recognized—in a clearly Schleiermacherian vein—that *Elias* also incorporated a "symbolic element":

> The oratorio, by its nature, is not necessarily either Christian or churchlike. Subjects from the Old Testament have actually provided the prime material for oratorios from Handel on down to the present day, and one can surely not say of them, in general, that they are foreign to us. We find ourselves in a territory that, from the standpoint of Christian education, is not only well known but, more significantly, is rendered symbolic by its preparation for Christianity, and offers the artist the advantage of a firm foundation on which to build. This symbolic element in the Old Testament, as a subject for Christian contemplation, is found throughout *Elijah*, too, in the passages throughout that not only advance the action, but also draw together into a general outlook the ideal content of elements that would otherwise appear as merely external events, especially at the conclusion, where the reference to Him who will come is given verbal expression.[78]

This somewhat contradictory review shows that, while recognizing Mendelssohn's intention to make *Elias* religiously relevant to Christians, Jahn was ultimately unable to let go of his broader historical expectations for the work and appreciate Mendelssohn's allegorical approach. By contrast, I would argue that by accepting *Elias* as an allegorical work and interpreting the "series of situations" in that light, the Christology generally detected in the oratorio's final numbers readily emerges in nearly every aspect of the piece.[79] Among *Elias*'s Christological elements are its overall structure and ordering, which, in a manner similar to *Messiah*, roughly parallel the gospel narrative, thereby suggesting to the listener that the events of Elijah's life closely resembled those of Christ's. Intricately and essentially connected with this design are the often subtle changes made to the biblical story of Elijah, to bring it further in line with the gospel story and to allow the parallels in table 5.2 to emerge.

In order to demonstrate this process, I will look at three clusters of Christological content in *Elias*: Obadiah's call to repentance, Elijah's encounter with the widow, and Jezebel's incitement of the mob against Elijah. In addition to examining these clusters as they appear in the published score (GA), my analysis will trace them back to their earliest incarnations, which is essential, given that *Elias*'s Christological content is often more evident in the drafts.

Of the changes Mendelssohn made to the original biblical narrative of Elijah as given in 1 and 2 Kings, by far the most sweeping—and indeed the one that most suggests an intentional Christological program—involves the character of Obadiah. In *Elias*, Obadiah assumes a strong resemblance to John the Baptist (Mt. 3:1–12; Mk. 1:1–8; Lk. 3:1–18; Jn. 1:19–34), as he both calls the people to return to God and demonstrates the same unwavering faith in Elijah that John shows in Christ. In the published version of *Elias*, Mendelssohn establishes these two aspects of Obadiah's basic character in his opening recitative and aria (GA 3–4).

TABLE 5.2. Christological Overview of *Elias*

Scenes from Mendelssohn's *Elias*	New Testament Counterparts
Backdrop: The drought and the suffering of Israel (GA Introduction–2)	Backdrop: The Roman occupation and the suffering of Israel
Call to the people to return to God by Obadiah (3–5)	Call to the people to return to God by John the Baptist (Mt. 3:1–12; Mk. 1:1–8; Lk. 3:1–18; Jn. 1:19–34)
Elijah sent to the wilderness (Cherith's brook), tended to by ravens and angels (6–7)	Jesus goes to the wilderness to be tempted by the devil, tended to by angels (Mt. 4:1–11; Mk. 1:12–13; Lk. 4:1–13)
The inexhaustible barrel of meal and cruse of oil; Elijah raises the widow's son (8–9)	Jesus feeds the multitudes (Mt. 14:15–21, 15:32–38; Mk. 6:35–44, 8:1-9; Lk. 9:10–17; Jn. 6:1–14); Jesus recalls the Elijah raising (Lk. 4:26); Jesus raises the widow's son (Lk. 7:11–15)
Challenge of Ahab and the Priests of Baal (10–18)	Jesus overthrows the moneychangers' tables at the temple (Mt. 21:12–13; Mk. 11:15–17; Lk. 19:45–46)
Relief from the drought (19–20)	Jesus heals the blind and lame at the temple (Mt. 21:14–15); Jesus as giver of the living water (Jn. 4:10, 7:38); John baptizes with the "water of repentance" (Mt. 3:11)
Part II introduction (21–22)	
Queen Jezebel plots and incites the mob to kill Elijah (23–24)	The Pharisees plot and incite the mob to kill Jesus (Mt. 26:1–5, 27:20; Mk. 14:1–2, 15:11; Lk. 22:1–2; Jn. 11:47–53, 18:14)
Elijah's wilderness journey, "It is enough" (25–29)	Jesus at Gethsemane (Mt. 26:36–46; Mk. 14:32–42; Lk. 22:40–46)
Elijah at Mount Horeb, "Behold, God the Lord passed by" (30–35)	Jesus at Gethsemane/The Transfiguration (Mt. 17:1–8; Mk. 9:2–8; Lk. 9:28–36; 2 Pt. 1:16–18)
Elijah's ascension (36–39)	Jesus' ascension (Mk. 16:19; Lk. 24:50–53)
Prophecy of coming of Christ (40–42)	Prophecy of the second coming of Christ (Mt. 24; Revelation)

Zerreißet eure Herzen, und nicht eure
Kleider! Um unsrer Sünden willen hat
Elias den Himmel verschlossen durch das
Wort des Herrn! So bekehret euch zu
dem Herrn, eurem Gott, denn er ist
gnädig, barmherzig, geduldig und von
grosser Güte und reut ihn bald der Strafe.

Rend your hearts and not your
garments! For your transgressions
Elijah has sealed the heavens through the
word of the Lord! So return to
the Lord your God, for He is merciful,
compassionate, patient, and full of
goodness, and repent to Him of the evil.

"So ihr mich von ganzem Herzen suchet,
so will ich mich finden lassen," spricht
unser Gott. Ach! dass ich wüsste, wie ich
ihn finden und zu seinem Stuhle
kommen möchte!

"If with all your hearts you truly seek me,
I shall allow myself to be found," says our
God. Oh! that I knew how I might find
Him, and might come before His
throne![80]

Obadiah continues in this vein through both his plea for Elijah to pray for rain (GA 19) and his warning to Elijah of Jezebel's plans to kill him (GA 25). In 1 Kings, however, Obadiah plays an extremely minor role, appearing in but a single passage (1 Kg. 18:3–16). He never calls the people to repentance, and although he "revered the Lord greatly" and saved scores of God's prophets from Jezebel's wrath (1 Kg. 18:3–4, 13), he is essentially Ahab's servant, and as such his fear of his master overpowers his faith in Elijah ("as soon as I have gone from you, the Spirit of the Lord will carry you whither I know not; and so, when I come and tell Ahab and he cannot find you, he will kill me" [1 Kg. 18:12]).

The decision to make Obadiah a Baptist-like "voice crying in the wilderness" extended back to Mendelssohn's and Klingemann's initial outline (Text I, fol. 42r), in which he was assigned both a pious aria that preaches repentance and a recitative that implies his allegiance to Elijah through his pronouncement of Elijah's curse.

Obadjah <u>Recit</u> [I Kön.] *Cap* 17. v. 1.
["Und es sprach Elia, der Thisbiter, aus
den Bürgern Gilleads, zu Ahab: So wahr
der Herr, der Gott Israels, lebt, vor dem
ich stehe, es soll diese Jahre weder Thau
noch Regen kommen, ich sage es denn."]

Obadiah <u>Recit</u> [1 Kg.] *Ch.* 17. v. 1.
["And so spoke Elijah the Tishbite, of
people of Gilead, to Ahab: As the Lord
the God of Israel lives, before whom I
stand, neither dew nor rain shall come
these years, except by my word."]

<u>Aria</u> fromm,—[B]ekehrung. Betet!

<u>Aria</u> pious,—Repentance. Pray!

Schubring, no doubt following the Mendelssohn/Klingemann outline, also planned an aria in which Obadiah would call for repentance in a Baptist-like fashion (Text III, fol. 1v), and eventually opted for both a recitative and aria (Text IV, fol. 4r), some of whose text would find its way into the final score. In his own first prose draft of the libretto (Text VI, fol. 1r), Mendelssohn adopted nearly all of Schubring's text and added a chorus based on a biblical passage of his own choosing (Job 23:3) that would also find its way into the final version of Obadiah's aria:

Obadja	*Obadiah*
Rufet zu dem Herrn. . . . Er wolle unser Trauern in Freude verkehren, und uns trösten und erfreuen nach dieser Betrübniß.	Call to the Lord. . . . He will turn our mourning into joy, and comfort and gladden us in this distress.
So ihr mich von ganzem Herzen suchet, so will ich mich finden lassen, spricht der Herr.	If with all your hearts you truly seek me, I shall allow myself to be found, says the Lord.
Chor	*Chorus*
Ach, daß ich wüßte wie ich ihn finden, und zu seinem Stuhle kommen möchte. Herr sei nicht ferne von mir.	Oh! that I knew how I might find Him, and might come before His throne. Lord, be not far from me.

Mendelssohn's casting of Obadiah in a role analogous to John the Baptist facilitated his depiction of Elijah as an Old Testament Christ. There are, of course, actual connections made in the Bible between Elijah and the coming of the Messiah and Elijah and the Messiah himself. The most significant evidence for the first type of connection (i.e., Elijah as the Messiah's herald) comes from two Malachi prophesies: "Behold, I will send you Elijah the prophet before the great and terrible day of the Lord comes" (Mal. 4:5) and "Behold, I send my messenger [i.e., Elijah] to prepare the way before me" (Mal. 3:1). Writing in his influential *Christology of the Old Testament* (*Christologie des Alten Testaments*), Ernst Wilhelm Hengstenberg commented in 1829 that while opinion was divided as to whether these prophecies had already been fulfilled (and if so, by whom), the Lutheran church had always maintained that they referred to John the Baptist.[81]

Hengstenberg agreed with the church's assessment that Elijah had returned in the form of John the Baptist (downplaying, as the church did, John's own denial of being Elijah [Jn. 1:21]).[82] He admitted, however, that numerous connections also exist between Elijah and Christ, including the fact that both were tempted in the desert for forty days, and both raised a widow's son.[83] These connections were evident to the authors of the New Testament themselves. Matthew, for instance, noted that crowds following Christ identified him as either Elijah or "one of the prophets of old" (Mk. 6:15; 8:27–28), while Luke, at one point, both depicts Jesus as Elijah and equates the disciples with Elisha, who inherited Elijah's power—power the disciples also believed they possessed ("Lord, do you want us to bid fire come down from heaven and consume them, as Elijah did?" [Lk. 9:54]).[84] Ultimately, Mendelssohn's basis for associating Elijah with Christ rather than John the Baptist was quite straightforward: as he wrote in his second letter to Klingemann on the topic of a new oratorio, "Elijah, and his ascent to heaven in the end, would be the most beautiful [subject]."[85] The ascension is of obvious Christological import, since Elijah stands alone as the only Old Testament prophet depicted as ascending into heaven.

With the ascension set as *Elias*'s Christological focal point, Mendelssohn began making the changes to the biblical story of Elijah necessary for it to coincide more closely with the gospel narrative and for his protagonist to better resemble Jesus himself. Mendelssohn accomplished this in part by limiting the number of depictions of Elijah's wrath (eliminating, most notably, Elijah's encounter with King Ahaziah [2 Kg. 1:1–18]). Instead, he focused on those episodes that show Elijah in a more merciful light (such as his raising of the widow's son and his prayers for rain), as well as those that recall some of the more essential elements of the gospel story (as seen in table 5.2). While all of *Elias*'s scenes demonstrate this to varying degrees in both the published version and the earlier drafts, two are of particular interest: the raising of the widow's son in Part I and the scenes of Part II in which Elijah is betrayed.[86]

As both Hengstenberg and the biblical concordances of Mendelssohn's era readily acknowledged, the most obvious connections between Elijah and Christ involve Elijah's encounter with a widow, an episode that ties into several events in the New Testament, all of which Mendelssohn highlighted in *Elias*. The first parallel appears just after Elijah meets the widow. In the biblical account (1 Kg. 17:10–16), Elijah requests food, causing the widow to complain of having barely enough for one last meal for herself and her son. Elijah then tells her to make a cake for him and then for herself and her son, adding that "the barrel of meal shall not waste, neither shall the cruse of oil fail, until the day that the Lord sends rain upon the earth." This incident recalls Jesus' numerous feedings of the multitudes, during which his disciples likewise complain of having only enough food for themselves. Jesus, like Elijah, tells them to begin distributing the food, which never runs out (Mt. 14:15–21, 15:32–38; Mk. 6:35–44, 8:1–9; Lk. 9:10–17; Jn. 6:1–14). The more obvious and central parallel between the stories, however, involves the raising of the widow's son, a miracle performed both by God through Elijah's prayer (1 Kg. 17:17–24) and by Christ himself (Lk. 7:11–15). Christ, in fact, mentions Elijah's encounter with the widow ("and Elijah was sent . . . to Zarephath, in the land of Sidon, to a woman who was a widow," Lk. 4:26), immediately after his return from the temptation in the desert.[87]

In their initial outline, Mendelssohn and Klingemann listed both the oil-cruse and raising miracles (Text I, fol. 42r), which Klingemann then set in his prose draft using most of the original 1 Kings text (Text II, fol. 34r, 35r). Mendelssohn found this too long, however, and wrote "Short" (*Kurz*) next to a bracket encompassing the text of the oil-cruse segment. Schubring (Texts III, fol. 1v, and IV, fol. 4v) followed Mendelssohn's directive, glossing over this first miracle in a brief recitative sung by Elijah. Knowing full well its Christological significance, however, Schubring created an extensive dramatic scene for the raising (curiously set at the opening of Part II of his libretto [Text V, fol. 1r]). Despite the remarkable similarity of Schubring's text to what Mendelssohn would eventually set in both the Birmingham and final scores, Mendelssohn chose instead to abandon the scene; no mention of it appears in any of his next three drafts for Part I (Texts VI, VIII, and X). In light of a pattern first observable in *Paulus*, Mendelssohn's decision to exclude the event may have stemmed from a reluctance to introduce two new minor characters into the oratorio.[88] (Indeed, Mendelssohn's eventual choice to include the scene led to criticism from Jahn and others for this very reason.) Schubring, however, was adamant about incorporating some reference to the encounter with the widow, noting in his comments on Text X that "this story, which is also mentioned in the New Testament by Christ, may not remain completely untouched. Luke 4:26."[89] Mendelssohn apparently agreed, but due to the late date of Schubring's comment (January 9, 1846, by which time Mendelssohn's plans for Part I were nearly finalized), he seems to have skipped writing his own textual draft for the scene. Instead, he began immediately to compose musical sketches (Text XVI, p. 5–12, 27, 58, 59–60) that were based extensively on Schubring's textual suggestions. From there, he went straight to the version that appears in the Birmingham score (below), whose text differs only slightly from the published edition.

No. 10. Recit:
Alto Solo | Der Engel
Elias, nun da der Bach vertrocknet ist, so mache dich auf und gehe gen Zarpath und bleibe daselbst, denn dort habe ich einer Witwe geboten, daß sie dich versorge; und ihr soll nichts mangeln durch das Wort des Herrn.

No. 11.
The Widow. | Soprano Solo[90]
Hilf mir du Mann Gottes mein Sohn ist Krank, daß kein Odem mehr in ihm blieb. Du bist zu mir hereingekommen, daß meiner Missethat gedacht und daß mein Sohn getödtet werde. Hilf mir du Mann Gottes. Es ist kein Odem mehr in ihm. Doch so du wollest, so möchte ihm noch geholfen werden.

Elias.
Gib mir her deinen Sohn! Wende dich zu ihr, Herr mein Gott! Wende dich zu ihr und sei ihr gnädig, und hilf dem Sohne deiner Magd. Herr mein Gott, laß die Seele dieses Kindes wieder zu ihm kommen!

[Die Witwe]
Wirst du denn unter den Todten Wunder thun? Werden die Gestorbnen aufstehn und dir danken?

No. 10. Recit:
Alto Solo | The Angel
Elijah, now the brook is dried up, so arise and go to Zarephath and abide there, for I have commanded a widow there that she should provide for you; and she shall want for nothing, through the word of the Lord.

No. 11.
The Widow | Soprano Solo
Help me, man of God, my son is [so] sick that no breath remains in him. Have you come to me to call my sin to remembrance and to slay my son? Help me, man of God. There is no breath left in him. But if you so desire, you may still be of help to him.

Elijah
Give me your son! Turn unto her, Lord my God! Turn unto her and be merciful to her, and help the son of Your handmaid. Lord, my God, let the spirit of this child return to him!

[The Widow]
Will you perform miracles on the dead? Will those who have died arise and thank you?

[*Elias*]
Herr, mein Gott, lasse die Seele dieses
Kindes wieder zu ihm kommen.

[*Elijah*]
Lord, my God, let the spirit of this child
return to him.

[*Die Witwe*]
Der Herr erhört deine Stimme, die Seele
des Kindes kommt wieder, es wird
lebendig!

[*The Widow*]
The Lord has heard your voice, the soul
of the child returns, he is
alive!

[*Elias*]
Siehe da, dein Sohn lebet!

[*Elijah*]
Behold, your son lives!

[*Die Witwe*]
Nun erkenne ich, daß du ein Mann
Gottes bist und des Herrn Wort in
deinem Mund ist Wahrheit. Wohl dem,
der den Höchsten fürchtet.

[*The Widow*]
Now I recognize that you are a man of
God and the word of the Lord in
your mouth is the truth. Happy is he
who fears the Almighty.

No. 12. Chor
Wohl dem, der den Höchsten fürchtet,
der auf Gottes Wegen geht.
Denn sein Geschlecht wird gesegnet sein.
Den Frommen geht das Licht auf in der
Finsterniß, von dem Gnädigen,
Barmherzigen und Gerechten.

No. 12. Chorus
Happy is he who fears the Almighty,
who travels on God's paths.
For his kind shall be blessed.
To the pious comes light in the
darkness from the merciful,
compassionate, and righteous one.

Despite the rapid sequence of events that led to the development of the Birmingham score, Mendelssohn still managed to find ways to imbue the widow's scene with theological depth beyond the obvious parallels to Jesus' feeding of the multitudes and raising of the widow's son. For instance, Mendelssohn chose a text for the *Wohl dem* chorus (Ps. 112:4, 128:1) that includes the common Messianic image of light shining in the darkness. Bartholomew's English version of the chorus (adapted from the King James Bible) includes an additional link to the gospels through an unmistakable textual connection to the beatitudes (Mt. 5:3–12; Lk. 6:20–22), in that the opening line of the chorus ("Blessed are the men who fear him: they ever walk in the ways of peace") structurally matches each of Christ's blessings. (While this connection is implied in the German version, the textual parallel is far weaker, since the Luther Bible of Mendelssohn's time begins each blessing with *Selig seyd* ["Blessed are"], not *Wohl dem* ["Happy is he"], as in Mendelssohn's chorus.) Aside from incorporating thematic and textual parallels to the New Testament, Mendelssohn also made Jesus' personality recognizable in his Old Testament counterpart by imbuing Elijah with Christlike compassion through his plea for God's mercy on the "son of Your handmaid" (a text he took from Psalm 86:16), and by depicting Elijah's unceasing prayer in the face of the widow's derision (an element also not present in the 1 Kings narrative).

No doubt because of the rush with which he assembled the widow's scene for the Birmingham score, Mendelssohn chose to revise it significantly before publication, a process that included composing one textual and two musical sets of drafts (Texts XXI, XXIV, and XXV). While Mendelssohn tackled a number of problems he and others had with the scene (recall that Eduard Bendemann had recommended removing the scene entirely), one effect of his changes was to make the association between Elijah and Christ even more concrete. For instance, Mendelssohn added prominent mention of the widow's weeping (by including three times in mm. 26–49 an adaptation of Psalm 6:7, "I drench my couch with my tears the whole night long" [*Ich netze mit meinen Thränen mein Lager die ganze Nacht*]). This prominent passage recalls the widow's weeping during the parallel gospel incident ("And when the Lord saw her, he had compassion on her and said to her, 'Do not weep,'" Lk. 7:13). Also added was a third plea from Elijah for the return of the boy's soul (the Birmingham score had only two); not only does this better reflect the original account (1 Kg. 17:20–21), but it also allows the listener to recall Jesus' threefold prayer at Gethsemane to have the cup of suffering pass from him. (Mendelssohn also invoked this image through Elijah's threefold prayers for rain [GA 19] and for death to take him [GA 26], neither of which appears three times in 1 Kings.) Undoubtedly, the most important Christological addition to the published version of the widow's scene was Christ's "greatest commandment" (Mt. 22:37; Mk. 12:30; Lk. 10:27; originally from Dt. 6:5)— "You shall love the Lord your God with all your heart, and with all your soul, and with all your might"—which Elijah uses to answer the widow's question of how to repay the Lord for His mercy.

Elias	*Elijah*
Siehe da, dein Sohn lebet!	Behold, your son lives!
Die Witwe	*The Widow*
Nun erkenne ich, daß du ein Mann Gottes bist, und des Herrn Wort in deinem Munde ist Wahrheit! Wie soll ich dem Herrn vergelten alle seine Wohlthat, die er an mir thut?	Now I recognize that you are a man of God and the word of the Lord in your mouth is the truth! How shall I repay the Lord for all of the blessings he bestows upon me?
Elias	*Elijah*
Du sollst den Herrn deinen Gott liebhaben von ganzem Herzen,	You shall love the Lord your God with all your heart,
Elias und die Witwe	*Elijah and the Widow*
Von ganzer Seele, von allem Vermögen; Wohl dem, der den Herrn fürchtet!	With all your soul, with all your might; happy is he who fears the Lord.

A third way in which Mendelssohn enhanced the Christological program of *Elias* was through the scenes in Part II that together create what could be called a "Passion of Elijah." To set the stage for this "passion," Part II of the published score begins with the aria "Hear ye, Israel" (*Höre, Israel*), which invokes images of God as "redeemer" (*So spricht der Herr, der Erlöser Israels*) and "comforter" (*Ich, ich bin euer*

Tröster), images that, while not uniquely Christian, are strongly associated with Christ and the Holy Spirit, respectively. Significantly, Mendelssohn had made his Christological intentions even more obvious earlier, in the tenor recitative that opened Part II of Birmingham score: "Elijah has come already, and they did not know him, but did to him whatever they pleased" (*Es ist Elias gekommen, und sie haben ihn nicht erkannt, sondern haben an ihm gethan, was sie wollten*). As Mendelssohn noted in his last complete libretto draft of the part (Text XIII, fol. 13r–v), this text derives from Matthew 17:12, in which Jesus identifies John the Baptist as the Elijah who was to come. But rather than attempting to identify Elijah with John, Mendelssohn incorporated this passage to suggest similar ones that describe Christ's suffering—including Isaiah 53:3 ("He was despised and rejected by men; a man of sorrows, and acquainted with grief") and, especially, John 1:11 ("He came to his own home, and his own people received him not"), thereby preparing the listener for the passion-like episodes to come. Mendelssohn's inclusion of the text also reveals that he was well aware of Elijah's implications for the New Testament and was attempting to integrate this greater meaning throughout the work. In the end, however, he removed the passage from the published score, perhaps feeling it too incongruous with the Old Testament flavor he hoped to maintain.[91]

In the published score, the Elijah "passion" begins with Jezebel's meeting with an undefined group of people, in which she discusses the prophet's recent actions (GA 23–24). Since no such discussion takes place in the biblical narrative (which only mentions Jezebel's vow to avenge the slain prophets of Baal [1 Kg. 19:2]), Mendelssohn had free reign in writing the scene. In the end, he chose to emphasize two Christological elements: the perception that Elijah was attempting to usurp the king's authority, and Jezebel's incitement of the mob to turn against the prophet.

Jezebel's charge that Elijah was trying to challenge Ahab's power clearly parallels the accusation by the Pharisees that Jesus, in identifying himself as the Christ, had called himself a king and thus threatened Caesar's authority. (This is most directly expressed in Luke 23:2: "We found this man perverting our nation, and forbidding us to give tribute to Caesar, and saying that he himself is Christ, a king.") In the published score of *Elias*, Jezebel makes a series of similar accusations against Elijah, asking the people, "Have you heard how he prophesied against the king of Israel?" (*Habt ihr's gehört wie er geweissagt hat wider den König in Israel?*) and "What kind of kingdom would Israel be if Elijah had power over the king's power?" (*Was wäre für ein Königreich in Israel, wenn Elias Macht hätte über des Königs Macht?*).

Jezebel's efforts to turn the people against Elijah recall Matthew 27:20, Mark 15:11, and John 18:14, in which the chief priests and elders convince the mob assembled before Pilate to demand both Barabbas' release and Jesus' crucifixion. In *Elias*, Mendelssohn accomplished a similar transformation of the people's views through Jezebel's accusations against the prophet, each of which slowly raises the people's ire until they can no longer contain themselves and cry out, "He must die!" (*Er muß sterben!*).

Elijah's challenge of Ahab's authority stood at the heart of every textual draft of the scene since the first outline (with the exception of Schubring's [Text V]), but Jezebel's manipulation of the mob and its Christological implications were only fully realized during the extensive revisions Mendelssohn made after the Birmingham premiere. In the original outline (Text I, fol. 44r), and subsequently in Klingemann's and Schubring's prose drafts (Text II, fol. 39r; Text V, fol. 1r), the mob consisted of servants of Baal who cry for revenge for their fallen brethren. In composing his own early drafts, Mendelssohn restricted the drama to Jezebel and Ahab, with Ahab calling for his servants or guards to "seize and kill Elijah" (Text XI, fol. 11r). Although a chorus also sings in most of Mendelssohn's versions of the scene, they reflect only on the barbarity of Jezebel's and Ahab's actions and are never physically present. The Birmingham score, however, begins to resemble the published version in that the chorus, or mob, *is* physically part of the scene and follows the orders of Jezebel to find and kill the prophet. But unlike the published version, the mob in the Birmingham score requires no manipulation: from Jezebel's very first accusation (which actually becomes the third in the published version) they cry out, "He must perish!" While the Birmingham version does establish a parallel to the people's admonishment of Christ, it does not attempt to establish simultaneously a New Testament connection for the cause of their change of heart (i.e., coercion by the authorities). Mendelssohn began trying to create such an association in the textual and musical drafts written after Birmingham (Texts XXI–XXIII; XXIV, p. 13–16), all of which contain the same gradual intensification of the crowd's anger as in the published version, which is conveyed by means of their "We have heard it" response to each of Jezebel's accusations (see ex. 5.3 for the music).

Coming as it does immediately after Jezebel's incitement of the people, *Elias*'s next scene, Elijah's wilderness journey (GA 25–29), extends the parallel to Christ's passion by alluding to Christ's visit to Gethsemane (Mt. 26:36–46; Mk. 14:32–42; Lk.: 22:40–46). In the synoptic gospels, Jesus' visit to the garden begins by his asking the disciples who accompanied him (Peter, John, and James) to remain behind while he goes off to pray. Once alone, according to Matthew's and Mark's account, Christ prays three times to God that "this cup may pass" from him, after which, in Luke's account, an angel appears and strengthens him so that he may carry out God's will. In the published version of Elijah's wilderness journey, Mendelssohn evokes all these elements, beginning with Obadiah's warning Elijah about Jezebel's agitation of the mob, followed by Elijah's order that Obadiah (like Jesus' disciples) remain behind while he goes off to the wilderness (GA 25), neither of which appears in the 1 Kings narrative.

Obadja	*Obadiah*
Du Mann Gottes, lass' meine Rede etwas	Man of God, may my words hold some
vor dir gelten! So spricht die Königin:	value for you! So says the queen:
Elias ist des Todes schuldig; und sie	Elijah is worthy of death; and they
sammeln sich wider dich, sie stellen	gather together against you, they place
deinem Gange Netze, und ziehen aus,	nets in your path, and go forth that they

dass sie dich greifen, dass sie dich tödten.	may seize you, that they may kill you.
So mache dich auf und wende dich von	So arise and turn away from them,
ihnen, gehe hin in die Wüste! Der Herr,	go forth into the wilderness! The Lord
dein Gott wird selber mit dir wandeln, er	your God Himself will travel with you,
wird die Hand nicht abthun, noch dich	His hand will not forsake you, nor
verlassen. Ziehe hin und segne uns auch!	leave you. Depart, and bless us also!
Elias	*Elijah*
Sie wollen sich nicht bekehren! Bleibe	They have no wish to repent! Stay
hier, du Knabe, der Herr sei mit euch! Ich	here, boy, the Lord be with you! I
gehe hin in die Wüste.	go forth into the wilderness.

Without any kind of pause or extended interlude to represent the journey (a logical choice, since Christ made none when he left the three disciples and went to pray alone), this scene then leads into Elijah's plea for his suffering to end ("It is enough" [*Es ist genug*]), which he, like Christ, repeats three times in close succession (ex. 5.1).

After his prayer, Elijah sleeps, during or after which angels appear to remind him that God will strengthen him (GA 27–29), an occurrence that mirrors Luke's account of Jesus in the Garden (Lk. 22:43).

Rezitativ (Tenor)	*Recitative (Tenor)*
Siehe, er schläft unter dem Wachholder,	Behold, he sleeps under the juniper tree
in der Wüste; aber die Engel des	in the wilderness; but there the angels of
Herrn lagern sich um Die her, so ihn	the Lord encamp around all those who
fürchten.	fear Him.
Terzett (Drei Engel)	*Trio (Three Angels)*
Hebe deine Augen auf zu den Bergen von	Lift your eyes up to the mountains, from
welchen dir Hülfe kommt. Deine Hülfe	whence comes your help. Your help
kommt vom Herrn, der Himmel und	comes from the Lord, who made heaven
Erde gemacht hat. Er wird deinen Fuss	and earth. He will not let your foot
nicht gleiten lassen, und der dich behütet,	be moved, and He who protects you
schläft nicht.	will not slumber.
Chor	*Chorus*
Siehe, der Hüter Israels schläft noch	Behold, the protector of Israel neither
schlummert nicht. Wenn du mitten in	sleeps nor slumbers. Though you walk in
Angst wandelst, so erquickt er dich.	the midst of trouble, he will refresh you.

As with Obadiah's warning and Elijah's order for him to remain behind, the three-fold nature of Elijah's *Es ist genug* prayer does not appear in the Bible. And although a single angel comes to deliver food (1 Kg. 19:5–7), it is not the spiritual nourishment specified in the New Testament or implied in Mendelssohn's text.

While the parallels to Christ's passion in the published version of this scene are readily apparent, the earliest drafts demonstrate even more clearly Mendelssohn's Christological intent. As in all of the drafts of the Part II libretto, Klingemann's and Mendelssohn's initial outline (fol. 44r) mentions not only Elijah's wilderness jour-

EXAMPLE 5.1. Elias, *GA 26, mm. 10–30.*

ney, but also that Elijah would be strengthened by an angel (singing "Fear not, I am with you" [*Fürchte dich nicht, ich bin bei Dir*]). The outline also indicates Mendelssohn's and Klingemann's intention to interpret this event Christologically by having Elijah, just before his departure, shake the dust from his feet (*er schüttelt den Staub von* [*seinen*] *Füßen*) in response to his persecution by the servants of Baal. While this action never appears in the Old Testament, Jesus suggests (Mt. 10:14 and Mk. 9:5) that his apostles make this symbolic gesture when leaving a place in which they were not favorably received (as Paul later did upon leaving Antioch [Acts 13:51]). Indeed, Mendelssohn considered the inclusion of this text so important that when Klingemann omitted it from his prose draft, Mendelssohn added it again in the right-hand margin (fol. 39r). By the time Mendelssohn wrote his own first prose draft several years later, however, he had decided against the action, perhaps believing it more evocative of Paul—who actually made the gesture—than of Christ.

Mendelssohn's depiction in the published score of God's appearance to Elijah at Mount Horeb (GA 30–35) evokes two New Testament events—Christ at Gethsemane (continuing the passion parallel from the previous scene) and Christ's transfiguration. In the biblical accounts of the transfiguration (Mt. 17:1–8; Mk. 9:2–8; Lk. 9:28–36; 2 Pt. 1:17), Jesus traveled to an isolated mountain with his disciples Peter, John, and James (all of whom would later accompany him to Gethsemane), where Elijah and Moses stood beside him while God appeared in a cloud overhead and declared, "This is my son, in whom I am well pleased: listen to him." Although the transfiguration occurs much earlier in the gospel narrative than the visit to Gethsemane, the similarities between the two events (e.g., the same three sleepy apostles, the isolated setting) made it easy for Mendelssohn to combine them, and the mountaintop appearance of God in both the New Testament and 1 Kings narratives makes the parallel even stronger.

The scene begins with Elijah still in the wilderness, continuing to complain of the seeming futility of his efforts as the angels provide comfort (GA 30–32). Further evoking Christ at Gethsemane, this first section of the scene closes with a chorus based on the gospel quotation "He that shall endure to the end shall be blessed" (*Wer bis an das Ende beharrt, der wird selig* [Mt. 24:13]), a text suggested by Schubring (Text V, fol. 1v) and one that Mendelssohn first incorporated into the libretto in his second Part II draft (Text IX, fol. 15r).

The second part of the scene (GA 33–35) evokes the transfiguration through the appearance of God in a voice (1 Kg. 19:11–18) and the seraphim's singing of Isaiah 6:2–3 ("Holy, Holy, Holy is God the Lord," otherwise known as the *Sanctus*).

Chor	*Chorus*
Der Herr ging vorüber. Und ein starker Wind, der die Berge zerriss, und die Felsen zerbrach, ging vor dem Herrn her, aber der Herr war nicht im Sturmwind. Der Herr ging vorüber: und die Erde erbebte, und das Meer erbrauste, aber der Herr war nicht im Erdbeben. Und nach dem Erdbeben kam ein Feuer, aber der Herr war nicht im Feuer. Und nach dem Feuer kam ein stilles, sanftes Sausen. Und in dem Säuseln nahte sich der Herr.	The Lord passed by. And a mighty wind that rent the mountains and broke the rocks went before the Lord, but the Lord was not in the tempest. The Lord passed by; and the earth quaked, and the sea heaved, but the Lord was not in the earthquake. And after the earthquake came a fire, but the Lord was not in the fire. And after the fire came a still, small whisper. And in the whisper onward came the Lord.
Rezitativ (Alt)	*Recitative (Alto)*
Seraphim standen über ihm, und Einer rief zum Andern:	Seraphim stood over him, and one cried to another:
Quartett (Sop., Alt), Chor [Sanctus]	*Quartet (Sop., Alto), Chorus* [Sanctus]
Heilig, heilig, heilig ist Gott der Herr Zebaoth. Alle Lande sind seiner Ehre voll.	Holy, Holy, Holy is God the Lord Sabaoth. All lands are full of His glory.

These two elements function together to recall both the voice of God and the glory surrounding His appearance at Christ's transfiguration. The *Sanctus* plays a crucial role in establishing the Christological parallel, as it not only stands in for the voice of God, but also represents a fundamental component of the Protestant and Catholic Eucharist liturgies.[92]

This recitative and the two surrounding choruses may, by themselves, seem to parallel the transfiguration only superficially. In earlier versions of the scene, however, the link to the transfiguration was much clearer, but it was softened as part of Mendelssohn's attempt to retain *Elias*'s Old Testament character. Schubring first suggested a connection between God's appearance to Elijah and Christ's transfiguration in the letter accompanying his partial Part II draft (Text V), in which he asked if, for his next installment, he could use God's appearance in the "whisper" as a "transition . . . to his [Elijah's] transfiguration, so as to hint at the New Covenant, where, of course, Elijah holds great significance as forerunner and comrade of Christ on the mount of transfiguration."[93] Mendelssohn agreed, noting in his reply that the "connection from the soft whisper to the transfiguration . . . seems to me even necessary for our goals and quite beautiful."[94] In his next letter, Schubring provided a more specific description of his vision of the scene:

> I thought that just as Elijah came to Christ on the Mount of the Transfiguration (Matt. 17), so Christ might come to Elijah and transfigure him; could show him from afar the streams of peace which flow over the heavenly Canaan. These three persons—Him, Elijah, and the heavenly choir of angels—might suffice, with suitable dramatic alteration, to transform the earth into heaven, until Elijah is taken away.[95]

Although Mendelssohn generally approved of the idea of a transfiguration parallel, he apparently found the directness of Schubring's vision and the introduction of additional characters unappealing. Instead, he attempted to integrate more subtle transfiguration references, beginning with his second Part II draft (Text IX, fol. 15r–v), in which God identifies himself with the simple declaration, "I am the Lord your God, who brought you out of the land of Egypt, out of the house of bondage" (Ex. 20:2 et al.), a moment strikingly similar to that in which God identifies Christ during the transfiguration ("This is my beloved Son, in whom I am well pleased" [2 Pt. 1:17]). This is then followed with God's instructions to Elijah, after which an aria proclaims, "Hear, Israel, hear the voice of the Lord!" and the choir announces what Christ considered the two greatest commandments, almost exactly as they appear in Matthew 22:37–39 and Mark 12:30–31. The scene then concludes with a shortened version of Christ's declaration in Matthew 22:40 that "[t]his is the whole of the law and the [message of the] prophets."

Chor	*Chorus*
Und siehe der Herr ging vorüber. . . .	And behold, the Lord passed by. . . .
Und nach dem Feuer kam ein stilles,	And after the fire, there came a still,
sanftes Sausen.	soft whisper.
Ich bin der Herr dein Gott der dich aus	*I am the Lord your God, who brought you*
Aegyptenland geführt hat, aus dem	*out of the land of Egypt, out of the*
Diensthause.	*house of bondage.*
Rec.	*Recit.*
Da das *Elias* hörte, verhüllte er sein	And when Elijah heard it, he wrapped his
Antlitz mit seinem Mantel. Und der Herr	face in his mantle. And the Lord
sprach zu ihm[:] gehe wieder durch die	said to him[:] go back through the
Wüste gen Damaskus. . . .	wilderness towards Damascus. . . .
Arie	*Aria*
Höre, Israel, Höre des Herrn Stimme!	Hear, Israel, hear the voice of the Lord!

Chor	Chorus
Du sollst den Herrn deinen Gott lieb haben	*You shall love the Lord your God*
von ganzem Herzen, von ganzer Seele, von	*with all your heart, with all your soul, and*
allem Vermögen; denn er ist der Herr.	*with all your might; for He is the Lord.*
Du sollst deinen Nächsten lieben wie dich	*You shall love your neighbor as*
selbst, denn er ist der Herr.	*yourself; for He is the Lord.*
Das ist das ganze Gesetz und die	*This is the whole of the law and the*
Propheten.	*[message of the] prophets.*

Mendelssohn retained both God's declaration of His identity and Christ's commandments in his next draft (Text X, fol. 4r–v), but also added several references to light and the sun to his description of God's appearance.

Der Engel.	The Angel.
Gehe herauf, tritt auf den Berg vor den	Go up, step onto the mount before the
Herrn. Seine Herrlichkeit erscheint über	Lord. His glory will shine upon you.
dir.	

Arie.	Aria.
Deine Sonne wird nicht mehr untergehn,	Your sun will never set again,
noch dein Mond seinen Schein verlieren.	nor will your moon lose its shine.
Denn der Herr wird dein ewiges Licht	For the Lord will be your everlasting
sein, und die Tage deines Leidens sollen	light, and the days of your suffering shall
ein Ende haben.	come to an end.

Chor.	Chorus.
Und siehe der Herr ging vorüber. . . .	And behold, the Lord passed by. . . .

References to light and the sun appear prominently in all the accounts of the transfiguration; to use Matthew 17:2 as an example: "And he was transfigured before them, and his face shone like the sun, and his garments became white as light." Although in future drafts Mendelssohn decided to do away with the *Deine Sonne wird nicht mehr untergehn* aria—as well as Christ's commandments—he retained the reference to God's shining glory through to the final version (GA 33), where, followed by the chorus of angels singing the *Sanctus*, it invokes the grandeur and glory of the transfiguration. Mendelssohn added to this an additional association with Christ's visit to Gethsemane, a recitative (GA 36) in which Elijah resigns himself to carry on and suffer for the will of God: "You are my Lord, and I must suffer for Your sake" (*Du bist ja der Herr, ich muß um deinetwillen leiden*). The statement, which Mendelssohn first contemplated in Text XI (fol. 12v) but did not set until the published score, recalls Matthew 26:39 et al. ("My Father, if it be possible, let this cup pass from me; but not as I will, rather as You will"), as well as Jesus' words to Ananias regarding Saul of Tarsus (Paul) in Acts 9:16 ("I will show him how much he must suffer for my name's sake"), a text Mendelssohn set in *Paulus* (GA 18).

In early January 1846, just before writing this final incarnation of the scene, Mendelssohn sent a copy of the nearly complete libretto (Text X) to Schubring for review. Schubring's corrections included numerous comments on the transfiguration; most prominently, he inserted a scene in which Elijah appears at the New Testament event itself. But since this new episode could not fit seamlessly beside God's appearance to Elijah at Horeb, Schubring placed it after Elijah's ascension (fol. 5v), where it becomes part of a larger narrative of Elijah's New Testament incarnations, first as John the Baptist (represented by a recitative sung on Matthew 3:2, "Repent, for the kingdom of heaven is at hand"), and then as himself at Christ's transfiguration (as witnessed by Peter, John, and James).

Recit.
Es ist eine Stimme des Predigers in der Wüste: Bereitet dem Herrn den Weg, macht auf dem Gefilde eine ebene Bahn unserm Gott. Thut Buße, das Reich Gottes ist nahe herbei gekommen. Denn die Herrlichkeit des Herrn soll geoffenbaret werden.

Recit.
It is a voice of a preacher in the wilderness: prepare the way for the Lord, make straight in the desert a highway for our God. Repent, for the kingdom of God is at hand. For the glory of the Lord shall be revealed.

Terzett (Petrus, Johannes, Jacobus)
Und wir sahen seine Herrlichkeit als des eingebornen Sohnes voller Gnade und Wahrheit. Sein Angesicht leuchtete wie die Sonne und seine Kleider waren weiß wie das Licht und Mose und Elia erschienen bei ihm in Klarheit da wir mit ihm waren auf dem heiligen Berge. (biblical citations omitted)

Trio (Peter, John, James)
And we beheld his glory, as of the only begotten Son full of mercy and truth. His face shone like the sun and his garments were as white as light and Moses and Elijah appeared with him in glory, for we were with him on the holy mountain.

Having moved the transfiguration parallel to the end of the work, Schubring suggested that for His Mount Horeb appearance God declare himself to be the "Good Shepherd" of John 10:14 by means of an aria based on that passage and a chorus based on Psalm 23 ("The Lord is my shepherd"), thus evoking the Johannine image of the eternal Christ ("He was in the beginning with God; all things were made through him," Jn. 1:2–3).

Mendelssohn did not adopt any of these suggestions, but they are noteworthy in that they illustrate both his overall symbolic goals for the oratorio and the fundamental difference between his and Schubring's approaches to the Elijah story. (It was, in fact, this difference that led to the disintegration of their partnership in early 1839 and remained unresolved after the reinstatement of their collaboration in 1845.)

By suggesting John's "I am the good shepherd" text (among others), Schubring attempted in both his own libretto drafts and his corrections to Mendelssohn's to create a narrative in which Johannine theology (i.e., that Christ has existed since the beginning of the world) stood at the core. An even clearer example of this is Schubring's initial idea for a transfiguration scene, in which Christ and a heavenly choir transfigure Elijah.[96] Indeed, throughout his involvement in the *Elias* project,

Schubring pushed Mendelssohn to incorporate blatant Christological symbolism in the oratorio by including such material in his drafts and by marking for deletion those of Mendelssohn's passages that, in his mind, had no clear New Testament or Lutheran significance. (Schubring rejected, for example, Mendelssohn's intention in draft X [fol. 4v] to identify God as He "who led you out of Egypt," perhaps because of Luther's declaration that "God never led us out of Egypt, but only the Jews."[97])

While Mendelssohn certainly intended to make *Elias* a Christological work, he believed it important to retain the work's Old Testament flavor, something he stressed in his comments to Schubring about the transfiguration scene addition: "[T]he passages which you provided for the close of the whole (namely, the trio between Peter, John, and James) are too historical and too far removed from the perspective (*Haltung*) of the (Old Testament) whole."[98] Mendelssohn therefore remained insistent that any Christological material that he incorporated into *Elias* also had to fit into an Old Testament context, a criterion that Christ's transfiguration (for example) clearly did not meet. On the other hand, Mendelssohn's rule did allow him to contemplate including references to Christ's "greatest commandments" since the commandments themselves originate in the Old Testament (Dt. 6:5; Lv. 19:18). Similarly, Mendelssohn could and did experiment with the idea of referring to God as a shepherd (Text XVI, p. 76, 95–97), but could not refer to him as the "Good Shepherd" or use the John 10:14 text Schubring suggested since both refer too specifically to Christ. Instead, he considered using a parallel passage from Ezekiel 34:12, "As a shepherd seeks out his flock when some of his sheep have been scattered abroad. So will I seek out my sheep" (*Wie ein Hirt seine Schafe suchet, wenn sie von ihm verirrt sind, wenn sie von ihm verirrt sind. Also will ich euch suchen*).

In many respects, Schubring's last-minute suggestions espoused a method of infusing *Elias* with New Testament significance that was not all that different from the overt and often jarring methods adopted by Mendelssohn's contemporaries. To cite a single example, Carl Loewe's 1834 oratorio *The Brazen Serpent* (*Die eherne Schlange*) ends with the leaders of five Israelite camps clairvoyantly remarking that their formation—at each of the four compass points, with one group in the center—resembles the cross at Golgotha, where "there nodded, so heavy and sacred, the head of the Son of Man." Indeed, Mendelssohn likely had *Die eherne Schlange* and other similarly awkward works in mind when he turned away from Schubring's path and chose to adopt a more Handelian model for his Christological program. Nevertheless, Mendelssohn's affection for the works of the Baroque masters may have pulled him too far in the other direction. For as Handel and Jennens did with *Messiah*, Mendelssohn ultimately created in *Elias* a musical riddle, in which listeners with a strong New Testament competence would be able to unravel the work's Christological program. Given that the riddle has, to date, not been readily recognized, Mendelssohn may have attributed to his audience a biblical knowledge more in keeping with Handel's time than his own. It is equally possible, however, that Mendelssohn underestimated the degree to which his own audiences—as well as history—would view him as a Jewish composer looking to create a Jewish work.

THE JEWISH IMAGE IN ELIAS

As noted in the previous chapter, in preparing *Paulus* for publication Mendelssohn revised the work in order (among other things) to temper some of its more virulent anti-Semitic scenes. This move to treat Jews and Judaism with greater sympathy continued in *Elias* and indeed became a central issue during the work's creation. The drafts demonstrate that Mendelssohn struggled with the problem, vacillating between more positive and negative versions of his libretto with respect to Judaism, until striking a balance that allowed him to carry out his Christological program without needlessly disparaging the Jews or the Jewish faith in the process.

Mendelssohn's solution involved keeping the image of the Jews vague, often by not specifically identifying them in scenes where they might be viewed negatively. As a result, the people (*das Volk*) become universalized—it is not only the Jews who stray from God but all people—rendering *Elias* not only an allegory for the life of Christ, but also a metaphor for the need for reform in the present. (As such, it recalls Mendelssohn's description of the character of Elijah as "a genuine prophet through and through, such as we could use again in our own day."[99]) In situations where vagueness was not an option, however, Mendelssohn made certain that some plausible reason stood behind the Jews' actions (e.g., Jezebel's coercion) and that there were always some Jews who remained steadfast in their faith.

Just as the changes to the character of Obadiah and the addition of his call to repentance help Mendelssohn define *Elias*'s Christological program, so too do they demonstrate Mendelssohn's conflict concerning his handling of the Jewish image in his work, as well as provide an example of his eventual solution to the problem. The development of the chorus that follows Obadiah's call is particularly revealing in this regard. In the published version of the chorus (GA 5), the people react first with frustration and anger at having to suffer under God's curse, but then suddenly change their tone and find value in Obadiah's message, recognizing that those who obey God's commandments will receive his blessing.

Aber der Herr sieht es nicht, er spottet unser. Der Fluch ist über uns gekommen, er wird uns verfolgen, bis er uns tödtet: Denn ich der Herr dein Gott, ich bin ein eifriger Gott, der da heimsucht der Väter Missethat an den Kindern, bis in's dritte und vierte Glied derer die mich hassen. Und thue Barmherzigkeit an vielen Tausenden, die mich liebhaben und meine Gebote halten.	Yet the Lord does not see it, he mocks us. The curse has come upon us, he will persecute us, until he kills us: For I the Lord your God, I am a jealous God, who afflicts the fathers' sins on the children to the third and the fourth generation of those that hate me. And [I] bestow mercy to the many thousands that love me and keep my commandments.

The depiction of the Jews resulting from this sudden shift is fairly positive: a discontented people, but one that has not lost its faith in God. Admittedly, the chorus has a somewhat schizophrenic quality, appearing almost to consist of two separate groups: the first having abandoned their hope in God and the other having retained it. This problematic effect likely stems from some of the chorus's earlier incarnations, in which two separate groups—the servants of Baal and the servants of Jehovah—did in fact participate.

Mendelssohn's and Klingemann's initial concept (Text I, fol. 42r) was to have a chorus of the servants of Baal mock Obadiah's plea ("Why pray?" [*Wozu beten?*]), sandwiched between two choruses in which the people express their outrage and despair. From this, Klingemann extrapolated two choruses in his prose draft (fol. 35v), the first of which proclaims the victory of the sun-god ("The sun is too powerful for your God; the Lord of the skies has the upper hand" [*Die Sonne ist eurem Gott zu mächtig, der Herr der Himmel hat die Oberhand*]), while the second chorus remarks that the curse of the Lord (Jehovah) rests upon them ("The curse of the Lord rests upon us!" [*Der Fluch des Herrn ruht auf uns!*]). Schubring likewise incorporated two groups into his drafts of the scene (Text III, fol. 1v and Text IV, fol. 4r–v), but specified that the first should echo Obadiah's sentiments, while the second was to be introduced by Ahab and Jezebel. As in the Klingemann draft, these two figures mock Obadiah and rejoice in their service to Baal, a sentiment the second chorus then echoes. For the most part, Mendelssohn followed this example in his first prose draft (Text VI, fol. 1r) by accompanying Obadiah's call with a chorus echoing his sentiments ("Oh! that I knew how I might find Him, and might come before His throne. Lord, be not far from me." [*Ach, daß ich wüßte wie ich ihn finden, und zu seinem Stuhle kommen möchte. Herr sei nicht ferne von mir.*]). Significantly, however, he replaced Schubring's group of Baal-followers with a single individual: it is Jezebel alone who protests, "Who is the Almighty, that we should serve him? And how are those who call on him better off? Leave us, we wish to know nothing of His ways" (*Wer ist der Allmächtige, daß wir ihn dienen sollten? Und was seid ihrs gebessert, die ihr ihn anrufet? Hebt euch von uns, wir wollen nichts von seinen Wegen wissen*).

In his next draft (Text VII, fol. 7v)—and in a musical sketch based upon it (XVI, p. 79–84)—Mendelssohn experimented with the decidedly more anti-Semitic approach of following Obadiah's call with a unified chorus of doubters, positioning Obadiah as the sole faithful one.

[*Obadja*]	[*Obadiah*]
Zerreißet Eure Herzen und nicht eure Kleider. Um unsrer Sünde willen hat Elias den Himmel verschlossen durch das Wort des Herrn. Ja, warum habt ihr ihn erzürnt durch eure Bilder und unnützen Gottesdienste, und dem Baal einen Altar	Rend your hearts and not your garments. For our transgressions Elijah has sealed the heavens through the word of the Lord. Oh why have you angered him through your idols and useless rituals, and built an altar to Baal

errichtet und ihm gemacht einen Hain, und verlasset den Herrn, unsern Tröster!	and made a grove for him, and abandoned the Lord, our comforter!

Chor

Wer ist der Allmächtige, daß wir ihm dienen? Was sind wir's gebessert, so wir ihn anrufen? Wer ist der Allmächt'g[e?]

Chorus

Who is the Almighty, that we should serve him? How are we better off that we should call upon him? Who is the Almighty?

Obad[ja]

Es ist der H[er]r der Gott Israels; er kann euer Trauern in Freude verkehren, und euch trösten und erfreuen in der Betrübniß.

Obadiah

He is the Lord, the God of Israel; He can turn your mourning into joy, and comfort and gladden you in times of distress.

Chor

Es ist umsonst, daß man Gott dienet. Was nützet es, daß wir sein Gebot halten? Und hartes Leben führen: Er siehet es nicht, und der Gott Jakobs achtet es nicht.

Chorus

It is meaningless to serve God. What good does it do that we keep his law? And lead a hard life: He does not see it, and the God of Jacob does not heed it.

Ob[adja]

Der Herr merkt und hört es, und denen die seinen Namen fürchten soll aufgehn die Sonne der Gerechtigkeit.
(biblical citations omitted)

Obadiah

The Lord heeds and hears, and for those who fear His name shall rise the sun of righteousness.

That the chorus would be identified as Jewish is ensured by Obadiah's comment that they had "abandoned the Lord, our comforter" and by the chorus's own reference to the Almighty as "the God of Jacob."

Mendelssohn abandoned this experiment when he wrote his next draft (Text VIII, fol. 5r; see fig. 5.1), which, for the most part, conveys the same image of the Jews as that in the published score (i.e., discontent, but faithful). When he first wrote the draft, however, he left out Obadiah's plea entirely, choosing instead the following chorus, which echoes the published version of the people's response to Obadiah's call.

Der Himmel über unserm Haupte ist ehern, und die Erde unter uns eisern! Der Fluch ist über uns gekommen. Der Herr wird uns verfolgen bis er uns umbringe, bis wir vertilgt sind.	The heavens above our heads is brass, and the ground under us iron! The curse has come upon us. The Lord will persecute us until he kills us, until we are destroyed.
[D]er Herr dein Gott ist ein eifriger Gott, der da heimsuchet der Väter Missethat an den Kindern! und thut Barmherzigkeit an diesen die ihn lieb haben und seine Gebote halten.	*The Lord your God is a jealous God, who afflicts the fathers' sins on the children! and bestows mercy to those that love him and keep his commandments.*

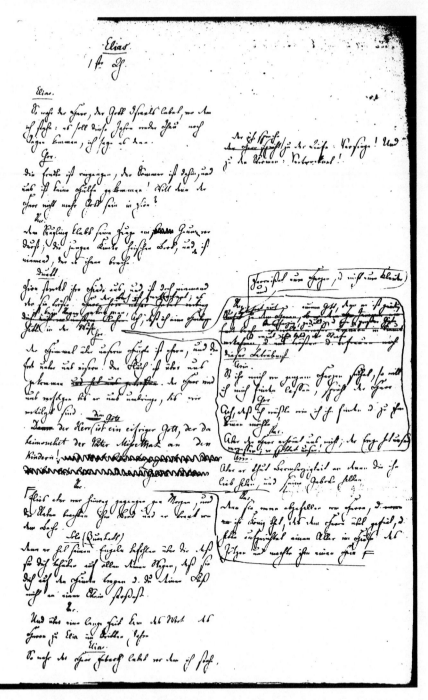

FIGURE 5.1. Elias, *Text VIII* (*GB-Ob MS. M. Deneke Mendelssohn c. 27*), fol. 5r, *showing some of Mendelssohn's intense work on Obadiah's call.*

He later revised the draft, however, putting back both Obadiah's call and the chorus that echoed his plea. Also added as part of this revision was a recitative which claimed that the people had strayed from God: "For they had fallen away from the Lord, and their king did that which displeased the Lord" (*Denn sie waren abgefallen vom Herrn, und ihr König that, das dem Herrn übel gefiel*). Mendelssohn seems to have rapidly abandoned this idea in his next Part I draft (Text X, fol. 1r–v), adopting instead what is essentially the published text. Aside from a few insignificant deletions, Mendelssohn would continue to use this revised text—which calls *all* people to God and does not specifically accuse the Jews of faithlessness—throughout the remaining versions of the work.

As with Obadiah's call, Jezebel's pursuit of Elijah at the opening of Part II (GA 23–24) is revealing of both Mendelssohn's Christological program and his handling of the Jewish image.[100] As a cursory glance at the published version of the scene shows, the identity of the chorus that eventually joins the queen in calling for Elijah's death is left vague: Are they those who returned to Jehovah during the earlier challenge scene or just some straggling followers of Baal? Since all of Baal's prophets were slaughtered at the end of the challenge scene and those who followed them were supposedly converted, a listener could easily conclude that they are converted Jews, suggesting the faithlessness of that group.

The drafts demonstrate, however, that this was not Mendelssohn's intent. Even in his original outline, he and Klingemann clearly specified the group as a "Chorus of Baal-servants" (*Chor der Baalsdiener*), who call for revenge for their slaughtered brethren (*Räche unsre Brüder*), an example followed in both Klingemann's and Schubring's prose drafts (II, fol. 39r; V, fol. 1r). Mendelssohn apparently realized that including a chorus of Baal-servants here would either be inconsistent with the results of the challenge scene or could be misinterpreted as the continuing faithlessness of the Jews. In his next four drafts (VI, fol. 3v; IX, fol. 15r; X, fol. 3v [shown below]; and XI, fol. 11r), he therefore lets Jezebel and Ahab plot alone against Elijah, leaving the chorus of newly converted Jews to deride them.

Was trotzest du denn, du Tyrann, daß du kannst Schaden thun? Der Herr hat geredet, so höre, und merke auf, und trotze nicht. Wer stolz ist, den kann er demüthigen, und dem Gericht des Allmächtigen, der alle Dinge sieht, kannst du doch nicht entfliehen.	Why do you boast, O tyrant, that you can commit mischief? The Lord has spoken, so hear, and pay heed, and do not boast. Whosoever is proud, He can humble, and from the judgment of the Almighty, who sees all things, you cannot flee.

Perhaps in an effort to contribute drama to the work, Mendelssohn added a chorus to carry out Ahab's orders to kill Elijah in his next draft of the scene (Text XIII, fol. 13r).

Der König	*The King*
Ziehet hin zu allen Völkern und Königreichen, und suchet Elias, daß wir seiner Seele thun wie er den Propheten.	Go forth to all the peoples and kingdoms and seek out Elijah, that we may do to him as he did to the prophets.

Chor	Chorus
Greifet ihn und tödtet ihn, wie er die Propheten Baals getödtet hat.	Seize him and kill him, as he killed the prophets of Baal.

Here too, however, Mendelssohn apparently wanted to avoid conveying the idea of a widespread public rebellion that included the Jews. He therefore also incorporated into the scene a chorus sung by or sung to the faithful that quotes God's promise of salvation for the righteous in response to Jezebel's accusations.

Die Königinn	The Queen
Was wäre für ein Königreich in Israel, wenn Elias thut, wie ihm gefällt? [D]ie <u>Götter</u> thun mir dies und das, wo ich nicht morgen seiner Seele thue, wie er den Seelen dieser Propheten. Er hat sie mit dem Schwert erwürgt. [E]r soll des Todes sterben.	What kind of kingdom would Israel be if Elijah can do as he pleases? The <u>gods</u> do this and that to me, if tomorrow I do not do to him what he did to these prophets. He slaughtered them with the sword. He shall die.

Chor	Chorus
Fürchte dich nicht, ich bin mit dir. Weiche nicht, denn ich bin dein Gott. Ich stärke dich, ich helfe dir auch, ich erhalte dich durch die rechte Hand meiner Gerechtigkeit.	Fear not, I am with you. Be not dismayed, for I am your God. I will strengthen you, I will help you also, I will preserve you through the right hand of My righteousness.
Ob tausend fallen zu deiner Seite und hunderttausend zu deiner Rechten so wird es doch dich nicht treffen. (biblical citations omitted; underline original)	If thousands fall at your [left] side and a hundred thousand at your right, still it will not strike you.

Admittedly, while the chorus that responds to Ahab's order in this draft is likely intended to be a group of soldiers and servants, their identity remains undefined. Therefore, in his first set of revisions to the draft (written to the right of the original material), Mendelssohn established that they are new priests ordained by Ahab (an act for which Elijah chastises him), who echo the king's call for Elijah's death.

Aber der König und sein Haus kehrten sich nicht von ihrem bösen Wege, und machten Priester der Höhen und verfolgten den Mann Gottes.	But the king and his house did not turn from their evil ways, and they made priests of the Most High and persecuted the Man of God.

Chor	Chorus
Fürchte dich nicht, ich bin mit dir. . . . [chorus text is same as above]	Fear not, I am with you. . . . [chorus text is same as above]

[Elias]	[Elijah]
Hast du dich von deinem bösen Wege gekehrt, König? Hast du nicht Priester	Have you turned from your evil ways, king? Have you not made priests

der Höhen gemacht von den Geringsten des Volkes? [U]nd Unthat gethan über alle die vor dir gewesen sind? Darum wird der Herr Unglück über dein Haus führen und der H[er]r wird *Israel* schlagen, wie das Rohr im Wasser bewegt wird.

of the Most High out of the lowest of the people? And committed misdeeds greater than any who came before you? Therefore the Lord will bring misfortune upon your house, and the Lord will smite Israel, as a reed is shaken in the water.

[*Chor der Priester*]
Laßt uns ihm thun, wie er gethan hat. Er soll des Todes sterben; Seele um Seele, Auge um Auge, das ist das Gesetz. Hat er sie nicht geschlachtet am Bache Kison? Er soll des Todes sterben. Hat er nicht den Himmel verschlossen und die theure Zeit über uns gebracht? Er soll des Todes sterben.
(biblical citations omitted)

[*Chorus of Priests*]
Let us do to him as he has done. He shall die; a soul for a soul, an eye for an eye, that is the law. Did he not slaughter them at Kishon's brook? He shall die. Did he not close the heavens and bring the lean years [of famine] upon us? He shall die.

But these changes have some disturbing implications. First, these new (albeit politically chosen and motivated) priests were not of Baal, but of Jehovah, and second, they dogmatically quote the law ("a soul for a soul, an eye for an eye, that is the law") in a manner reminiscent of the Jews in *Paulus*. Mendelssohn's recognition of these anti-Semitic leanings may have spurred him to eliminate any mention of the priests in his second set of revisions of the draft (written on its last page, fol. 14v). This, however, left nothing to establish the chorus's identity, a situation that, again, allows for the assumption that they are the newly converted Jews.

Die Königinn
Er ist ein Mensch gleichwie wir! Er hat alle Propheten Baals mit dem Schwert erwürgt. Die Götter thun mir dies und das, wo ich nicht morgen um diese Zeit deiner Seele thue, wie dieser Seelen einer. Er ist des Todes schuldig.

The Queen
He is a human being just like us! He slaughtered all of the prophets of Baal with the sword. The gods do this and that to me, if by tomorrow about this time I do not do to him as he did to one of them. He is worthy of death.

Chor
Er ist des Todes schuldig. Laßt uns ihm thun, wie er gethan hat. Er schlachtete sie am Bache Kison; er ist des Todes schuldig. Er hat den Himmel verschlossen und die theure Zeit über uns gebracht. Er ist des Todes schuldig! Er ist des Todes schuldig.

Chorus
He is worthy of death. Let us do to him as he has done. He slaughtered them at Kishon's brook; he is worthy of death. He closed the heavens and brought the lean years [of famine] down upon us. He is worthy of death! He is worthy of death.

Despite this solution's shortcomings, Mendelssohn based the Birmingham score upon it, no doubt in part due to time constraints. He seems, however, to have tried to counter possible anti-Semitic interpretations by providing the Jews with a reason to rebel: Elijah's threat (expanded from Text XIII) that "the Lord shall smite Israel, as a reed is shaken in the water" (Text XVIII, no. 28).

The Birmingham score also contained musical elements that reflected negatively upon the Jews. Foremost among these was the musical resemblance of the setting of "He is worthy of death" (*Er ist des Todes schuldig*) to the Jews' dogmatic cry of "Here is the Lord's temple!" (*Hier ist des Herren Tempel!*) used in *Paulus* against Paul and his followers (ex. 5.2a, b). Given *Paulus*'s tremendous popularity, such a quotation would have been easily recognized and might even have been interpreted as a kind of "Jews' motive" that spanned the works, creating an association between the members of the *Elias* chorus and the negatively depicted Jews in *Paulus*. While reminiscence motives were common within oratorios (including *Elias*, in which the "curse motive" from the introduction reappears frequently, and *Paulus*, with its repeated stoning choruses), it was not uncommon to find motivic connections among oratorios, such as those connecting the three oratorios of Friedrich Schneider's *Christus* cycle (*Christus das Kind* [1829], *Christus der Meister* [1827], and *Christus der Erlöser* [1838]).[101] Such connections also appear among Mendelssohn's sacred works: both Psalm 42 (*Wie der Hirsch schreit*, op. 42) and Psalm 43 (*Richte mich, Gott*, op. 78, no. 2) close with identical text and music.

While the music in the Birmingham score suggests Jews similar to those in *Paulus*, the negative association is significantly strengthened by the text, whose last sentence, "He is worthy of death" (*Er ist des Todes schuldig*) derives from both Jeremiah 26:11 (like most of the rest of the chorus) and Matthew 26:66, where the High Priests use it to condemn Christ. Such usage is reminiscent not only of the stoning choruses of *Paulus*, but also of the crucifixion (*Kreuzige ihn!*) choruses of the Bach Passions, and was most likely adopted as part of *Elias*'s Christological program, as the first textual draft for the published version (Text XXI), which quotes more of Matthew 26:66, suggests.

Text XXI, reproduced as in original

Königinn	*Queen*
Wir	We
[^]~~Ihr~~ habten es mit ~~euch~~unsern Ohren gehört, wie er geweissaget gegen diese Stadt; ~~was dünkt [euch,] ist er nicht des des Todes schuldig?~~	[^]~~You~~ have heard it with your ears how he has prophesied against this city; ~~what do you think, is he not worthy of death?~~
Chor	*Chorus*
Er muß sterben.	He must die.
Königinn	*Queen*
Er ist des Todes schuldig.	He is worthy of death.

Matthew 26:65–66

Da zerriß der Hohepriester seine Kleider, und sprach: Er hat Gott gelästert;	Then the high priest tore his robes, and said: He has blasphemed against God;

EXAMPLE 5.2a. Elias *Birmingham score* (*GB-Bp MS 1721*), *no. 28, mm. 16–23.*

EXAMPLE 5.2b. Paulus, *GA 37, mm. 1–7.*

was dürfen wir weiter Zeugniß!	what further evidence do we need!
Siehe, jetzt habt ihr seine Gotteslästerung	Behold, you have now heard his
gehöret. Was dünket euch?	blasphemy. What do you think?
Sie antworteten, und sprachen:	They answered and said:
Er ist des Todes schuldig.	He is worthy of death.

As the cross-out in the draft shows, however, Mendelssohn chose to reject the *Was dünkt euch* textual parallel shortly after writing it. Moreover, the music of the published version of this scene limits the phrase *Er ist des Todes schuldig* to a single utterance each by Jezebel and the chorus.

Although these changes tempered *Elias*'s anti-Semitic content, Mendelssohn was clearly concerned about their effect on the work's Christological program. He therefore chose a different method of alluding to the High Priests' incitement of the mob against Christ. Rather than build on textual connections, Mendelssohn instead focused on the incitement process itself by having Jezebel manipulate the mob against Elijah. This solution had the twofold benefit of reinforcing Mendelssohn's Christological program, while simultaneously providing a justification for the actions of the Jews. Indeed, Mendelssohn had already provided for this possibility in the Birmingham score by including Elijah's threat ("And the Lord shall smite Israel"). In the published version and its drafts (Texts XXI–XXIV), Jezebel uses this threat *against the state* (as opposed to *against God*, an important distinction) to turn the people slowly against Elijah: "Have you heard how he has prophesied against this people?" (*Habt ihr's gehört, wie er geweissagt hat wider dieses Volk?*). The people calmly and quietly (*piano*) agree that they have ("We have heard it" [*Wir haben es gehört*]), but, unlike in the Birmingham score, they are not yet resolved to attack the prophet. Jezebel then asks the people if they have heard how Elijah had spoken against the king ("How he has prophesied against the king of Israel" [*Wie er geweissagt hat wider den König in Israel?*]), thus accusing him of a second count of the (secular) crime of treason, to which the people —already angered and growing louder—confirm her claim ("We have heard it") (ex. 5.3a).

Jezebel then asks why such a man, who snubs his nose at the king's authority, should be allowed to speak for God: "Why is he permitted to prophesy in the name of the Lord? What kind of kingdom would Israel be if Elijah had power over the king's power?" (*Warum darf er weissagen im Namen des Herrn? Was wäre für ein Königreich in Israel, wenn Elias Macht hätte über des Königs Macht?*). This particular accusation clearly reveals Jezebel's attempt to manipulate the people, since she pretends offense at Elijah's prophesying in the name of a God in whom she herself does not believe (as demonstrated in the next sentence, "The gods do this and that to me"), but in whom her audience clearly does. Moreover, she carefully words the accusation so as not to challenge the obvious fact that God has endowed Elijah with authority. Throughout her tirade, then, Jezebel restricts her accusations against Elijah to his perceived misuse of that authority and to secular crimes, all of which represent acts of treason against the state. Jezebel's accusations whip the crowd into a frenzy (something Mendelssohn represents in the score through a crescendo of tremolo strings and a timpanic roll), leading them to cry out, "He must die!" (ex. 5.3b).

Once Jezebel has successfully incited the people, she continues to list Elijah's abuses of his power: murder of the prophets of Baal, depriving the people of rain, and creating the famine. Now recognizing Elijah's treason, the people conclude that such a man should have neither God's power nor the authority to speak in His name.

EXAMPLE 5.3a. *Elias, GA 23, mm. 30–38.*

EXAMPLE 5.3b. Elias, *GA 23, mm. 44–56.*

Wehe ihm! er muss sterben! Warum darf er den Himmel verschliessen? Warum darf er weissagen im Namen des Herrn? Dieser ist des Todes schuldig! Wehe ihm, er muss sterben, denn er hat geweissagt wider diese Stadt, wie wir mit unsern Ohren gehört. So ziehet hin, greifet ihn, tödtet ihn!

Woe to him, he must die! Why may he be permitted to close the heavens? Why may he prophesy in the name of the Lord? This man is worthy of death! Woe to him, he must die, for he has prophesied against this city, as we have heard with our ears. So go forth, seize him, kill him!

While the Jews' anger, at least in the light of Jezebel's accusations, now appears justified, it still leaves the listener with the impression that all the Jews have rebelled against Elijah, something Elijah himself would seem to confirm in *Es ist genug* (GA 26).

EXAMPLE 5.3b. (continued)

| Ich habe geeifert um den Herrn, um den Gott Zebaoth, denn die Kinder Israels haben deinen Bund verlassen, und deine Altäre haben sie zerbrochen, und deine Propheten mit dem Schwert erwürgt. Und ich bin allein übrig geblieben, und sie stehn danach, dass sie mir mein Leben nehmen! | I have been very jealous for the Lord, for the God of Hosts, for the children of Israel have abandoned your covenant, and broken your altars, and slain your prophets with the sword. And I alone am left, and they lie in wait to take my life from me! |

To counter this image, Mendelssohn drafted and included in the published version a choral recitative sung by the angels after their *Sanctus* (Text XXIII; Text XXIV, p. 34; GA 36), that declares that Elijah may now depart, for "the Lord yet has left to Him seven thousand in Israel, knees which have not bowed to Baal" (*Noch sind übrig geblieben siebentausend in Israel, die sich nicht gebeugt vor Baal*). With this addition, *Elias* closes having made clear that despite Jezebel's and Ahab's efforts, there were many

EXAMPLE 5.3b. (continued)

Jews who remained steadfastly faithful to their God. Perhaps more important, however, the scene now leaves the listener with the impression that because of Jezebel's manipulation, those who did stray are deserving of some level of understanding.

As Jezebel's scene poignantly demonstrates, Mendelssohn did not intend to write a philo-Semitic work when he composed *Elias*. However, unlike *Moses* and *Paulus*, *Elias* contains little of the blatant anti-Semitic content that could have helped Mendelssohn distance himself from his Jewish roots. *Elias* instead represents Mendelssohn's first real attempt to find a method of publicly declaring the depth of his Christian faith without having simultaneously to sully the Jewish image. As we have seen, this was an arduous process, one that caused the composer to vacillate among various Christological symbols, contemplate a range of adaptations of the somewhat negative biblical account, and create versions of the libretto which depicted the Jews with varying degrees of sympathy. In the end, Mendelssohn's solution was imperfect; it required that the negative images be balanced by more positive ones or that the Jews' actions be justified in some manner. Even in its final incarnation, *Elias* demonstrates Mendelssohn's lingering ambivalence toward his Jewish heritage and the tentativeness with which he made these first steps toward accepting it. *Christus* would represent yet another step in this direction, but ultimately, it was a journey Mendelssohn would not have the opportunity to complete.

Christus

Now when Jesus was born at Bethlehem, in the Jewish lands . . .
—*Matthew 2:1, as quoted in Mendelssohn's* Christus

As R. LARRY TODD HAS NOTED, the Mendelssohn oratorio fragment known as *Christus* is a composition whose history "remains shrouded in mystery,"[1] a result of a scarcity of drafts and correspondence describing Mendelssohn's work on the score. Well documented, however, is the emergence of Mendelssohn's concept for the work, which he discussed with numerous colleagues for nearly a decade before finally settling on the plan he was in the process of executing when he died on November 4, 1847. Mendelssohn launched this plan in 1844 with the help of Christian Karl Josias von Bunsen, the Prussian ambassador to London and a talented theologian whom Mendelssohn first met while in Italy in 1831.[2] Mendelssohn's enlistment of Bunsen—the man responsible for bringing him back to Berlin in 1841 to serve King Friedrich Wilhelm IV—is no doubt the source of *Christus*'s relatively invisible development, for two reasons. First, Bunsen's extensive ambassadorial duties likely prevented him from working with Mendelssohn on the libretto with the same intensity as those who had contributed texts for *Paulus* and *Elias*. Second, given that only a single letter from Bunsen (and none from Mendelssohn) survives that discusses the *Christus* libretto, any conversations the men had regarding the text probably took place in person, either during Mendelssohn's visits with Bunsen in London or during Bunsen's visit to Berlin during Mendelssohn's tenure there as *Generalmusikdirektor für kirchliche und geistliche Musik*.[3] Mendelssohn's decision, upon agreeing to work with Bunsen, not to discuss the project further with his other regular correspondents (including his earlier libretto contributors) followed the pattern he had established with his other oratorios: once he had established a relationship with a contributor, he stopped providing details to the others, perhaps concerned that they might feel slighted by his abandonment of their work.

Aside from a lack of correspondence, an additional impediment to the study of *Christus* is the total loss of Bunsen's and Mendelssohn's libretto drafts. These drafts, which were in the possession of the composer's grandson Albrecht Mendelssohn Bartholdy in Hamburg, were destroyed in a fire early in the twentieth century.[4] Despite this loss and the overall scarcity of information, however, *Christus* still reveals a great deal about Mendelssohn's evolving attitude toward his Jewish heritage. Indeed, a comparison of the score fragment with the original biblical texts from which it derived reveals a clear intention on Mendelssohn's part to protect the Jewish image. As with *Elias*, Mendelssohn realized that disparagement of the Jews was not an indispensable component of a retelling of the Christ story, nor was it necessary in order for him to prove the sincerity of his Christian faith.

The Genesis of *Christus*

The concept for the oratorio that would eventually be known as *Christus* first emerged in 1838. As noted in the previous chapter, Mendelssohn had at this time temporarily abandoned the idea of composing an oratorio on the subject of Elijah, as his two librettists, Karl Klingemann and Julius Schubring, had each failed to compile a suitable text. This did not discourage Mendelssohn from continuing his search for a viable oratorio subject, however, especially since the late 1830s witnessed the growing popularity of *Paulus*, which was becoming widely known through both performances and private readings of the newly published score. As a result, Mendelssohn began to receive a steady stream of oratorio libretti from resourceful *Paulus* admirers who had managed to track him down. Among the first was the *Elijah* draft written by the Reverend James Barry (sent in January 1838 by Charles Greville) discussed in the last chapter. The following November, Mendelssohn received another unsolicited collection of texts from Lutheran pastor Karl Sederholm in Moscow, which the author described as being for a "large piece of church music . . . that would include *all* of the key events of Christendom and in which all Christian feelings would find their expression."[5] But despite Sederholm's categorization of the work as "church music," the collection consisted mostly of selections from Milton (in English), Metastasio (in Italian), and the Roman Breviary (in Latin).[6] The negligible use of biblical text and the lack of any dramatic argument in the libretto were no doubt among the reasons Mendelssohn chose not to use it. The concept of a work that encompassed the "key events of Christendom" evidently struck a chord with Mendelssohn, however, inspiring him to pursue similar topics.

In the summer of 1839, Mendelssohn approached the Frankfurt theater coach and music journalist Carl Gollmick for assistance in preparing an oratorio entitled *Erde, Hölle und Himmel* (*Earth, Hell and Heaven*)—the original title of what would eventually be known as *Christus*. As Gollmick recalled in his autobiography:

> That . . . conversation had, in the end, the result that Mendelssohn wanted material for an oratorio which sought [to describe] the three highest principles of moral existence, "Earth, Heaven and Hell."[7] After I had first written *this material of extremes* in prose and divided it up into scenes, I turned . . . the manuscript over to my friend Gambs, who then poetically set all of these parts after the biblical texts.[8]

The libretto Gollmick purportedly provided is lost, making it impossible to determine its influence on *Christus*. But since the surviving *Christus* fragment is a historical work rather than the moral tale Gollmick describes, and since Mendelssohn continued to search for a librettist after the summer of 1839, it seems unlikely that he used any of Gollmick's material.

That same summer, Mendelssohn conducted the Lower Rhine Music Festival in Düsseldorf, at which time he likely discussed the idea of an *Erde, Hölle und Himmel* oratorio with English music critic Henry Fothergill Chorley, who was in attendance.[9] Chorley apparently agreed to help and shared his thoughts with the composer in a letter dated November 3, 1839. This letter indicates that, as he had with Gollmick, Mendelssohn described his vision of the oratorio to Chorley in the vaguest terms, perhaps again mentioning only the "three highest principles of moral existence." Chorley attempted to compensate for this lack of direction by providing a historical narrative revolving around the parable in Luke 16:19–31 of the rich man (Dives) and the poor man (Lazarus).[10] Mendelssohn considered the proposal, but quickly rejected it, writing to Karl Klingemann two months later that "Chorley's idea of Lazarus does not really appeal to me."[11] A month after that, Mendelssohn told Chorley of his concerns regarding the Lazarus subject:

> I have not been able to form an exact idea of what you intend the whole to be; the fact is, that I did not quite understand what part both figures should act in hell or in heaven, because I do not quite understand the part they act on earth. . . . I only find Dives very rich and Lazarus very poor, and as it cannot be only for his riches that one is burning in hell, while the other must have greater claims to be carried to Abraham's bosom than his poverty alone. . . . Perhaps you have another view of the whole; pray let me know it.[12]

Mendelssohn likely requested additional information more out of politeness than genuine interest; as his skeptical tone and his comment to Klingemann suggest, he had already abandoned the idea by this time and, indeed, never mentioned it again in his correspondence with Chorley.

Within a few days of writing Chorley, Mendelssohn asked Julius Schubring to help with *Erde, Hölle und Himmel*.[13] Schubring accepted the invitation, and became especially enthusiastic about the project upon reading a possible source for the "Hell" segment. "A short while ago," he wrote Mendelssohn:

> the idea [for an *Erde, Hölle und Himmel* oratorio] became once again very exciting to me when I read the apocryphal gospel of Nicodemus, which contains a truly poetic portrayal of Christ's descent into Hell (which, according to common belief, took place between the death and resurrection of the Lord).[14]

In the same letter, Schubring also provided Mendelssohn with a suggestion for a Christological creation story for the "Earth" segment:

As for the content of "Earth," it could begin with the glory of the Creation. Ps. 19, Ps. 104 (v. 24) and the like; then the appearance of sin handled as the disturbance of a number of happy conditions; then redemption through Christ, sanctification on Earth; it would close with a call to faith and a warning about Hell.[15]

Of these suggestions, it was Schubring's mention of the Gospel of Nicodemus that most intrigued Mendelssohn, who replied:

You have written me a most important word with your apocryphal Nicodemus and with his journey through Hell—I believe it will lead me down a straight path to the completion of my idea of composing a large work about Hell and Heaven, and will be the pillar that I have sought for so long. Where can I read this Nicodemus (even if only in a poor excerpt)? It has most likely not been translated; and what are the main subjects of his Gospel? In the worst case, I would have to make the effort of reading it in Greek, although I would rather not.[16]

In his next letter to Schubring, written the very next day, Mendelssohn continued to display enthusiasm for the Gospel of Nicodemus, which he described as being "very much on my mind," and about which he again requested information.[17] If Schubring ever responded to Mendelssohn's request, the letter has been lost. It is also quite possible, however, that Schubring never responded to Mendelssohn's inquiries because of his greater interest in Mendelssohn's idea for a possible oratorio on John the Baptist (*Johannes*).

Schubring's enthusiasm for this alternative subject clearly surpassed that for *Erde, Hölle und Himmel,* judging by the extensive detailed suggestions he made for *Johannes'* content.[18] In their correspondence over the next week, the two men discussed *Johannes* intensely, as Mendelssohn was considering composing it to fulfill a recent commission from the city of Leipzig for its 1840 celebration of the 400th anniversary of Gutenberg's invention of movable type.[19] Mendelssohn abandoned this idea, however, choosing instead to fulfill his commission by transforming his unfinished symphony in B-flat into the *Lobgesang* (Symphony no. 2).[20] This decision coincided with the sudden end of his discussion of his oratorio plans with Schubring, an event likely precipitated by a fundamental disagreement about which elements of the Baptist story a *Johannes* oratorio should include, as well as the appropriateness of performing the oratorio at the Leipzig festival.[21] A similar disagreement also probably emerged regarding *Erde, Hölle und Himmel.* For although Mendelssohn was excited by Schubring's suggestion of the Nicodemus gospel, Schubring's overall vision for the work—judging from the surviving score—differed substantially from Mendelssohn's. As Schubring summarized in his memoirs:

Regarding the oratorio of *Christus,* he never exchanged a word with me; on the other hand, we had often previously talked about St. Peter and John the

Baptist. What I told him of the account given in the gospel of Nicodemus concerning the descent of Christ into Hell, interested him in an extraordinary degree, and, from what escaped him, I am inclined to believe he intended turning it, sometime or other, to musical account.[22]

(Schubring clearly did not realize that *Christus* and *Erde, Hölle und Himmel* were one and the same, and that he had actually been cut out of the loop regarding the future development of the libretto.)

At some point Mendelssohn apparently discussed his *Erde, Hölle und Himmel* concept with *Paulus* contributor Julius Fürst as well. Although no mention of the project appears in Fürst's letters to Mendelssohn, the only surviving plans for the oratorio in Mendelssohn's hand are on a single folio containing an undated outline with the heading *Fürsts Plan*. Written just above this is Mendelssohn's own brief, unfinished outline, which bears some similarity to the Fürst plan.[23] Both demonstrate that one of Mendelssohn's concepts for *Erde, Himmel und Hölle* involved producing not a biblical work per se, but rather something similar to Goethe's *Faust* or Dante's *Divine Comedy*: a work that combined a postbiblical setting with sacred text and legend (extracted, perhaps, from apocryphal texts) to create a more contemporary (but still biblically styled) drama. This concept is most readily evident in the "Earth" segments described in Mendelssohn's and Fürst's outlines, which present all the stages of earthly life (e.g., baptism [*Taufe*], marriage [*Ehe*], and death [*Tod*]), as well as some possible calamities (e.g., war [*Krieg*] and plague [*Pest*]). Indeed, the inclusion of these latter elements suggests that Mendelssohn and Fürst had planned for a Last Judgment oratorio similar to those popular during the 1810s and 1820s. This was certainly Fürst's objective: Part II of his outline is even entitled "Day of Judgment" (*Tag des Gerichts*). Mendelssohn's inclusion of the common apocalyptic signs of war and plague in the "Earth" segment of his own outline similarly suggests an intention to depict the last days of the world. Ultimately, however, neither Mendelssohn's nor Fürst's outline bear any resemblance to Mendelssohn's actual *Christus* score, as neither depicts Christ's life, limiting their usefulness in determining Mendelssohn's intentions.

In addition to soliciting his friends for libretto and plot suggestions, Mendelssohn asked them about other contemporary settings of the subject of Christ. Some of these works were already known to him, such as Friedrich Schneider's 1827 *Christ, the Master* (*Christus der Meister*).[24] Schubring was familiar with only one other—another work from Schneider's *Christus* cycle, *Christ, the Child* (*Christus das Kind*, 1829)—and added that, in his opinion, there did not yet exist any quality Easter oratorios; even *The Resurrection and Ascension of Jesus* (*Die Auferstehung und Himmelfahrt Jesu*), written in 1807 by Mendelssohn's former teacher Carl Friedrich Zelter, he found "of little value."[25] Mendelssohn continued making inquiries as late as 1842, when he contacted music journalist Otto Jahn (who wrote on *Paulus* that same year),[26] requesting that he procure for him a copy of the printed textbook of the 1825 *Christus* oratorio by Georg Christian Apel, Jahn's former teacher.[27] On April 5, Jahn mailed Mendelssohn a handwritten copy of the booklet,[28] as no spare published copies remained in Apel's possession.[29] Once again, Apel's text was not a source for *Christus*; Mendelssohn was interested only in reviewing the manner in which the Christ story had been set.

With the exception of his contact with Otto Jahn, Mendelssohn made little progress on *Erde, Hölle und Himmel* between 1840 and 1844, at which point he turned to Bunsen for help. As noted earlier, little evidence survives regarding the nature of their arrangement. However, the April 8, 1844, letter from Bunsen that accompanied his partial draft demonstrates fairly conclusively that it was his libretto—which he originally wrote on his own initiative sometime around 1830—that served as the primary outside textual source for *Christus*. This letter, which partially summarizes the libretto, indicates clearly that Bunsen's text, like the surviving *Christus* fragment, was based on the gospels' account of Christ's life:

> Here you have the draft written out up until the resurrection: the rest is contained in the drafts that I wrote ten to fifteen years ago, and which I therefore would like to see again when I am back in London, where we will meet. I still have not had time to write down the chorales in the second section: Specifically, I think they belong between Jesus['] words on the cross. . . . The whole [libretto] can be worked out; but here and there we would have to do without sustained narrative transitions.[30]

In fact, that Mendelssohn settled upon Bunsen's libretto as a textual source for *Erde, Hölle und Himmel,* and—more important—then adapted the libretto to create his own text (continuing the pattern he had established in *Paulus* and *Elias*) is corroborated by an entry in Queen Victoria's diary, written on the occasion of Bunsen's visit in December 1847:

> Before dinner Ld. Palmerston brought up Bunsen, who came with a letter from the King of Prussia. . . . Bunsen much regrets [the death of] Mendelssohn, whom he had known very well. He had settled & arranged with him the text for a new Oratorio of "Earth, Hell & Heaven" & said it had been wonderful to see how beautifully Mendelssohn chose the text from scripture.[31]

Although Mendelssohn could have begun composing what we now call *Christus* any time after Bunsen began handing over his libretto on April 8, 1844, it seems unlikely that any serious work occurred before April 1847,[32] by which time Mendelssohn had fully completed *Elias,* a project that had preoccupied him since the summer of 1845. The *Christus* fragment was one of the pieces found on Mendelssohn's desk shortly after his death on November 4, 1847. The score was untitled, unnumbered, unbound, and consisted of a small set of pieces on the nativity and a larger set on the passion.[33]

Until recently, these scenes (the birth and the passion of Christ) were thought to be the first two of what would eventually have been a three-part work (the final section presumably being "the resurrection").[34] But Mendelssohn's and Bunsen's continual reference to the work as *Erde, Hölle und Himmel*—not to mention the brevity of the two surviving scenes—makes this unlikely. As R. Larry Todd has hypothesized, these two scenes are instead probably components of the oratorio's first part, "Earth,"[35] which most likely would have concluded with a resurrection scene, as Bunsen's April 8, 1844, letter implies. However, the exact organization of the part is impossible to determine, as is whether the chorale that closes the posthumously published fragment even belongs to it. (Its text, "He takes upon his back the load that weighs me down" [*Er nimmt auf seinen Rücken die Lasten, die mich drücken*], provides a fitting end to the passion scene, however, suggesting that it probably does belong.) Also unclear is how much more music Mendelssohn intended to compose for the "Earth" part—or even for the surviving scenes. Since no standardized numbering system exists for the score, the one used here (table 6.1) reflects these uncertainties. Each new number represents a movement that begins on a clean folio (i.e., one that does not include the end of the previous movement) and before which Mendelssohn could have intended to insert additional music. (For example, since No. 4a begins at the top of a new page, Mendelssohn could have planned to insert additional music—a chorale perhaps—between it and No. 3j.)

The title by which the work is known today, *Christus*, almost certainly did not originate with either Bunsen or Mendelssohn. As Queen Victoria's diary entry describing Bunsen's visit reveals, even a month after Mendelssohn's death, Bunsen was not referring to the oratorio by its current title. In fact, another of the Queen's diary entries, written six months earlier on the occasion of Mendelssohn's final visit to England, suggests that the composer himself did not embrace the *Christus* title:

> We had the great treat of hearing Mendelssohn play, & he stayed an hour with us, playing some new compositions. . . . For some time he has been engaged in composing an Opera & an Oratorio, but has lost courage about them. The subject for his Opera is a Rhine Legend [*Die Lorelei*] & that for the Oratorio, a very beautiful one depicting Earth, Hell, & Heaven, & he played one of the Choruses out of this to us, which was very fine.[36]

Rather, the source of the title *Christus* was most likely Felix's younger brother, Paul, who used it to describe to visitors to the Mendelssohn home shortly after the composer's death what appeared (in its unfinished form) to be a "Christ" oratorio. A letter written by Mendelssohn's friend Ignaz Moscheles strongly suggests this possibility:

> His brother [Paul] explained to me that among Mendelssohn's papers was a plan for an oratorio: *Christus*. Two pieces [i.e., scenes] are already complete. Felix is supposed to have said that he wanted to save up his best energy for this work!![37]

TABLE 6.1. The numbering system used in this chapter for *Christus* (reflects foliation)

[Scene One: The Birth of Christ]

1a. *Recitative* (*Soprano*)	Now when Jesus was born at Bethlehem
	(*Da Jesus geboren war zu Bethlehem*)
1b. *Trio* (*Tenor, 2 Basses*)	Where is the newborn King of the Jews
	(*Wo ist der neugeborne König der Juden*)
2. *Chorus*	A star shall come forth out of Jacob
	(*Es wird ein Stern aus Jakob aufgehn*)

[Scene Two: The Passion of Christ]

3a. *Recitative* (*Tenor*)	And the entire crowd arose
	(*Und der ganze Haufe stand auf*)
3b. *Chorus*	We found this man leading the people astray
	(*Diesen finden wir, daß er das Volk abwendet*)
3c. *Recitative* (*Tenor*)	Pilate said to the high priests and to the people
	(*Pilatus sprach zu den Hohenpriestern und zum Volk*)
3d. *Chorus*	He has stirred up the people
	(*Er hat das Volk erregt*)
3e. *Recitative* (*Tenor*)	But Pilate said: I find no guilt in him
	(*Pilatus aber sprach: Ich finde keine Schuld an ihm*)
3f. *Chorus*	Away with this one and release Barabbas to us!
	(*Hinweg mit diesem und gib uns Barabbam los!*)
3g. *Recitative* (*Tenor*)	Then Pilate cried again to them
	(*Da rief Pilatus abermals zu ihnen*)
3h. *Chorus*	Crucify, crucify him!
	(*Kreuzige, kreuzige ihn!*)
3i. *Recitative* (*Tenor*)	Pilate said to them: Take him yourselves
	(*Pilatus spricht zu ihnen: Nehmet ihr ihn hin*)
3j. *Chorus*	We have a law
	(*Wir haben ein Gesetz*)
4a. *Recitative* (*Tenor*)	Then he handed him over
	(*Da überantwortete er ihn*)
4b. *Chorus*	You daughters of Zion
	(*Ihr Töchter Zions*)
5. *Chorale*	He takes upon his back
	(*Er nimmt auf seinen Rücken*)

THE JEWISH IMAGE IN *CHRISTUS*

As my discussion of the genesis of *Christus* has demonstrated, many of the sources that might appear to have played a role in the libretto's creation actually had little or no influence. None of the libretti or ideas submitted to Mendelssohn before his collaboration with Bunsen resemble the piece as it stood at the time of his death. In fact, since the Bunsen drafts are themselves lost, there exists but a single source with which Mendelssohn's text can be compared for the purpose of this study: the Bible itself. Fortunately, Mendelssohn set *Christus* in a manner similar to Bach's *Christmas Oratorio* and Passions, in that he adopted a narrative style and attempted to set the biblical text verbatim whenever possible. As a result, a comparison between the surviving score and the original Bible text reveals a great deal about Mendelssohn's changing attitude toward his Jewish heritage.

Of the minor changes Mendelssohn made to the original Bible text for his setting of *Christus*, especially illuminating are those instances in which he retained or deleted the words "Jews" (*Juden*), "Jewish" (*jüdische*), and "Hebrew" (*Ebräisch*). For the Christmas segment of the work, Mendelssohn took the text for all of no. 1 nearly verbatim from Matthew's gospel (Mt. 2:1–2). As a result, Mendelssohn's libretto, like the gospel, recounts the story of the "newborn King of the Jews" (no. 1b, *Wo ist der neugeborne König der Juden*), who has been born "at Bethlehem, in the Jewish lands" (no. 1a, *Da Jesus geboren war zu Bethlehem im jüdischen Lande*). While both of these statements clearly attest to Jesus' Jewish birth, Mendelssohn reinforced this fact with a chorus (no. 2), whose first sentence derives from the Messianic prophecy in Numbers 24:17: "A star shall come forth out of Jacob, and a scepter shall rise out of Israel, which shall crush princes and cities" (*Es wird ein Stern aus Jakob aufgehn, und ein Szepter aus Israel kommen, der wird zerschmettern Fürsten und Städte*).[38] Mendelssohn's inclusion of this particular prophesy no doubt derived from the fact that the Bibles of his era identified it as a parallel to Matthew 2:2, which relates the star's appearance and its signaling of the Messiah's birth and which is sung by the wise men in the preceding trio (no. 1b, "Where is the newborn King of the Jews, we have seen his star" [*Wo ist der neugeborne König der Juden, wir haben seinen Stern geseh'n*]).

In the passion segment, Mendelssohn again set the biblical text nearly verbatim (in this case from the gospels of Luke and John), but with one significant exception: he deleted the words "Jewish," "Jews," and "Hebrew" from the three places where they would have appeared.

Mendelssohn's *Christus*	Luther Bible (1824)
3d. Chor Er hat das Volk erregt damit daß er gelehret hat hin und her im ganzen Lande und hat in Galiläa angefangen bis hieher!	Er hat das Volk erreget, damit, daß er gelehret hat hin und her im ganzen *jüdischen* Lande, und hat in Galiläa angefangen, bis hieher. (Lk. 23:5)

He has stirred up the people with	He has stirred up the people with
what he has taught	what he has taught
throughout all the lands,	throughout all the *Jewish* lands,
beginning in Galilee,	beginning in Galilee,
until this place.	until this place. (Lk. 23:5)

3i. Recit.

Pilatus spricht zu ihnen:	Pilatus spricht zu ihnen:
Nehmet ihr ihn hin und kreuziget ihn,	Nehmet ihr ihn hin, und kreuziget ihn;
denn ich finde keine Schuld an ihm.	denn ich finde keine Schuld an ihm.
Da antworteten sie:	*Die Juden* antworteten ihm: (Jn. 19:6–7)
Pilate said to them:	Pilate said to them:
Take him yourselves and crucify him,	Take him yourselves and crucify him;
for I find no guilt in him.	for I find no guilt in him.
They answered:	*The Jews* answered him: (Jn. 19:6–7)

4a. Recit.

Da überantwortete er ihn	Da überantwortete er ihn,
daß er gekreuzigt würde	daß er gekreuziget würde.
sie nahmen Jesum und führten ihn hin	Sie nahmen aber Jesum, und führeten ihn hin. Und er trug sein Kreuz, und ging hinaus zur Stätte, die da heißet
zur Schädelstätte,	Schädelstätte,
	welche heißet auf *Ebräisch* Golgatha. (Jn. 16–17)
es folgte ihm aber nach	es folgete ihm aber nach
ein großer Haufe Volks und Weiber	ein großer haufe Volks, und Weiber,
die klagten und beweineten ihn.	die klagten und beweineten ihn. (Lk. 23:27)
Then he handed him over	Then he handed him over
to be crucified.	to be crucified.
[T]hey took Jesus, and led him	They took Jesus, and led him away. And he carried his cross, and went out to the place that is called
to the place of skulls,	place of skulls,
	which is called in *Hebrew* Golgatha. (Jn. 16–17)
there followed him	[T]here followed him
a great multitude of people, and women,	a great multitude of people, and women,
who bewailed and lamented him.	who bewailed and lamented him. (Lk. 23:27) (Emphasis added)

The combined effect of these changes recalls a pattern observed in *Elias*. While the Bible clearly identified the crowd calling for Jesus' crucifixion as consisting of Jews, in *Christus* it is simply referred to as "they" (*sie*), "the people" (*das Volk*) or "the crowd" (*das Haufe*). By keeping the identity of Christ's accusers vague, while simultaneously retaining the references to Jesus' Jewish birth, *Christus* goes out of its way to treat the Jews more sympathetically.

A second manner in which Mendelssohn lessened the passion scene's anti-Semitic content (again by following the *Elias* model) relates to the pattern of gospel usage in the oratorio. Over the course of the scene, Mendelssohn subtly shifts from one gospel narrative (Luke) to another (John), thereby establishing some justification for the mob's actions. For the scene's first seven numbers (3a–3g), Mendelssohn sequentially drew his text from Luke's passion (Lk. 23:1–21), omitting only Jesus' appearance before Herod (Lk. 23:6–15). (This segment, if included, would have interrupted the dramatic crescendo that develops between Pilate, Jesus, and the mob). The text of the eighth number (3h, "Crucify, crucify him!" [*Kreuzige, kreuzige ihn!*]) appears in both the gospels of Luke (23:21) and John (19:6) and was thus able to serve as a pivot point between the books. Mendelssohn took advantage of this and based the three numbers that follow (3i–4a) on the gospel of John (19:7, 16–17). In so doing, he included in chorus 3j the rationale for the mob's call for Jesus' death, as it appears in John 19:7: "We have a law, and by that law he ought to die, because he has made himself the Son of God" (*Wir haben ein Gesetz, und nach dem Gesetz soll er sterben, denn er hat sich selbst zu Gottes Sohn gemacht*). (Luke's gospel contains no such justification, only further cries for Jesus' crucifixion and the release of Barabbas.) Of course, this rationale in itself does not spare the Jews from blame. But since Mendelssohn had already altered the text of the recitative that introduces the chorus from "The Jews answered him" to "They answered," the identity of the mob is ambiguous at best. Interestingly, the mob's motive for presenting Jesus to Pilate in the first place conveys a similar universality. In no. 3b, the crowd does not accuse Jesus of claiming to be the Messiah, but rather of attempting to supersede Caesar by forbidding the giving of tribute and by calling himself "Christ, a king"— a secular, rather than sacred title.

After the *Wir haben ein Gesetz* chorus, the Evangelist explains how Pilate turned Jesus over to the crowd, who led him out to the "place of skulls" (*Schädelstätte*). For the remainder of the scene, Mendelssohn returns to Luke's passion account, and in so doing points out the number of people who remained loyal to Jesus (see text of No. 4a above)—a caveat not present in John's gospel. Such a strategy mirrors Mendelssohn's efforts in *Elias*, where, as noted in the last chapter, he not only attempted to justify the mob's actions, but also made a point of indicating that a significant number of Jews remained steadfast in their faith.

THE UNIVERSALITY OF *DAS VOLK*

By obscuring the traditional role of the Jews in the *Christus* fragment, Mendelssohn managed to create an effect similar to what occurs in *Elias*: namely, the identity of the people (*das Volk*) becomes, by virtue of the very lack of specificity, universal. As noted in the previous chapter, Mendelssohn seems to have had this goal in mind when he first conceived of the character of Elijah, whom he wanted to depict in a timeless manner, so that the listener might recognize elements of modern-day life in the work (such as what Mendelssohn called "the court rabble and popular rabble").[39] He also accomplished this universality in *Elias* through Obadiah's call to repentance, which, by the time it reached its final incarnation, was no longer directed solely at the Jews but was instead a call to *all* the people, thereby conforming to the Lutheran tradition of universal blame for sin.[40] On the whole, however, this universal blame was only imperfectly expressed in *Elias*, since there continued to exist scenes in which responsibility for the various sins against God or Elijah was specifically assigned to either the priests of Baal or the Jews. In the *Christus* fragment, however, Mendelssohn was more consistent: the removal of any reference to the Jews in the passion segment leaves Christ's persecutors unspecified and allows for a more universal interpretation.

It is worth noting that the chorale that has traditionally been used to close the passion segment in *Christus* (no. 5) represents not only an attempt to universalize the blame for Christ's suffering on the cross (another Lutheran tradition),[41] but does so by following the model of Bach's *St. Matthew Passion*, a work whose narrative structure likely served as a model for *Christus*. There, Bach turns the crucifixion into a contemporary event (i.e., all Christians cause Christ's suffering in perpetuity through sin) through his setting of the fifth verse of the chorale "O world, behold your life" (*O Welt, sieh' dein Leben*). This chorale appears after Jesus announces that one of the apostles has betrayed him, to which eleven of them respond, "Lord, is it I?" (*Herr, bin ich's?*). Then, before the narrative continues, the present-day congregation admits through the chorale their own complicity in the betrayal through their sin (ex. 6.1). Given the lack of concrete identification of the mob in *Christus*, Mendelssohn's inclusion of the very next verse of this same hymn—a verse that associates Jesus' heavy cross with the sins of all mankind—suggests that he intended to convey the same sense of universal guilt as in Bach's work (ex. 6.2).

Mendelssohn, however, accomplished this not only through his choice of verse—which likewise describes the crucifixion as a contemporary event—but also through the melody, which would have reminded the listener of the other verses of *O Welt, sieh' dein Leben*, all of which similarly describe Christ's suffering. (It is also worth noting that Mendelssohn's version of the melody bears a far greater resemblance to Bach's than to the original hymn tune, suggesting that the *St. Matthew Passion* may have been more than just a conceptual model.)

Despite *Christus*'s multitiered evocation of universal guilt in the passion segment's final chorale, it remains doubtful whether this image would have been sufficiently vivid to prevent Christian listeners from reverting to a more contemporary (and therefore more anti-Semitic) understanding of the gospel story, which placed the blame for the crucifixion squarely on the Jews. Nor does it seem likely that the omission of the words "Jew," "Jewish," and "Hebrew" from the passion narrative

EXAMPLE 6.1. *J. S. Bach,* St. Matthew Passion, *no. 10.*

It is I, I should atone,
with hands and feet
bound in Hell.
The scourges and the bonds,
and that which you endured,
so too my soul deserves.

EXAMPLE 6.2. *Christus, no. 5, mm. 1–12 (first verse).*

He takes upon his back
the load [i.e., sins] that weighs me down
to the point of collapse;
He becomes accursed
so I may receive blessings,
O how merciful is He!

would have sufficed to prevent his listeners from making similar connections. The question remains, then, as to why Mendelssohn would have troubled himself with these protective gestures if they were unlikely to have been recognized by most of his audience.

Conclusion
Matters of Perspective

Because *christus* was never completed, it is difficult to draw
definitive conclusions about its treatment of the Jews. It is probably safe to say, however, that whether Christian audiences would have interpreted the people (*das Volk*)
in the universal sense Mendelssohn intended would have depended on each audience
member's religious perspective. While anyone curious about Jewish responsibility for
the crucifixion could have observed that, technically speaking, no such blame is assigned in *Christus*'s passion scene, this subtlety would probably have been lost on the
average Christian member of Mendelssohn's audience. Indeed, even though Christian listeners, upon hearing the passion scene's final chorale, would have been reminded
of the message of universal guilt for Christ's suffering, many would have been so familiar with both the story and contemporary anti-Semitic rhetoric that they would
have identified Christ's persecutors as Jewish automatically. Similarly, most Christian
listeners of *Elias* would have been predisposed to perceive the Jews in that work as
fulfilling their traditional New Testament function—this despite the fact that Mendelssohn deliberately avoided casting them in such an adversarial role.

In his earlier sacred libretti, however, Mendelssohn was not prepared to allow
his audiences even this limited flexibility in interpreting the motivations of the Jews.
In editing Bach's *St. Matthew Passion*, Mendelssohn kept all the anti-Semitic content that placed the blame for the crucifixion squarely on the Jews. And as a comparison between Mendelssohn's *Moses* and Adolf Bernhard Marx's oratorio *Mose*
reveals, Mendelssohn's decision to portray Moses as a Christlike figure led him to
depict the work's Jews in a corresponding New Testament manner, one that resonated with several anti-Semitic stereotypes of the day, such as that of a people incapable of true faith and as adherents to barbaric ritual. A convert to Christianity who
nonetheless retained a positive attitude toward his Jewish heritage, Marx found such
a representation distasteful and went out of his way to depict the Jews heroically in
his oratorio, often by making subtle alterations to Mendelssohn's own text.

Mendelssohn's *Paulus*, as we have seen, constitutes a turning point in the composer's attitudes, representing both the apex of his attempt to distance himself from

his heritage and the point at which his attitude began to change. But even the version of the work heard today is filled with common nineteenth-century stereotypes of the Jews as a "stiff-necked" people, dedicated to the word, rather than the spirit, of the law. As noted in chapter 4, anti-Semitic imagery is even stronger in *Paulus*'s numerous libretto drafts, a product, in my view, both of Abraham Mendelssohn's personal influence on the work and of contemporary oratorio trends. In response to these influences and pressures, Mendelssohn rejected less anti-Semitic alternatives offered to him by contributors such as Julius Fürst and Marx. As he had in *Moses*, Mendelssohn depicted Paul as a Christlike figure, a representation that, combined with Mendelssohn's heroic depiction of the Gentiles, resulted in an intensely negative characterization of the Jews throughout the work's development, all the way up through its Düsseldorf premiere. This frankly anti-Semitic content began to lessen, however, when the most powerful influence on the piece—Mendelssohn's father—died a few short months before the premiere. Once Mendelssohn had recovered from his grief, the discomfort surrounding his Jewish heritage instilled in him by his father began to dissipate. This development coincided with both the final revision of *Paulus* for publication and the establishment of Mendelssohn's career on a firm footing in Leipzig. As a result, the published score reveals a softening (although by no means an elimination) of the work's anti-Semitic content and, more important, the beginning of a new attitude on the composer's part, one no longer fueled by a need to demonize the Jews in order to prove the sincerity of his Christian faith.

Despite this shift in attitude, however, and contrary to prevailing opinion, Mendelssohn's subsequent (and most popular) oratorio, *Elias*, is not a philo-Semitic work, nor was it an attempt on the composer's part to embrace his Jewish heritage. As argued in chapter 5, it is essentially a Christian work throughout. Once again, Mendelssohn presented his protagonist as an Old Testament Christ by employing Christological imagery throughout the work and by constructing the piece so as to parallel the gospel narrative of the life of Christ. Significantly, however, this Christological program is not realized at the expense of the work's Jews. While the Jewish image in the work is by no means entirely favorable, both the final version and the drafts of *Elias* demonstrate an unmistakable effort on Mendelssohn's part to depict the Jews more sympathetically than he had in the past. In most instances he accomplished this by not placing them in an adversarial role (as they had been in both *Moses* and *Paulus*) and by ensuring that they remained distinct from those to whom he did assign that role—namely, the priests and followers of Baal. In those cases where the Jews could have been implicated (such as in Jezebel's scene), Mendelssohn made it clear that those Jews who had turned against Elijah had been manipulated to do so, and that others remained consistently faithful both to him and to Jehovah.

Although unfinished, *Christus* can be read as a continuation of Mendelssohn's efforts to spare the Jewish image in his oratorios, this time in what is traditionally the most anti-Semitic of biblical stories: the passion of Christ. Of special note in this regard is Mendelssohn's rigorously strict setting of the Luke and John gospel texts, with the significant exception of his omission of the words "Jews," "Jewish," and "Hebrew" when they appear in negative contexts. As a result, the presence and the role of the Jews is, as in *Elias*, kept vague. Mendelssohn consciously avoided assigning them their traditional role as the crucifiers of Christ and instead emphasized the Lutheran tradition that placed that blame equally on all sinners, past and present, Jew and Christian alike.

For Mendelssohn's listeners to have recognized those elements of the *Elias* and *Christus* libretti that represent an attempt on the composer's part to depict the Jews sympathetically would have required an acute sensibility. Specifically, it would have required that they be open to the possibility of a portrait of the Jews defined by something other than contemporary stereotypes, and, moreover, that they be willing to accept such a portrait. Given the growing anti-Semitic climate in Germany, such listeners would no doubt have been increasingly rare. What concerns me here, however, is not that such interpretations were common, but rather that they were possible at all—and, more important, that Mendelssohn intended them to be possible. Indeed, if I am correct in observing that Mendelssohn's construction of the *Elias* and *Christus* libretti represents an attempt to reconcile his Christian faith and his Jewish heritage, then he may very well have been counting on what could be called a strategy of dual perspective.[1] If Mendelssohn's audiences were predisposed to see his later oratorios as continuing to disparage the Jewish people, that was their interpretation. Mendelssohn ensured, however, that this was not the only interpretation these works would allow.

The enthusiastic acceptance of *Elias* by both Christians and Jews attests most conclusively to Mendelssohn's success in employing this strategy of dual perspective. Indeed, despite the work's Christological program and its obvious appeal to Christian audiences (including contemporary critical reviewers such as Otto Jahn), if anything the work has been embraced even more warmly by Jews, to whom the Christological program has evidently not been readily recognizable.[2] The oratorio even came to be performed in synagogues, including—in 1937—the Oranienburger Straße synagogue in Berlin, where, as Leon Botstein notes, "There was no doubt that . . . Jews believed they were hearing a Jewish work written by a German Jew affirming the greatness of Judaism."[3] This universal acceptance of *Elias* is made possible by the work's dual perspective. For those members of Mendelssohn's Christian audience expecting to find a less than favorable portrait of the Jews, there is much in *Elias* to satisfy their expectation: most notably, the (Jewish) people's rejection of Elijah. From the perspective of Jewish listeners, however, that rejection could be viewed as emanating not from the Jews at all, but rather from a benighted sect of Baal-followers. To Christians, the mention that only 7,000 remained faithful to Jehovah might seem a condemnation; to Jews, it can be taken as a triumph in the face of overwhelming adversity. To Christians, the opening chorus ("Help, Lord" [*Hilf, Herr*]) might conceivably resonate with the stereotype of the parasitic Jew; to Jews, it could serve as a symbol of the people's continuing faith in times of hardship.

It is, of course, impossible to say with certainty whether Mendelssohn's attempts to reconcile his Christian faith with his Jewish heritage by creating a variety of interpretive possibilities in his later oratorios would have been his final, ambiguous word on the subject or rather an intermediate step on the path toward a full, unambiguous embrace of his heritage. However, given the growth in the anti-Semitic movement shortly after Mendelssohn's death, it seems unlikely that he could have managed, had he lived longer, to treat the Jews much more sympathetically than he already had. Even had he lived, Mendelssohn would have been unable to prevent the anti-Semitic attacks launched against him after 1847; after all, Richard Wagner's 1850 essay *Judaism in Music* (*Das Judenthum in der Musik*) attacked both the living (Meyerbeer) and the dead (Mendelssohn).[4] The expectation, therefore, that Mendelssohn, in such an atmosphere, would have been able to compose oratorios like Handel's, in which the Jewish people are depicted heroically, is an unrealistic one. If he wished to survive professionally, he would have had to follow one of three paths: revert to the anti-Semitic depictions of the Jews evident in *Moses* and *Paulus*, continue the careful balancing act observed in *Elias* and *Christus*, or cease composing oratorios altogether. As mentioned at the outset of this volume, such an unappealing reality may not accord with the heroic images we may wish to entertain of great artists. But part of the reason Mendelssohn's religious music was accepted—even celebrated—in its time is that the composer recognized, acknowledged, and worked around the sensibilities of his audiences. In other words, he was willing to pay the price of assimilation.

Notes

Introduction

1. As Sander Gilman points out, Jewish assimilation through the abandonment of Yiddish and the adoption of High German as their primary language was not entirely successful. Many Jews continued to be identified by their Yiddish accent (a manner of speech the Germans called *Mauscheln*, a term based on the proper name *Moische*). Gilman, *Jewish Self-Hatred*, 139–48.

2. Quotation from Meyer, *Deutsch-jüdische Geschichte*, 2:180. (All English translations of German-language sources are the author's, unless otherwise noted.) In addition to closing Jews out of certain circles, the law prevented nonconverted Jews from holding any kind of state office, as well as most teaching positions (see ibid., 2:187).

3. Schoeps, *Deutsch-jüdische Symbiose*, 174. While atheism might seem to satisfy the requirement that Jews separate themselves from their religion in order to enter German society, non-Jews writing on the subject (including Wilhelm von Humboldt, Immanuel Kant, Friedrich Schleiermacher, Karl Streckfuß, and August Gfrörer) never mention this as a possible alternative. Some rationalists, such as Humboldt, even went so far as to suggest that Jews who wished to live atheistically should still allow themselves and their children to be baptized so as to better blend with predominantly Christian society. Such a suggestion was not meant hypocritically—most atheistic rationalists retained their Christian identity, becoming, in essence, nonobservant Christians. By the same token, Jews who lived atheistically would have continued to retain their Jewish identity, thereby falling short of the goal of separating themselves from Judaism. As a result, very few (at least based on the accounts of the more noted former Jews) adopted an atheistic lifestyle without at least a demonstratory baptism. See Meyer, *German-Jewish History*, 2:170–74.

4. That Mendelssohn saw himself as German and was proud of the fact can be seen in letters such as that of 25 August 1831 to Goethe, where he wrote, "I very much want to tell you how especially happy I am these days that I happen to be living at just this particular time and that I just happen to be a German" (Wolff, *Meister-Breife*, 29). For more on Mendelssohn's relationship to Schleiermacher, see chapter 2 of this book. Regarding his more overt attempts to assimilate, Mendelssohn appears to have succeeded, at least as far as was physically possible: contemporary writers often referred to Mendelssohn's Semitic appearance, but never indicated that he (or his father) ever spoke with any kind of accent—although a slight lisp is occasionally mentioned (see Nichols, *Mendelssohn Remembered*, 126, 139, 141, 185, 218, 225).

5. Schoeps, *Deutsch-jüdische Symbiose*, 178.

6. Meyer, *German-Jewish History*, 2:178.

7. Freudenberg, 25, in Todd, *A Life*, 59.

8. The German here (*eppes Rores*) is, as Eric Werner indicates, a kind of mock-Yiddish. E. Werner, *Neuer Sicht*, 39.

9. Letter of 21 October 1821 from Zelter to Johann Wolfgang von Goethe. Hecker, *Brief-wechsel*, 2:158.

10. Diary entries for 14 and 15 November 1840. Nauhaus, *The Marriage Diaries of Robert and Clara Schumann*, 31–32. Brackets Nauhaus's. An additional anti-Semitic episode involving Robert Schumann (albeit indirectly) occurred a few years later when Mendelssohn premiered Schumann's Second Symphony in Leipzig, after which the audience demanded an encore of Rossini's *William Tell Overture* that preceded it. The *Leipziger Tageblatt* described the encore choice as a "Mosaic" plot designed to undermine Schumann's symphony. See Todd, *A Life*, 532.

11. Richard Wagner's *Das Judenthum in der Musik* first appeared in the 3 and 6 September 1850 editions of the *Neue Zeitschrift für Musik* under the pseudonym "K. Freigedank" ("K. Free-thought").

12. A 14 November 1935 supplement to the infamous "Nuremburg Law" of 15 September 1935 that stripped German Jews of their citizenship defined a Jew as one who stemmed from three or more "fully Jewish" grandparents (i.e., those who were members of the Jewish religious community) and a *Mischling* ("half-caste" or partial Jew) as one with two "fully Jewish" grandparents. Walk, *Das Sonderrecht für die Juden im NS-Staat*, 127, 139.

13. Meyer, *German-Jewish History*, 4:395.

14. E. Werner, *New Image*, 43; Konold, *Felix Mendelssohn Bartholdy*, 75. A notable exception to this trend is R. Larry Todd's recent biography, *Mendelssohn: A Life in Music*.

15. Letter from July 1834 to Henriette von Pereira Arnstein. P. Mendelssohn Bartholdy, *Italy and Switzerland*, 201.

16. Letter of 13 July 1831 to Eduard Devrient. Devrient, *My Recollections*, 113.

17. Leon Botstein ("Aesthetics of Assimilation," 22) provides an example: "The texts Mendelssohn selected, the prominence played by the issues of conversion and graven images (in *St. Paul*), and the attraction to the figure of Elijah are markers of the extent to which Mendelssohn devoted his artistic energy to finding bridges between Judaism and Christianity." A somewhat older example appears in Kupferberg (*The Mendelssohns*, 252), who notes after his two-sentence discussion of Mendelssohn's psalm settings that "[i]t is in music like this that Felix and Moses Mendelssohn come together at the last."

18. Grove, "Mendelssohn," 2:304.

19. See, for example, E. Werner, *New Image*, 350–52 and Konold, *Felix Mendelssohn Bartholdy*, 193.

20. As Dinglinger (*Studien*, 26) points out, both Werner and Konold grant only minimal coverage to Mendelssohn's other Psalms. Kupferberg (*The Mendelssohns*, 252), however, is among the most guilty, ignoring even Mendelssohn's beloved Psalm 42 in favor of 114: "Above all, one would wish to encounter, as part of the Mendelssohn revival, a performance of his Psalms. Of the nine [*sic*] he set to music, at least one, Psalm 114 . . . is a masterpiece, a monumental eight-part choral work that impelled Sir George Grove to write. . . ."

21. Dinglinger (*Studien*, 170–85) documents an unbroken tradition of orchestral psalm composition from Bach and Handel to Mendelssohn and beyond; likewise, Dörffel's statistics of concerts held at the Leipzig Gewandhaus (1–79) demonstrate a strong tradition of

psalm motets and cantatas dating back to the organization's inception in 1781. For interpretations of Mendelssohn's Psalms as an ecclesiastical bridge, see, for example, Botstein, "Mendelssohn and the Jews," 213; Kupferberg, *The Mendelssohns*, 252; and Jacob, *Mendelssohn and His Times*, 233.

22. Two other works from this period, *Ich will den Herrn nach seiner Gerechtigkeit preisen* and *Tag für Tag sei Gott gepriesen*, also tend to get referred to as Psalms, but their texts are only psalm-like and do not appear to be based on actual Psalms.

23. Mendelssohn, ed. Zappalà, *Dreizehn Psalm-Motetten*, v–vi.

24. Abraham mentions this discussion in his letter to Felix of 8 July 1829. M. Schneider, *Mendelssohn oder Bartholdy?* 17.

25. Todd, *A Life*, 445, 468–69.

26. Brodbeck, "Winter of Discontent," 2–5.

27. Ibid., 6–10.

28. Ibid., 15–20.

29. Mendelssohn, ed. Todd, *Hör mein Bitten*, ii; Mendelssohn, ed. Zappalà and Mohn, *Neun Psalmen und Cantique*, 3; Todd, *A Life*, 542.

30. E. Werner, "The 100th Psalm," 54–57. According to the letters Werner himself reprints in his article, Psalm 100 of 1844 clearly does not match Fränkel's criteria: it lacks organ accompaniment and uses Luther's translation of the Psalm rather than Moses Mendelssohn's.

31. Todd, *A Life*, 468–69.

32. For discussions of Psalm 114 in this regard, see, for example, Botstein, "Mendelssohn and the Jews," 213; Kupferberg, *The Mendelssohns*, 252; and Jacob, *Mendelssohn and His Times*, 233.

33. Clostermann, *Mendelssohn Bartholdys kirchenmusikalisches Schaffen*, 58–59.

34. Dinglinger, *Studien*, 70; Konold, *Felix Mendelssohn Bartholdy*, 193. Mendelssohn himself added an actual Doxology to the version of Psalm 2 (op. 78, 1) he composed for the Berlin Cathedral Choir.

35. Some of the drafts written by Julius Schubring are published—without Mendelssohn's corrections or contributions and often with numerous errors—in Schubring, *Briefwechsel*. Arntrud Kurzhals-Reuter has also published short segments of various drafts in her book. Nearly all of the drafts discussed in this book are now available in Sposato, "The Price," vol. 2.

36. Langmuir, *Toward a Definition of Antisemitism*, 57. The discussion that follows has been heavily informed by the entirety of Langmuir's study.

37. The reader may notice that the issue of race has not been included here. This aspect of anti-Semitism (i.e., Jews as biologically inferior) was only embryonic during Mendelssohn's lifetime and was not regularly raised in contemporary anti-Semitic rhetoric.

38. For more on common early nineteenth-century Jewish stereotypes, see chapter 3.

39. Hensel, *Familie Mendelssohn*, 877.

40. Schünemann also claims, again with no supporting documentation, that academy director Carl Friedrich Zelter was not only (contrary to Eduard Devrient's account) very supportive of Mendelssohn's endeavor, but that he himself directed the majority of rehearsals. The entire account stands in strong contrast to one from fifty years earlier by Singakademie director Martin Blumner, who gladly gave Mendelssohn full credit not only for the performances but also for his editorial changes to the score. Schünemann, *Singakademie*, 73, 53–56; Blumner, *Geschichte der Sing-Akademie*, 76.

41. Letter of 8 July 1829 from Abraham to Felix. M. Schneider, 18.

Chapter 1

1. Jack Werner ("Mendelssohnian Cadence," 18) is one of the few scholars to actually put this assumption into print: "Though I have not come across any actual record of Mendelssohn's ever having attended a synagogue service, it is not unreasonable to assume that he may well have accompanied his parents on more than one occasion before his conversion."

2. Ibid., 17. The chant example below appears precisely as in Jack Werner's article (18). Werner did not cite a source for the example, which, strangely, is harmonized and includes dynamic markings. As Werner himself notes, however, the melody would have been chanted (sung monophonically) by the priests.

3. E. Werner, *New Image*, 470–71; *Neuer Sicht*, 497–98.

4. Riehn, "Das Eigene und das Fremde," 138, 143.

5. Steinberg, "Mendelssohn's Music," 40–42; Botstein, "Mendelssohn, Werner, and the Jews," 47–48, quotation from 48.

6. An attraction to Kant's "universal religion" was quite common among Jewish converts, as was the belief that Christianity and European civilization were inseparably bound together, a philosophy propagated by Abraham's friend, Wilhelm von Humboldt. Meyer, *German-Jewish History*, 2:178.

7. Hensel, *Mendelssohn Family*, 1:79–80. Some words in the final paragraph are italicized in this English translation, but are not so marked in the original and have therefore not been italicized here.

8. Letter of 8 July 1829 from Abraham to Felix. M. Schneider, *Mendelssohn oder Bartholdy?* 18–19.

9. On the relationship between Christianity and German national identity, see Katz, *From Prejudice to Destruction*, 76–78.

10. J. Mendelssohn, "Moses Mendelssohn's Lebensgeschichte," 53.

11. In Homberg's 1812 *Bne-Zion*, for example, several prayers appear for the monarch, whom he depicts as the embodiment of God's power on earth and whose orders must be obeyed without exception. In his words, "everything that the regent of a nation orders regarding civil and political matters has the same power of law and holiness as if laid down by a king in Israel or the former highest court of the Israelites (the Sanhedrin)" (Homberg, 177, quoted in Meyer, *German-Jewish History*, 2:253–54). Moses Mendelssohn had advocated obedience of civil laws in *Jerusalem* (133), but stopped short of allowing those laws to compromise the laws of faith. Moses' disagreement with Homberg on this subject is documented in his letter to Homberg of 22 September 1783 (M. Mendelssohn, *Gesammelte Schriften*, 13:133–34, cited in Lowenstein, *Berlin Jewish Community*, 53, 214 n. 64).

12. Geiger, *Geschichte der Juden in Berlin*, 1:103.

13. From 1750 until the Emancipation Edict of 1812, the rights and restrictions of Jews in Prussia were defined by the Revised General Code (*Revidiertes Generalprivilegien und Reglement*), which established six distinct classes of Jews. Abraham's class, the "generally privileged" (*Generalpriviligierte*), was the highest and was granted most of the same rights as Christian businessmen. Each of the five others had fewer and fewer rights, with the lowest being made up of servants who were only permitted to stay in Berlin for the duration of their employment. See Meyer, *German-Jewish History*, 1:148–49 and Lowenstein, *Berlin Jewish Community*, 10–13.

14. Gilbert, *Bankiers, Künstler und Gelehrte*, xxxix.

15. Jewish equality began to be curtailed in 1806, when Napoleon began to distrust the Jews—seeing them as a state within a state, rather than as "Frenchmen of the Mosaic faith"—and began at first to modify and then to eliminate their basic rights as guaranteed under the French constitution. Dubnow, *History of the Jews*, 4:543–56, 560–66, quotation from 553.

16. Hensel, *Mendelssohn Family*, 1:71; Treue, "Das Bankhaus Mendelssohn," 32.

17. Many of these privileges were actually not privileges at all, but omissions from and vague clauses in the law, some of which were more clearly defined—usually in the Jews' favor—later on. See Whaley, *Religious Toleration*, 88–110.

18. Ibid., 88–110.

19. Richter, *Mendelssohn*, 45; Treue, "Das Bankhaus Mendelssohn," 32.

20. For a more detailed discussion of the cottage, see Todd, *A Life*, 28.

21. Elvers, "Frühe Quellen," 18; Jacobson, "Von Mendelssohn," 256.

22. Hecker, 2:158, quoted in Elvers, "Frühe Quellen," 18.

23. Gilbert, *Bankiers, Künstler und Gelehrte*, xvii–xviii; Jacobson, *Judenbürgerbücher*, 54.

24. Treue, "Das Bankhaus Mendelssohn," 33 n. 1a; Hensel, *Mendelssohn Family*, 1:74.

25. The term "Jewish Quarter" should not be mistaken for a walled-in "Jewish Ghetto" (which, as Steven Lowenstein points out, did not exist in Berlin), nor should it be assumed that only Jews lived in the quarter, which was the center of medieval Berlin. The quarter, however, is where the city's "Judenstraße" was (and still is) located, around which lived the greatest number of the city's Jews. Lowenstein, *Berlin Jewish Community*, 16–18.

26. There has been much confusion regarding the dates for the various Mendelssohn addresses in Berlin, but two relatively recent articles clarify matters significantly. Manfred Kliem provides a wealth of information on Neue Promenade 7 and its surroundings in his article ("Berliner Mendelssohn-Adresse," 127, 135–36), while Cécile Lowenthal-Hensel ("Neues zur Leipziger Straße Drei," 141) notes in her article that the move to Neue Promenade is mentioned in a letter dated 18 February 1819 from Lea to her cousin Henriette von Pereira Arnstein. Peter Ward Jones has informed me, however, that other events mentioned in this letter clearly indicate that Lea misdated it, and that it was actually written in 1820. See also Todd, *A Life*, 73.

27. Jacobson, "Von Mendelssohn," 257; Todd, *A Life*, 15–16. Although Abraham may have taken on the additional surname because Prussia's Emancipation Edict of 1812 required all Jews without surnames to choose one, families with one already were encouraged to keep it. Instead, Abraham may simply have seen this as an opportunity to change his name with relatively little fuss and notice, since many such changes were taking place at that time. For a discussion of the laws regarding surname changes, see Bering, *Stigma of Names*, 35.

28. Jacobson, "Von Mendelssohn," 257.

29. Lesser, *Chronik der Gesellschaft der Freunde*, 8–9. The *Chronik* also shows (55–58) that Abraham resumed active membership immediately after his return from Hamburg, even serving a term as its president (*Vorsteher*), a position he took over from his brother when Joseph left Berlin in mid-1812 and held until January 1814.

30. Lowenstein, *Berlin Jewish Community*, 131. The openness of the Society to conversion is demonstrated in the 1842 history written by Society member Ludwig Lesser. In his chronicle of the organization's founding members (17–21), all of those who eventually converted—including Abraham—are listed by their adopted Christian names first, with their abandoned Jewish names printed underneath in parentheses.

31. Steinthal, *Nachtrag zur Chronik*, 9.

32. Ibid., 5–6; Todd, *A Life*, 429–30. Steinthal also records that Mendelssohn attended the 1842 celebration.

33. Dubnow, *History of the Jews*, 4:650–51.

34. Meyer, *German-Jewish History*, 2:27.

35. Lowenstein, *Berlin Jewish Community*, 124–125, 247 n. 28.

36. See Katz, *From Prejudice to Destruction*, 76–78.

37. Meyer, *German-Jewish History*, 2:27–30.

38. As R. Larry Todd has recently pointed out, additional testimony supporting this assessment appears in a review of a Berlin performance by the thirteen-year-old Mendelssohn, in which the author claims that the "boy was born and raised in our Lutheran religion." *Wiener Zeitschrift für Kunst* 7 (1822), cited in Todd, *A Life*, 30.

39. Elvers, "Frühe Quellen," 18. Dinglinger notes that at that time, the Jerusalems-Kirche served both the Lutheran and Reformed communities (with pastors from both on staff), but that the Reformed service was universally used for baptism; thus, Felix may technically have been baptized into the Reformed church (Dinglinger, "Glaubensform," 296). Such distinctions were essentially irrelevant, however, as the differences between the Reformed and Lutheran churches in Prussia were mostly minor liturgical ones, and those too eventually came to an end after the churches merged, a process led by Frederick Wilhelm III that began in earnest in 1817 (Macmillan, *Protestantism in Germany*, 175). Moreover, Felix's confirmation confession of 1825 demonstrates that he was trained in this nonsectarian (but still Lutheran-based) ideology (Brown, *Portrait*, 92–103; Klingemann, *Briefwechsel*, 358–62). In the interest of clarity, I will refer to him—as his contemporaries did (see the preceding note, for example)—as Protestant or Lutheran throughout this book.

40. Hensel, *Mendelssohn Family*, 1:75. Although Sebastian Hensel writes that "the children were brought up as Christians, secretly at first, not to hurt the feeling of their Jewish grandparents, especially old Madame Salomon," Bella Salomon (after 1812, Bella Bartholdy) was, in fact, the only surviving grandparent at the time the Mendelssohn children were baptized. That the family was determined to keep both the children's and, later, the parent's conversion a secret from her is also indicated in Wilhelm Hensel's 1 December 1823 letter to his sister Luise Hensel (Gilbert, *Bankiers, Künstler und Gelehrte*, 58).

41. Hensel, *Mendelssohn Family*, 1:74–75. Hensel includes here the charming story of the very young Fanny's successful plea for Jacob's and Bella's reconciliation.

42. Jacobson, "Von Mendelssohn," 257.

43. Kliem, "Die Berliner Mendelssohn-Adresse," 136.

44. Jacobson, "Von Mendelssohn," 257.

45. Curiously, although she herself never converted, in 1812 Bella Salomon changed her name to Bartholdy, the name her son Jacob had adopted before his conversion (Jacobson, *Judenbürgerbücher*, 93).

46. Abraham was probably not concerned about his membership in the *Gesellschaft der Freunde* when making his arrangements to be baptized since, as mentioned above, the group was very accepting of its many converted members.

47. The 1806 ledger for the Berlin branch of Joseph and Abraham's bank (J. & A. Mendelssohn) has been published in Elvers and Klein, *Mendelssohns in Berlin*, 134–35. As R. Larry Todd argues, the dissolution of Abraham's ties to the bank on 8 December 1821 may very well have paved the way for his conversion. Todd, *A Life*, 15–16, 575 n. 63.

48. Lowenstein, *Berlin Jewish Community*, 129.

49. Meyer, *German-Jewish History*, 2:178–80; Botstein, "Mendelssohn, Werner, and the Jews," 48.

50. For a discussion of the silence on Jewish issues that assimilated Jews believed was required for societal integration, see Jourdan, "Hidden Pathways of Assimilation," 100, 102.

51. Letter of 8 July 1829 from Abraham to Felix. M. Schneider, *Mendelssohn oder Bartholdy?* 18.

52. In addition to the errors in Werner's publications pointed out here, see Ward Jones, "Letter to the Editor," 27–30.

53. On the promising of the post to Mendelssohn, see Todd, *A Life*, 247, 264.

54. Little, "Mendelssohn and the Berlin Singakademie," 65–81. For Devrient's complete account of the Singakademie decision, see E. Devrient, *My Recollections*, 145–56. For other examples of Werner's selective reading of documents, see Sposato, "The Price," 1:40–45.

55. The exact meaning of "Hep" remains uncertain. One possibility is that it was an acronym for "Hierosolyma est perdita" (Jerusalem is lost) and originated during either the Crusades or the Thirty-Years War. Katz, *Die Hep-Hep-Verfolgungen*, 29 n. 63.

56. E. Werner, *New Image*, 28; see also E. Werner, *Neuer Sicht*, 36.

57. Varnhagen von Ense, *Denkwürdigkeiten*, 3:541–42. My thanks to Clive Brown and Peter Ward Jones for alerting me to this discrepancy. Michael Zywietz also discusses this error in his study (*Adolf Bernhard Marx*, 135).

58. E. Werner, *New Image*, 40; see also E. Werner, *Neuer Sicht*, 63.

59. See Felix's letter to Fanny of 27 July 1824 and to Paul of 7 July 1824 in Elvers, *Life in Letters*, 23–24 and Weissweiler, *Briefwechsel*, 24–26, respectively. My thanks to R. Larry Todd for alerting me to this discrepancy; see his *A Life*, 132 for his discussion of this issue.

60. E. Werner, "New Light," 560.

61. E. Werner, *Neuer Sicht*, 551.

62. Private correspondence of 3 June 1997 from Dr. Thomas Wach to me. He writes that "we have passed on all of the manuscripts in the family's possession to libraries and museums." None of the libraries he mentions (the New York Public Library, the Staatsbibliothek zu Berlin—Preußischer Kulturbesitz, and the Bodleian Library in Oxford) possess the diary.

63. Werner mentions both letters several times: *New Image*, 42–43; *Neuer Sicht*, 64; and "New Light," 562–63.

64. Letter of 23–24 June 1829 from the family to Felix, GB-Ob MS. M. Deneke Mendelssohn d. 27, no. 62; letter of 17 July 1829 from Felix to the family, US-NYp *MNY++, no. 72.

65. E. Werner, *New Image*, 38. See also E. Werner, *Neuer Sicht*, 62; and E. Werner, "New Light," 557.

66. Konold, *Felix Mendelssohn Bartholdy*, 75.

67. Indeed, according to Fanny, Abraham appears to have been quite upset about the situation, having grumbled about it for days before lashing out at Felix. See Fanny's diary entry of 11 July 1829. Klein and Elvers, *Tagebücher*, 19.

68. M. Schneider, *Mendelssohn oder Bartholdy?* 20.

69. E. Werner, "New Light," 556. The 8 July 1829 letter was originally printed by Albrecht Mendelssohn Bartholdy in the 31 January 1909 edition of the *Frankfurter Zeitung*. Shortly before Werner reprinted the letter (for the first time in English) in *New Image*, 36–38, Max F. Schneider reprinted it, along with Felix's reply (M. Schneider, *Mendelssohn oder Bartholdy?*

16–24). Werner does not seem to have been aware of Schneider's publication, however, even when he reprinted the letter in German in *Neuer Sicht*, 59–61.

70. M. Schneider, *Mendelssohn oder Bartholdy?* 20. Felix's reply of 16 July (a Thursday) begins: "I received your letter of July 8th on Tuesday." The Tuesday Felix mentions was 14 July, the day after his final London concert.

71. E. Werner, *Neuer Sicht*, 62.

72. Letter of 16 July 1829 from Felix to his father. M. Schneider, *Mendelssohn oder Bartholdy?* 20–24.

73. Fanny's diary entry of 30 July 1829. Klein and Elvers, *Tagebücher*, 19.

74. A "private letter" indicates a message not sent as part of one of the long letters the family wrote together on a regular basis to Felix.

75. Letter of 8 July 1829. Citron, *Letters*, 66–67.

76. Letter of 11 August 1829. Ibid., 68.

77. It is something of an irony—as well as a vindication of Felix's explanation for the English press's use of the name "Mendelssohn" (without Bartholdy)—that English speakers continually identify the composer in a similar manner. As in 1829, the name "Mendelssohn Bartholdy" remains a bit cumbersome for general use. That said, it is significant that the shortened name chosen both then and today is "Mendelssohn," and not what would reflect the more common choice in such two-part names, "Bartholdy," by which he was and is hardly ever called. Regarding the use of "Mendelssohn" during the composer's lifetime, I believe the English press itself provides the answer: the fame of Felix's grandfather, Moses Mendelssohn (as compared to the lack of any notable association with the name "Bartholdy"). The power of this association likely continued to influence references to the composer after his death, but less and less because of his grandfather's philosophical works and more and more because of his notoriety as a Jew. As Abraham noted in the 8 July 1829 letter (see pp. 35–36 below), the name "Mendelssohn" was synonymous with Judaism, a fact that anti-Semites used in their fight against the composer's music by referring to him (as Karl Blessinger does in his anti-Semitic treatise) simply as "Mendelssohn" and rarely, if ever, as "Mendelssohn Bartholdy." In the postwar interpretation, this trend continues, but in a philo-Semitic sense.

78. See E. Werner, "New Light," 562; E. Werner, "Family Letters," 10; E. Werner, *Neuer Sicht*, 64.

79. The manner by which Werner reaches his final version of this letter (as appears in *Neuer Sicht*, 64) reads like a one-person musicological game of "telephone," with each successive printing (beginning with "New Light," 562) straying farther afield from the original. See Sposato, "Creative Writing," 202–4.

80. Little should be read into Mendelssohn's use of Yiddish here, as German Christians regularly sprinkled Yiddish or mock-Yiddish words into their writings about Jews (as Zelter did when he noted that "it would be a truly rare thing (*eppes Rores*), if the son of a Jew [i.e., Mendelssohn] were to become an artist." Letter of 21 October 1821 from Zelter to Johann Wolfgang von Goethe. Hecker, *Briefwechsel*, 2:158.

81. *Times* (London, England), 17 July 1833, 1. The requirements for naturalization, as stated in the statutes, were "an unexceptional character," the ability to speak German well, "the adoption of a special family name," residence in Posen since 1815 (or permission from the government to settle there), and a skill in a trade or art.

82. *Times* (London, England), 17 July 1833, 2.

83. *Times* (London, England), 23 July 1833, 4. Mistaking "Mr. Finch" for "Mr. Finn" was one of two errors that slipped into Mendelssohn's report on the parliamentary vote that he

took from the *Times*. The second was reporting the number of votes in favor of the bill's passage as 187; the actual number was 189.

84. *Times* (London, England), 2 August 1833, 1–2; letters of 1–6 and 14–16 August 1833 from Abraham to the family in Berlin in Klein, "Abraham Mendelssohn Bartholdy," 114, 123. Abraham's position on the Civil Disabilities Act and the Posen statutes is difficult to discern. His letters on the subject (which also include that of 19–23 July 1833, ibid., 109–10) are skeptical and dispassionate and even appear to excuse the Posen restrictions.

85. Konold, *Felix Mendelssohn Bartholdy*, 75.

86. E. Werner, "New Light," 562.

87. Leon Botstein, "Aesthetics of Assimilation," 21.

88. As Paul Jourdan points out ("Hidden Pathways of Assimiliation," 107–12), Mendelssohn was acquainted with many prominent Jews in London, as well as with several politicians sympathetic to their desire for complete emancipation. Jourdan's conclusion, however, that "Mendelssohn's proximity to the Jewish cause in England affected him strongly" (111), transforming him from an interested bystander (similar to that which I have outlined here) into a fighter for the cause is problematic, as it relies on Eric Werner's description of the missing letter of 17 July 1829 from Felix to his sister Rebecka and on Werner's incorrect analysis of Abraham Mendelssohn's letter of 8 July 1829 to his son on the use of the name "Mendelssohn" in London concert programs (both discussed above).

89. P. Mendelssohn Bartholdy, *Briefe*, 72–73. Verified against the manuscript, US-NYp *MNY++, no. 218.

90. E. Werner, *Neuer Sicht*, 63. The 23 July 1833 letter is the second in a series of events that Werner sees as evidence of Mendelssohn's growing consciousness of his heritage, a transformation spurred by his being rejected for the post of Berlin Singakademie director. The first part of this supposed growth process is Mendelssohn's composition of a *Moses* libretto for his friend Adolf Bernhard Marx ("Is it a pure coincidence that in 1832, the year of the humiliation, he wrote the entire libretto of an oratorio, *Moses*, for his friend A.B. Marx?" *New Image*, 40–41). But aside from not mentioning that Mendelssohn's libretto was in exchange for one by Marx of *Paulus* (or that the idea for the exchange came from Marx), Werner's chronology is incorrect here. The *Moses* libretto, in its final form, is dated 21 August 1832 (D-Bsb MA MS 76); Mendelssohn was not rejected by the Singakademie until 22 January 1833.

91. Letter of 8 February 1831 from Felix to his family. Sutermeister *Briefe einer Reise*, 111.

92. Letter of 4 April 1831 from Felix to his family. Ibid., 132.

93. Letter of 16 June 1831. P. Mendelssohn Bartholdy, *Italy and Switzerland*, 188.

94. Elvers, *Life in Letters*, 56.

95. Schubring, "Reminiscences," 227.

96. Eric Werner claims that, as a sign of his belief in Schleiermacher's de-emphasis of the person of Jesus Christ and his own "identification with the Jewish lot," Mendelssohn never mentioned the names "Jesus" or "Christ" in his letters (*New Image*, 42; *Neuer Sicht*, 66). This is not entirely true, as they do appear occasionally; their rarity, however, is due more to the idiosyncrasies of the German language than any attempt to avoid the reference on Mendelssohn's part. Statements such as "Gott sei Dank," "Ach, Gott!," or "Ich danke dem Herrn," for example, are common German expressions (and appear frequently in Mendelssohn's correspondence), whereas no common expressions involve the names "Jesus" or "Christ."

97. Schumann, "Aufzeichnungen," 104, 105, 113.

98. Letter of 6 May 1831 from Hector Berlioz to a group of his friends. Searle, *Hector Berlioz*, 37.

99. Schubring, "Reminiscences," 227. For additional examples of both Felix and Fanny's attachment to Protestantism, see Dinglinger, "Glaubensform," 298–300.

100. Fanny's 8 June 1829 letter to Felix implies that the two siblings had numerous discussions on the subject of their family name, during which Felix had apparently mentioned his desire to leave the Bartholdy surname behind. Since Felix, in his reply to Fanny's letter, no longer showed any such desire, it seems likely that those conversations had taken place several years earlier, perhaps around the time Mendelssohn traveled to Paris with his father (1825) and asked him about the reasons behind the family's name change (see n. 103 below).

101. Hensel, *Mendelssohn Family*, 1:74.

102. The manuscripts of the two Psalm 119 settings are located in GB-Ob MS. M. Deneke Mendelssohn b. 5, fol. 69r–72v. The set has recently been published in an edition by Pietro Zappalà (*Dreizehn Psalm-Motetten*).

103. Abraham recounts the journey and his answers in his letter of 8 July 1829 to Felix, reprinted on pp. 35–36.

104. The document, which includes comments from Felix's religion instructor Friedrich Philipp Wilmsen dated 27 September 1825, may be found in Brown, *Portrait*, 92–103 and Klingemann, *Briefwechsel*, 358–62.

105. Letter of 8 July 1829 from Abraham to Felix. M. Schneider, *Mendelssohn oder Bartholdy?* 17–18. Schneider's transcription of this passage from the original manuscript (GB-Ob MS. M. Deneke Mendelssohn d. 27, no. 71) is accurate. Werner, however, adds a sentence in his 1963 English Mendelssohn biography (*New Image*, 37): after "enduring significance" (my translation), Werner added, "This, considering that you were reared a Christian, you can hardly understand." Werner did not add this text in his 1980 German edition.

106. Todd, *A Life*, 244.

107. Letter of 20 February 1840 from Felix to Joseph Mendelssohn, and letter of 23 February 1840 from Joseph to Felix. Altmann, "Moses Mendelssohn's gesammelte Schriften," 73–74, 77–79.

108. Joseph Mendelssohn's letter of 4 March 1840 provided Felix with information on the original publishers of some of Moses Mendelssohn's most significant works. It is clear, however, that by the time of the next letter (15 November 1840) Joseph had taken control of the project and was working closely with Brockhaus. Ibid., 79–88.

109. In his letter to Felix of 2 August 1845, Joseph wrote that he regretted not taking the opportunity to thank him publicly for his help anywhere in the edition. See Ibid., 87.

110. J. Mendelssohn, "Moses Mendelssohn's Lebensgeschichte," 1–56.

111. Letter of 3 February 1842 from Felix to Hofrath André Offenbach. L. Nohl, *Letters of Distinguished Musicians*, 445. Mendelssohn's 1835 home inventory (GB-Ob MS. M. Deneke Mendelssohn d. 30, no. 204) does support the composer's statement here, at least as far as his grandfather's published works are concerned, although it appears that by the late 1830s, he did possess a response written by Moses to a letter he received from Christian Dohm (GB-Ob MS. M. Deneke Mendelssohn c. 21, no. 9). According to his 1844 inventory, however, Mendelssohn's collection of his grandfather's published works had increased significantly between this 1842 letter and 1844 (see Ward Jones, "The Library," 294–321); he also appears to have acquired at least one more piece of Moses' personal correspondence (GB-Ob MS. M. Deneke Mendelssohn b. 2, no. 6) during the 1840s as well.

112. Steinthal, *Nachtrag zur Chronik*, 5–6.

Chapter 2

1. Mendelssohn's performance was heralded as occurring in the centenary year of the premiere, but it has since been discovered that the Passion was actually premiered in 1727. The work was then performed again in 1729, 1736, and ca. 1742.

2. See chapter 1 for my correction of Eric Werner's publication of the 23 July 1833 letter from Mendelssohn to his family, in which Werner incorrectly indicated that Mendelssohn identified himself as Jewish.

3. E. Devrient, *Erinnerungen*, 62.

4. E. Devrient, *My Recollections*, 14–15. In his recent biography, R. Larry Todd rightly argues that Devrient's claim that Mendelssohn received the score as a Christmas present in 1823 is most likely incorrect, given, among other things, the care the Mendelssohns took not to reveal their conversion to Felix's maternal grandmother, Bella. Todd instead supports Peter Ward Jones' view that Felix's fifteenth birthday on 3 February 1824—an event celebrated with particular pomp—was a far more logical occasion for the presentation of such a thoughtful (and no doubt expensive) gift. Todd, *A Life*, 122–24.

5. E. Devrient, *My Recollections*, 38–39.

6. T. Devrient, *Jugenderinnerungen*, 303–305. Brackets are original. Presumably, the evenings that Therese described were many, continuing into January 1829, at which point—according to her husband's account in the quotation which follows—Eduard approached Felix with his proposal.

7. E. Devrient, *Erinnerungen*, 49–52; translation after *My Recollections*, 47–49.

8. Letter of 22 March 1829. Hensel, *Familie Mendelssohn*, 237; translation after *Mendelssohn Family*, 1:170–71.

9. E. Devrient, *My Recollections*, 62–63.

10. Letter of Good Friday [17 April] 1829 from Zelter to Johann Wolfgang von Goethe. Hecker, *Briefwechsel*, 3:166.

11. Blumner, *Geschichte der Sing-Akademie*, 77.

12. E. Devrient, *Erinnerungen*, 48; translation after *My Recollections*, 46.

13. Schubring, "Reminiscences," 227.

14. Letter of 22 March 1829 to Karl Klingemann. Hensel, *Mendelssohn Family*, 1:171.

15. E. Devrient, *Erinnerungen*, 60–61.

16. E. Devrient, *My Recollections*, 39.

17. The analysis that follows draws on Mendelssohn's original handwritten copy of the *St. Matthew Passion* score (GB-Ob MS. M. Deneke Mendelssohn c. 68), the textbook from the Berlin premiere (D-Bsb Tb 70), and Martin Geck's study, *Die Wiederentdeckung der Matthäuspassion im 19. Jahrhundert*, especially pp. 36–40.

18. Marissen, "Religious Aims," 722–23, quotation from 722.

19. Technically, the final word of this passage, "keines," is also cut and replaced by "keins" at the end of the cut in the next recitative (33). Since this is more of a musical change than a textual one, I have simplified the description for clarity's sake.

20. Translations of passages from the Luther Bible are mine, after the Revised Standard Version Bible.

21. Marissen, "Religious Aims," 722.

22. Ibid., 722–23.

23. Nos. 37 and 10 are based on Paul Gerhardt's *O Welt, sieh hier dein Leben*, and nos. 46 and 3 are based on Johann Heermann's *Herzliebster Jesu*. Bach also repeats the *Herzliebster*

Jesu melody in no. 19, *O Schmerz*, but this piece uses the chorale melody in much the same manner as the opening chorus—as a coloring element for what is, in this case, primarily a solo movement. As such, it will be discussed along with the other arias and ariosos later in this chapter.

24. For more on the structural function of *O Haupt voll Blut und Wunden*, see Platen, *Matthäus-Passion*, 112–13.

25. Bachmann, *Geschichte der Berlin Gesangbücher*, 222. Bachmann notes that the canonical status of *O Haupt* was discussed by the commission assembling the 1829 *New Berlin Hymnal* (*Neue Berliner Gesangbuch*).

26. Geck, *Wiederentdeckung*, 38–39. In GB-Ob MS. M. Deneke Mendelssohn c. 68, the original text appears in ink, with the changed words crossed out in pencil and the new text written underneath.

27. Statistics for the discussion which follows are from Bachmann, *Geschichte der Berlin Gesangbücher*, 261–351.

28. In addition to the Bachmann statistics, see Dieterich, *Gesangbuch*.

29. Geck, *Wiederentdeckung*, 87–96. Quotation from Mosewius, 7, in Geck, *Wiederentdeckung*, 90.

30. D-Bsb Tb 70/3.

31. Hientzsch, 298ff., in Geck, *Wiederentdeckung*, 149–53, quotation from 150.

32. Smither, *History of the Oratorio*, 4: 79–81.

33. Marissen, "Religious Aims," 721.

34. Schubring, *Briefwechsel*, 15.

35. Letter of 7 May 1831 from Mendelssohn (in Naples) to his family. Sutermeister, *Briefe einer Reise*, 147.

36. Clements, *Pioneer of Modern Theology*, 29–32.

37. In his description of naturalist Alexander von Humboldt's lectures at the University, Mendelssohn lists the well-known University scholars in regular attendance, among whom was Schleiermacher. Letter of 5 February 1828 to Klingemann. Klingemann, *Briefwechsel*, 47.

38. Geck, *Wiederentdeckung*, 34, 49.

39. Letter of 19 February 1834 from Felix to Lea. Dinglinger, "Die Glaubensform," 301 n. 31.

40. Letter of 18 February 1834 from Fanny to Felix, Citron, *Letters*, 125. Felix also briefly mentioned Schleiermacher just a few days before the theologian's death in his letter of 5 February 1834 to Eduard Devrient. E. Devrient, *My Recollections*, 173–74.

41. Clements, *Pioneer of Modern Theology*, 33.

42. Schleiermacher, *The Christian Faith*, 578–81, quotation from 578.

43. Either to better balance the duties of the soloists or to compensate for the higher pitch of the nineteenth century, Mendelssohn reassigned three of the alto movements—nos. 5, 6, and 39—to the soprano.

44. These findings are based on the printed textbooks for these performances: D-Bsb Tb 70/1 (Berlin, 1829), 70/3 (Breslau, 1830), 70/6 (Berlin, 1835), 70/7 (Berlin, 1844), 70/2 (Berlin, 1830), and 70/4 (Berlin, 1831).

45. Letter of 21 October 1821. Hecker, *Briefwechsel*, 2:158. The connection of the words "eppes Rores" to Yiddish was first made by Eric Werner. See E. Werner, *Neuer Sicht*, 39.

46. Letter of 2 November 1830. Hecker, *Briefwechsel*, 3:373.

47. Martin Geck's study of Schelble's score (D-F Mus. ms. 147) includes a fairly complete list of cuts and other changes for, if not the first performance, the version he tradition-

ally performed there (see Geck, *Wiederentdeckung,* 75–82); for the textbook from Sämann's performance, see D-Bsb Tb 70/5 (Königsberg, 1832).

48. Geck, *Wiederentdeckung,* 75–79, 101–108.

49. For a discussion of early nineteenth-century anti-Semitic stereotypes, see chapter 3 of this book.

50. As the *St. Matthew Passion* itself demonstrates (see *Ich bins, ich sollte büßen* [no. 10], for instance), Bach was quite familiar as a church musician with the Lutheran concept of universal guilt, which maintained that all people, living and deceased, are responsible for Christ's crucifixion. It is certainly possible, then, that Bach intended "His blood be upon us and our children" to be interpreted in a universal—as opposed to anti-Semitic—manner. By Mendelssohn's day, however, the meaning of this line had clearly shifted, a product, I would argue, of an overall intensification in German anti-Semitism. Evidence of this can be found in the final moments of Carl Loewe's 1830 oratorio *The Destruction of Jerusalem* (*Die Zerstörung von Jerusalem*). As the Jews face defeat by the Romans, a high priest cries out, "What crime, O Lord, has your poor people committed?," to which spirit-voices respond, "His blood be upon us and our children!" Loewe's oratorio is discussed in further depth in chapter 3; see also the discussion of Louis Spohr's *Des Heilands letzte Stunde* in that chapter. For more on Luther's concept of universal guilt, see Althaus, *Theology of Martin Luther,* 211–17.

51. Geck's study includes a fairly comprehensive sampling of reviews and commentary on both of these performances, none of which complains of missing material. Geck, *Wiederentdeckung,* 75–86, 101–108, 149–166.

Chapter 3

1. Marx, "Memoirs," 212–13. Marx's objection to both the subject of St. Paul and Mendelssohn's vision for *Paulus* are discussed in the next chapter.

2. Marx, *Erinnerungen,* 2:171–73.

3. Alvensleben, "Über die Idee dramatischen Fortgangs," 73.

4. Letters of 4 February and 16 January 1833. Klingemann, *Briefwechsel,* 109–10, 107.

5. D-Bsb MA MS 76 (Text IV). That this manuscript represents Mendelssohn's copy of the libretto he sent to Marx (and not Marx's own copy) is evinced by Marx's claim that he kept the libretto Mendelssohn sent him "as a memento" ("Memoirs," 214), as well as by the lack of any of Marx's handwriting in the manuscript and the presence of some minor additions in Mendelssohn's hand. It would seem, therefore, that Mendelssohn wrote a presentation copy (Text IV), decided on some last-minute changes, and then made a fresh, pristine copy which he sent to Marx, keeping this penultimate copy for himself. Once Marx announced he would not be using the libretto, Mendelssohn most likely pulled out his own copy and crossed out the attribution. Marx's copy of the libretto remains lost.

6. Letter of 6 August 1834. Paul and Carl Mendelssohn Bartholdy, *Letters,* 45. For more on Mendelssohn's relationship with Marx, see Sposato, "The Price," 1:133–46 and Siegfried, "'Der interessanteste und problematischste seiner Freunde,'" 35–44.

7. Marx, *Erinnerungen,* 2:138.

8. T. Marx, *Marx' Verhältniß,* 22.

9. Eduard Devrient's account of this story (*Recollections,* 98–99) indicates that Marx wanted Mendelssohn to perform *Mose* at the Lower Rhine Music Festival (*Niederrheinisches Musikfest*), which Mendelssohn would direct in Düsseldorf in May 1839. Either the Gewandhaus in Leipzig or the *Musikfest* would have been an appropriate forum for the work,

but the latter seems the more likely, as a large-scale oratorio performance was an essential component of most music festivals and would have afforded the work far greater exposure (see Smither, *History of the Oratorio*, 4:40–53).

10. T. Marx, *Marx' Verhältniß*, 22–23.

11. Ibid., 24.

12. Werner, *New Image*, 40–41, quotation from 41. Werner also claimed that Mendelssohn wrote the libretto in response to his rejection for the Berlin Singakademie directorship, a rejection due in part to Mendelssohn's Jewish lineage. As noted earlier, however, it was Marx who approached Mendelssohn with a proposed exchange; moreover, *Moses* was completed before the Singakademie vote (August 21, 1832, vs. January 22, 1833). For more on Mendelssohn's candidacy for directorship of the Singakademie, see Little, "Mendelssohn and the Berlin Singakademie," 65–85.

For nineteenth-century German theologians, all of the Old Testament's importance lay in its prophecies. As Friedrich Schleiermacher wrote, "[except for prophecy,] almost everything else in the Old Testament is, for our Christian usage, but the husk or wrapping of its prophecy" (*The Christian Faith*, 62). Oratorios on Old Testament subjects were written in accordance with this philosophy, and as a result made a point of including some connection (either direct or subtle) to the New Testament. This practice may be readily observed in the works of the era's foremost oratorio composers: Friedrich Schneider, Sigismund Neukomm, Louis Spohr, Carl Loewe, and Mendelssohn. Christology in early nineteenth-century oratorio and, more specifically, Mendelssohn's *Elias* is discussed in chapter 5. For a more in-depth discussion of Christology in the *Moses* libretto, see Sposato, "The Price," 1:159–82.

13. There were a total of eight Moses oratorios written between 1800 and 1840 (with most appearing in the 1830s), making him the most popular Old Testament German oratorio subject of the early nineteenth century. The runners-up were David (with three settings), Abraham (three), Solomon (three), Jephtha (two), and Abel (two). Statistics assembled from Geck, *Deutsche Oratorien*, 9–38.

14. Although both Mendelssohn and Marx refer to the people in their texts as the "children of Israel" or "Israelites" (as is appropriate for this period in biblical history), contemporary German audiences would have viewed them as Jews. Therefore, the terms "Israelite" and "Jew" will be used interchangeably throughout this discussion.

15. Katz, *From Prejudice to Destruction*, 150; Rohrbacher and Schmidt, *Judenbilder*, 178–93, 289, 305–6, 313–20. These stereotypes are discussed in greater detail below.

16. Quoted in Katz, *From Prejudice to Destruction*, 150. For further examples of similar anti-Semitic writings, see also ibid., 60, 62, 149–50, and Meyer, *German-Jewish History*, 2:169–77.

17. Meyer, *German-Jewish History*, 2:169–77.

18. Rohrbacher and Schmidt, *Judenbilder*, 289, 305–6, 313–23.

19. Ibid., 178–93.

20. In his study of Marx's *Mose*, Michael Zywietz (*Marx und das Oratorium*, 262–82) also conducts a comparison between Marx's and Mendelssohn's texts (not including Mendelssohn's drafts). Zywietz, however, focuses on the handling of drama in the work.

21. Another reference to modern Christian services appears in *Mose*'s no. 7, a kind of proto-Kyrie in which Aaron recites a series of prayers for the people, after each of which they respond, "Lord, have mercy on us!" (*Herr, erbarme dich unser!*).

22. The mention of "gods" here, and indeed Mendelssohn's entire depiction of the Jews as cultish, may be a manifestation of Friedrich Schleiermacher's influence. Schleiermacher

noted that Judaism was not fully monotheistic during Moses' lifetime or even for some time afterward (*The Christian Faith*, 37).

23. Crum and Ward Jones, *Catalogue of the Mendelssohn Papers*, 3:77. See also the discussion of Loewe in chapter 4 of this book.

24. Loewe, *Die Zerstörung von Jerusalem*, 4.

25. Mendelssohn's acquaintance with Spohr's oratorio is discussed in chapter 4.

26. Rochlitz was actually unaware that Spohr had decided to compose a work based on his passion libretto, and so offered a revised version of the text to Mendelssohn, who was too busy with the composition of *Paulus* to accept. Mendelssohn apparently discussed the offer with Spohr during his October 1834 visit with the elder composer at his home in Cassel. In so doing, he sparked a dispute between Spohr and Rochlitz, who—very late in the composition stage—wanted Spohr to adapt his music to the significant changes he had made to the libretto. Spohr refused and Rochlitz eventually relented. See Brown, *Des Heilands letzte Stunden*, vi.

27. Schleiermacher, *The Christian Faith*, 37.

28. Smither, *History of the Oratorio*, 4:17–18. For a list of Handel vocal works Mendelssohn knew and a partial list of Handel performances during Mendelssohn's lifetime, see Loy, *Bach-Rezeption*, 168–79.

29. Smither, *History of the Oratorio*, 4:99; Geck, *Deutsche Oratorien*, 9–38.

30. Keferstein, "Das Oratorium," cols. 922–23; Heuser, "Oratorium und Oper," 162, 177, 207–208; Raff, "Aus Weimar," 6. These reviews are summarized in Smither, *History of the Oratorio*, 4:71–72.

31. Marx, *Erinnerungen*, 2:173.

32. Marx never disclosed his father's name in his memoirs, but Michael Zywietz (*Marx und das Oratorium*, 120) reveals the name in his study.

33. From what can be distilled from Marx's memoirs, Marx's father was particularly attracted to Voltaire's Deist belief in a higher power, as well as his disdain for ceremony, ritual, and belief in the supernatural. Voltaire was, however, no friend to the Jews, as Jacob Katz demonstrates. While Voltaire's dislike of all organized faiths prevented him from calling for the Jews' conversion, he instead believed that "when the society of man is perfected, when every people carries on its trade itself, no longer sharing the fruits of its work with these wandering brokers, . . . [the Jews] will assimilate among the scum of the other peoples." Katz, *From Prejudice to Destruction*, 34–47, quotation from 47. Marx's father, however, may not have been aware of Voltaire's views on this matter.

34. Marx, *Erinnerungen*, 1:1–10.

35. Ibid., 1:8–9, quotation from 9.

36. Ibid., 1:9–10.

37. For detailed discussions of the depiction of Christ as the "New Moses" in Matthew's gospel, see Teeple, *The Mosaic Eschatological Prophet*, 74–83, and the entirety of Allison's *The New Moses*.

38. The Luther Bibles of Mendelssohn's era generally included a built-in concordance: citations for parallel texts are indicated in smaller print immediately after the original passage. In the 1824 Bible used for this study (*Die Bibel, oder die ganze heilige Schrift. . .*), the citations that appear at Dt. 18:18 are Jn. 1:45, 7:16, 8:26, 8:40, and Heb. 3:2–3, 12:24.

39. For a discussion of this view of Protestantism, see Meyer, *German-Jewish History*, 2:168–80.

40. Shmueli, "Deutscher Musiker," 224, 226. See also Zywietz, *Marx und das Oratorium*, 123.

41. For more on Mendelssohn's relationships with Loewe and Spohr, see chapter 4.

42. Letter of 8 July 1829 to Felix. M. Schneider, *Mendelssohn oder Bartholdy?* 18.

43. Letter of 8 July 1829 to Felix. Ibid. In biographies written during his lifetime, Mendelssohn's descent from the great philosopher rarely failed to be mentioned. The 27 December 1837 issue of the *Allgemeine Musikalische Zeitung,* for example, contains an extensive Mendelssohn biography that begins, "Felix Mendelssohn-Bartholdy, grandson of the philosopher Moses Mendelssohn" (Fink, "Felix Mendelsohn Bartholdy," 845). See also chapter 1 for the association of Felix with his grandfather during his 1829 trip to England.

Chapter 4

1. Mendelssohn's visits to Schelble, starting in 1822, are recorded in Hensel, *Mendelssohn Family,* 1:113, 141, 272–73 and 2:21.

2. Letter of 13 November 1831 to Abraham Mendelssohn. E. Werner, *New Image,* 529. The nervousness apparent in this letter ("I hardly know how I can approach such a task") soon gave way to excitement in those that followed, but the nervousness eventually returned.

3. Ibid.

4. Letter of 20 December 1831. Klingemann, *Briefwechsel,* 90.

5. E. Werner, *New Image,* 283.

6. See Botstein, "Mendelssohn, Werner, and the Jews," and Steinberg, "Mendelssohn's Music." These articles were responses to my "Creative Writing" article in *The Musical Quarterly,* and were followed in the next issue of that journal by my counterresponse, "Mendelssohn, *Paulus,* and the Jews."

7. E. Devrient, *Erinnerungen,* 136–37; translation after E. Devrient, *Recollections,* 137–38.

8. Specifically, Devrient recommended Mendelssohn contact Pastors Albert Baur and Julius Schubring (E. Devrient, *Recollections,* 139). Although Mendelssohn and Baur (who had been Schubring's classmate—see Todd, *A Life,* 194) remained in contact during the *Paulus* years, the composer chose not to involve him in the composition of the libretto. As for Schubring, Mendelssohn would, in fact, enlist his help that summer. It also appears that Karl Klingemann was involved in the later stages of the libretto's assembly. In his 4 February 1833 letter to Klingemann, Mendelssohn mentioned that before he began composing any music, he wanted Klingemann to "ratify" (*ratifizieren*) the text (Klingemann, *Briefwechsel,* 110). According to Mendelssohn's 11 November 1834 letter to his mother (US-NYp *MNY++, no. 211), Klingemann did this during Mendelssohn's late spring 1833 London visit. What Mendelssohn showed him, however, is unclear; at the time of their meeting, he would have had Texts I, II, IIIa, and IV (see table 4.1) in his possession, but he may also have begun work on Text V. As for Klingemann's comments, all of them seem to have been provided verbally, as no corrections or suggestions for *Paulus* appear in his correspondence, nor are there any existing drafts or markings in Klingemann's hand. My thanks to Siegwart Reichwald for providing me with transcriptions of this and some of the other unpublished letters from the New York Public Library collection (US-NYp) examined in this chapter.

9. The surviving version of Text I is that which Mendelssohn sent to Schubring on 22 December 1832. Upon its receipt, Schubring edited the draft slightly, adding citations to some of Mendelssohn's textual fragments. He also placed parentheses around those citations that were incorrect, as several of them—particularly in Paul's departure speech—refer to places that do not exist in the Bible. In Part III (which later became Part II), for example, appears the citation "(2 Cor. 2, 24)," but chapter two of 2 Corinthians contains only seventeen verses.

These errors further suggest that the draft Mendelssohn sent to Schubring was probably a duplicate of his original, since the errors were most likely the result of mistakes in copying.

10. See Sposato, "The Price," 2:71–92.

11. The only specifics about Fürst's contributions in Mendelssohn's correspondence appear in his letter to Fürst of 20 July 1834, in which Mendelssohn thanks him for his "passages for 'St. Paul'" (see P. and C. Mendelssohn Bartholdy, *Letters*, 37–38). This singular mention of Fürst is likely responsible for the incorrect assessment by several writers (including Kurzhals-Reuter [*Oratorien*, 47] and Reimer ["Textanlage," 45]) that he provided Mendelssohn with only a few biblical citations.

12. Letter 20 July 1834 to Fürst. P. and C. Mendelssohn Bartholdy, *Letters*, 37–38.

13. Letter of ca. 1 August 1834. Citron, *Letters*, 151.

14. *The Jewish Encyclopedia*, 1st ed. (1901–06), s.v. "Fürst, Julius"; *Encyclopedia Judaica*, 1st ed. (1971), s.v. "Fuerst, Julius."

15. My assessment of the timing of Mendelssohn's appeal to Fürst is based on Fürst's first draft (Text IIIa) and its similarity to the one Mendelssohn requested of Devrient. For both, Mendelssohn appears not to have insisted on the inclusion of chorales. (Mendelssohn gave Devrient the option of using hymn texts, but did not require their inclusion.) Since the inclusion of chorales was an integral part of the requests he made of Adolf Bernhard Marx and Julius Schubring that summer, their absence in Fürst's libretto suggests that Mendelssohn discussed the project with him around the time he wrote to Devrient. Fürst's libretto also enables us to extrapolate the approximate date of *Paulus*'s original outline—i.e., the lost model for Text I—as late spring 1832, since his text follows the outline closely.

16. Marx, "Memoirs," 213–14. Mendelssohn considered writing a *Petrus* oratorio shortly after *Paulus* was fully completed, but abandoned the idea in favor of *Elias*. See chapter 5.

17. Marx, "Memoirs," 214.

18. Schubring, *Briefwechsel*, 20.

19. Letter of 22 December 1832. Schubring, *Briefwechsel*, 21–22.

20. Letter of 22 December 1832. Schubring, *Briefwechsel*, 22.

21. Ibid.

22. Marx, "Memoirs," 213. See also chapter 3.

23. Letter of 10? March 1833 to Schubring. Schubring, *Briefwechsel*, 37.

24. Letter of 27 March 1833 to Schubring. Schubring, *Briefwechsel*, 39.

25. Schubring, "Reminiscences," 230.

26. Letter of 27 March 1833 to Schubring. Schubring, *Briefwechsel*, 39.

27. In terms of dating the arrival of Fürst's text, both Schubring's draft (Text II) and the letter Mendelssohn sent to Schubring on 22 December 1832 (Schubring, *Briefwechsel*, 21–25) requesting it indicate that Mendelssohn did not yet possess a prose libretto from Fürst (or anyone else, for that matter). But Marx's libretto (Text IV), dated 15 March 1833, clearly borrows from both Fürst's and Schubring's texts, suggesting that Mendelssohn probably received Fürst's libretto around January 1833. Upon its receipt, Mendelssohn apparently sent copies of both it and Schubring's text to Marx to supplement the copy of the original outline (Text I) Marx may have already had.

28. It is unclear whether Mendelssohn passed along to Marx the corrections and comments he made on Fürst's draft.

29. As with Fürst, Marx's contribution to *Paulus* has been underappreciated. Kurzhals-Reuter (*Oratorien*, 144), for example, believed that Marx reneged on the exchange arrangement

and did not provide Mendelssohn with a complete draft. Aside from the missing chorales, however, Marx's draft is a complete prose libretto.

30. Letter of 27 March 1833. Schubring, *Briefwechsel*, 39.

31. The request appears on Text IIIa, fol. 6r.

32. On 6 September 1833, Mendelssohn wrote to Schubring asking for his comments on and further contributions to a text of Mendelssohn's own arrangement; at no point does he mention Marx or Fürst, and he establishes himself firmly in the role of librettist throughout the letter. Schubring, *Briefwechsel*, 40–42.

33. Letter of 20 July 1834. P. and C. Mendelssohn Bartholdy, *Briefe*, 45.

34. Rochlitz wrote the libretto for Spohr's *Des Heilands letzte Stunde.*

35. Letter of 15 July 1834 to Schubring. Schubring, *Briefwechsel*, 68; translation after Elvers, *A Life in Letters*, 198.

36. Letter of 25 February 1835 to Friedrich Rochlitz. K. Mendelssohn-Bartholdy, *Goethe and Mendelssohn*, 189.

37. Schubring, "Reminiscences," 227, 230.

38. The draft accompanied Mendelssohn's letter of 6 September 1833; see Schubring, *Briefwechsel*, 40–42.

39. Letter of 14 September 1833 from Schubring. Schubring, *Briefwechsel*, 44.

40. Letter of 15 July 1834 to Schubring. Elvers, *Life in Letters*, 197.

41. The date composition began can be roughly established through Mendelssohn's letters of 28 March 1834 to his father and 2 May 1834 to his mother. In the first, Mendelssohn mentions his plan to begin composition around Pentecost (May 18), while in the second, he mentions having already completed two numbers. US-NYp *MNY++, nos. 187, 190.

42. Letter of 17 December 1834. GB-Ob MS. M. Deneke Mendelssohn d. 29, no. 334.

43. Letter of 23 December 1834. P. Mendelssohn Bartholdy, *Letters*, 60–61.

44. Letter of 8 October 1835. Schubring, *Briefwechsel*, 95–96.

45. Reichwald, *Musical Genesis*, 29–40.

46. Letter of 6 December 1835. Schubring, *Briefwechsel*, 99–100; translation after P. and C. Mendelssohn Bartholdy, *Letters*, 86.

47. Letter of 11 December 1835 from Schubring. Schubring, *Briefwechsel*, 103.

48. In his letter of 25 August 1832 to Schubring, Mendelssohn wrote that he expected to finish the work the following spring. Schubring, *Briefwechsel*, 20.

49. Mendelssohn received offers to premiere the work in the winter of 1834 and the fall of 1835 in Frankfurt with Schelble, and one for Pentecost 1835 in Cologne. See his letter of 6 June 1834 to his mother (US-NYp *MNY++, no. 201), and his letters of 30 November 1834 and 26 March 1835 to Klingemann (Klingemann, *Briefwechsel*, 154–55, 173).

50. Letter of 15 July 1834. Elvers, *Life in Letters*, 198.

51. Letter of 6 August 1834. Schubring, *Briefwechsel*, 79; translation after P. and C. Mendelssohn Bartholdy, *Letters*, 44–45.

52. K. Mendelssohn-Bartholdy, *Goethe and Mendelssohn*, 115. For more on the Horsley family, see Wilson Kimber, "Family, Friendship, and Community," 57–60.

53. See, for example, letters of 26 June 1835 to Klingemann (Klingemann, *Briefwechsel*, 182) and 13 August 1835 to Moscheles (F. Moscheles, *Letters*, 136–37).

54. Letter of 13 August 1835. F. Moscheles, *Letters*, 136–37.

55. Müller, *Mendelssohn*, 7. As Müller points out and as Mendelssohn mentions in his 26 March 1835 letter to Klingemann (Klingemann, *Briefwechsel*, 173), the composer was to give Schelble a copy of the score in May 1835 in anticipation of the fall performance, but prepa-

rations were nowhere that far along. For an analysis of Mendelssohn's progress on the score in the latter half of 1835, see Reichwald, *Musical Genesis*, 31–32.

56. Letter of 11 November 1835 from Abraham. GB-Ob MS. M. Deneke Mendelssohn d. 30, no. 148.

57. Letter of 23 November 1835. US-NYp *MNY++, no. 251. Felix sent the original letter (plus a note) to his mother after his father's death.

58. Letter of 6 December 1835. Schubring, *Briefwechsel*, 99–100. The relevant segment of this letter is reprinted later in this chapter.

59. Müller, *Mendelssohn*, 7.

60. US-NYp *MNY++, no. 298.

61. Of all the *Paulus* sources, the PL-Kj MN Bd. 55 piano-vocal score (Texts XI and XVI) is the most problematic. While most of the score mirrors the "Düsseldorf full score" (Text XIII), it also contains versions of numbers that clearly predate and postdate it (thus its dual designation as both Text XI and XVI). In the former category are the dozens of segments marked with corrections that Mendelssohn incorporated into the Düsseldorf score. Also in this category are alternative versions of pieces (such as *Vertilge Sie* and the chorale *Wachet auf*), and aborted attempts at pieces, such as an unfinished opening chorus to Part II, *Die Nacht ist Vergangen* (which is followed by an alternative version—perhaps the very first version—of *Der Erdkreis ist nun des Herrn*). Segments of the piano-vocal score that postdate the Düsseldorf score include Recitative 24, which describes Paul's baptism and preaching of Christ, and Recitative 32 (*Paulus aber und Barnabas sprachen frei und öffentlich*), both of which match the published score.

While many sections of the piano-vocal score may well be reductions from their full-score incarnations, other sections (such as *Die Nacht ist Vergangen* and the alternative versions of *Vertilge Sie* and *Der Erdkreis ist nun des Herrn*) survive only in this source. And although these too may be reductions from now lost full scores, it seems equally likely that these movements were composed in piano-vocal score before being orchestrated, a possibility strengthened by the appearance of "H.D.m." (*Hilf Du mir*)—the prayer Mendelssohn wrote on many of his first drafts—on the first page of the piano-vocal score's version of *Sei getreu bis in den Tod*. Given this evidence that Mendelssohn used the piano-vocal score to work out the initial versions of some pieces, and the lack of any other sources to prove otherwise, I have chosen to label this score as "compositional" and have dated it to match the statements in Mendelssohn's letters, indicating he began composing the music in April 1834.

62. The processes by which Mendelssohn arrived at the final versions of both the Düsseldorf and published scores are highly complex and outside the scope of this book. See the entirety of Reichwald's study on *Paulus*'s musical genesis.

63. Mendelssohn attests to the existence of this now lost score in his letter of 30 March 1836 to Ferdinand von Woringen, and his letter of 16 April 1836 to the festival organizers. Reichwald, *Musical Genesis*, 22–23.

64. See, for example, Fanny's letters of 30 July and 19 December 1836 to Felix. Citron, *Letters*, 208, 225–26.

65. My thanks to Peter Ward Jones for his assistance with *Paulus*'s publication history.

66. See, for example, E. Werner, *New Image*, 288.

67. Letter of 8 July 1829 from Abraham to Felix. M. Schneider, *Mendelssohn oder Bartholdy?* 20.

68. See chapter 3 for specifics on the anti-Semitic content of these works.

69. Crum and Ward Jones, *Catalogue of the Mendelssohn Papers*, 3:77, 290.

70. There seems to have been very little correspondence between Schneider and Mendelssohn during this time. Mendelssohn first introduced himself to Schneider in his 7 March 1829 letter, in which he invited Schneider to the premiere of the *St. Matthew Passion* (Elvers, *Life in Letters*, 53). Mendelssohn does not appear to have written to him again until 21 March 1836, when he wrote a very formal letter to accompany the return of Schneider's symphony scores, noting that he had been able to perform only one of them, and that he would not be able to perform Schneider's latest oratorio (ibid., 220–21). Finally, in his 6 December 1838 letter to Schubring, Mendelssohn described his correspondence with Schneider as "diplomatic," which was "not at all to my liking" because of its purely business-like nature (Schubring, *Briefwechsel*, 148). Mendelssohn also does not seem to have owned any of Schneider's works, with the exception of a single aria contained within a larger vocal collection (Crum and Ward Jones, *Catalogue of the Mendelssohn Papers*, 3:2).

71. Bitter, *Loewes Selbstbiographie*, 105–6.

72. Ranft, *Lebenschronik*, 16.

73. In his letter of 17 February 1827 to his family, Mendelssohn announced his arrival in Stettin (US-NYp *MNY++, no. 35); the concert with Loewe took place on 20 February, and Mendelssohn likely remained in town for a few days afterward.

74. Dusella, *Oratorien Carl Loewes*, 53–54.

75. Geck, *Wiederentdeckung*, 98–99.

76. Bitter, *Loewes Selbstbiographie*, 194.

77. Letter of 28 February 1834. Citron, *Letters*, 163 n. 1.

78. Letter of 19 July 1822 from Mendelssohn to Zelter. Elvers, *Life in Letters*, 12; Todd, *A Life*, 98.

79. Hensel, *Mendelssohn Family*, 1:124.

80. Letter of 14 April 1829 to his family. Elvers, *Life in Letters*, 56. The relevant segment of this letter is reprinted in chapter 1.

81. Letter of 6 October 1834 to his family. US-NYp *MNY++, no. 209.

82. See, for example, Mendelssohn's 8 March 1835 letter to Spohr and his 14 March 1841 letter to Charlotte Moscheles in Selden-Goth, *Letters*, 237–38, 300.

83. Letter of 13 December 1836 to Spohr. Elvers, *Life in Letters*, 230–32.

84. Spohr dedicated a piano sonata to Mendelssohn in early 1842 and Mendelssohn returned the honor in early 1846 with his Piano Trio no. 2 in C minor (op. 66). Spohr, *Autobiography*, 242; Elvers, *Life in Letters*, 273–74.

85. Letter of 6 August 1834 to Schubring. Schubring, *Briefwechsel*, 79.

86. For the contents of Mendelssohn's music library, see Crum and Ward Jones, *Catalogue of the Mendelssohn Papers*, vol. 3.

87. Letter of 10 March 1835 to Felix. Selden-Goth, *Letters*, 241.

88. Letter of 12 March 1836 to Musikfest director Otto von Woringen. Grossmann-Vendrey, *Musik der Vergangenheit*, 81.

89. Mendelssohn does not appear to have discussed the *Moses* libretto he wrote for Marx with his father. This is not surprising, since Abraham disapproved of Marx (see E. Devrient, *Recollections*, 98).

90. Letter of 23 December 1834. P. and C. Mendelssohn Bartholdy, *Letters*, 61.

91. Letter of 6 December 1835. Schubring, *Briefwechsel*, 99–100; translation after P. and C. Mendelssohn Bartholdy, *Letters*, 85–86.

92. Letter of 4 February 1836 from Fanny Hensel to Karl Klingemann. Hensel, *Mendelssohn Family*, 2:2.

93. Letter of 23 November 1835 to his mother. US-NYp *MNY++, no. 251.

94. In addition to the full score, Mendelssohn had to prepare a piano-vocal score and send a copy of the full score to Simrock for the preparation and printing of the parts for the premiere.

95. Meiser, "Das Paulusbild bei Mendelssohn," 261.

96. Throughout this chapter, the word "Gentiles" and its English and German synonym "heathen" (*Heiden*) are used (by Mendelssohn, his *Paulus* libretto contributors, and myself) in the biblical sense of meaning non-Jews who had yet to accept Christianity.

97. Lull, *Luther's Basic Theological Writings*, 139.

98. Ibid., 138.

99. Schleiermacher, *The Christian Faith*, 60–61.

100. Ibid., 62.

101. Butler and Jones, *Lives of the Saints*, June: 41.

102. As noted in the Introduction, August Wilhelm Bach was Mendelssohn's organ teacher from 1820 to 1822.

103. Statistics and list of Boniface oratorios assembled from Geck, *Deutsche Oratorien*, 9–38. Smither's tabulation (*History of the Oratorio*, 4:104) lacks Keller's *Bonifacius*, but shows that Boniface remained a fairly popular subject in the second half of the century, with five more settings appearing between 1860 and 1888. Schubring's work on Schneider's oratorio may have had a direct influence on his work for Mendelssohn, since he pursued *Bonifacius* simultaneously with the later stages of *Paulus* (see Schubring's letter of 31 July 1834 to Mendelssohn in Schubring, *Briefwechsel*, 71).

104. Statistics and list of *Paulus* oratorios assembled from Geck, *Deutsche Oratorien*, 9–38. See also Smither, *History of the Oratorio*, 4:95.

105. Geck, *Deutsche Oratorien*, 14. Although Mendelssohn knew Grell, Grell's oratorio probably had little or no impact on *Paulus*, as the two were not close friends and no evidence exists to suggest that Mendelssohn heard the work (or even that it was ever performed).

106. Regarding Elkamp, Mendelssohn wrote to Ignaz Moscheles on 5 September 1835: "Who is Mr. Elkamp who is writing a 'Saint Paul'? Have you seen anything of his, and has it any merit or not?" F. Moscheles, *Letters*, 138.

107. Schweitzer, *Paul and His Interpreters*, 2.

108. Marx, "Memoirs," 213.

109. Schweitzer, *Paul and His Interpreters*, 9–10. Some of the other contemporary works Schweitzer mentions include those of J. A. W. Neander (1832), H. E. G. Paulus (1831), and W. M. Leberecht De Wette (second edition, 1838).

110. Fink, "Paulus," 502.

111. Schrader, *Apostel Paulus*, 2:9–10; Hemsen, *Apostel Paulus*, 5.

112. Schrader, *Apostel Paulus*, 2:15; Hemsen, *Apostel Paulus*, 3–4. The two theologians differed on the reason behind Paul's eventual adoption of his heathen name. Schrader believed that the Holy Spirit instructed him to use the name Paul as a sign of being owned by God, in much the same way—to use his example—that a slave would be given a new name upon being purchased. Hemsen, on the other hand, believed Paul began to go by his heathen name once he started preaching to the Gentiles, thus continuing his pattern of using the appropriate name for each audience.

113. For an analysis of the evolution of the anti-Semitic image for the entire oratorio, see Sposato, "The Price," 1:266–316.

114. The omission of the words "not only at Ephesus but also" from this passage is in

accordance with Mendelssohn's instructions in his outline to not include the name of the city: "Einige wiegeln das Volk auf (Ap. G. 19, 26–27 ohne Angabe der Stadt)."

115. The text and music are identical in the Düsseldorf and final version scores, with the minor exception of Mendelssohn's replacement of the words "schrieen laut" with "riefen gegen ihm."

116. For a discussion of common nineteenth-century stereotypes of Jews, see chapter 3.

117. Reimer, "Textanlage," 66–67. See also Reimer, *Vom Bibeltext*, 80.

118. Letter of 6 October 1830 to his father. US-NYp *MNY++, no. 121. The specifics of the poetry volume Hauser gave Mendelssohn remain uncertain as Mendelssohn apparently did not retain the book in his private library (see Ward Jones, "The Library of Felix Mendelssohn Bartholdy"). However, based on a unique error in this volume that found its way into the first version of *Die erste Walpurgisnacht*, Peter Krause speculates that Hauser's gift was most likely volume 7 of *Goethe's neue Schriften*, published in Berlin by Ungar in 1800. See Krause, "Mendelssohns dramatische Kantate," 103–4.

119. Letter of 16 October 1830 to Zelter. P. Mendelssohn Bartholdy, *Reisebriefe*, 41.

120. Letter of 7 May 1831 to his family. Sutermeister, *Briefe einer Reise*, 147.

121. While a few Lieder were written to texts from other sources, all of the numerous sacred works from this period—with the single exception of the chorale cantata *O Haupt voll Blut und Wunden* (a text nearly every German Lutheran knew intimately)—are based either on the Latin Vulgate (the only Bible available to him) or Luther's chorales.

122. Letter from March 1831 to Hauser. Hanslick, 26, in Krause, "Mendelssohns dramatische Kantate," 104.

123. The dates appear in the manuscript score: PL-Kj MN 37.

124. Krause, "Mendelssohns dramatische Kantate," 105.

125. Ibid., 108–20.

126. Kramer, "*Felix culpa*," 76.

127. The physical setting is not revealed in the poem itself, but rather in Goethe's letter to Zelter of 3 December 1812, in which he responds to Zelter's request for information on the historical backdrop of the story. As Tobias Fichte points out in his discussion of the letter, Goethe's comments also reveal why the poem is called the "The *First* Walpurgis-Night": Goethe intended the story to depict the origin of the witch manifestation legends associated with the Harz mountains. Fichte, "Rituality, Authenticity and Staging," 121–22, 132 n. 8.

128. See, for example, Kramer, "*Felix culpa*," 79; E. Werner, *New Image*, 203 and *Neuer Sicht*, 231; Botstein, "Songs without Words," 566–68; and the entirety of Metzger's article ("Noch einmal").

129. Metzger, "Noch einmal," 94. Botstein supports Metzger's view, adding, "The most remarkable example of Mendelssohn's residual psychological loyalty to his Jewish heritage was the secular cantata *Die erste Walpurgisnacht*." Botstein, "Aesthetics of Assimilation," 22.

130. Prandi, "Kindred Spirits," 135–46.

131. Seaton, "Romantic Mendelssohn," 398–99.

132. Letter of 22 February 1831 to his family. Hellmundt, "Arbeit an seiner Kantate," 101.

133. Letter of 5 March 1831 to Goethe. Fichte, "Rituality, Authenticity and Staging," 120.

134. Melhorn, "Mendelssohn's *Die erste Walpurgisnacht*," 50–52.

135. Hensel, *Mendelssohn Family*, 1:131. The translation of Goethe's *Faust* (Part I, lines 4395–4399) is also from Hensel.

136. Eckermann, 251 in Szeskus, "'Die erste Walpurgisnacht,'" 172.

137. Letter of 22 February 1831 to his family. Hellmundt, "Arbeit an seiner Kantate," 101;

translation from Prandi, "Kindred Spirits," 144. Brackets and ellipses are Prandi's. See also Mendelssohn's letters of 5 March 1831 to Goethe, 27 April 1831 to his family, 13 July 1831 to E. Devrient, 14 July 1831 to his family, and 28 August 1831 to Goethe. Hellmundt, "Arbeit an seiner Kantate," 101–5.

138. Melhorn, "Mendelssohn's *Die erste Walpurgisnacht*," 54. See also Hensel, *Mendelssohn Family,* 1:133–34.

139. Marx, "Memoirs," 217.

140. See, for example, Kramer, "*Felix culpa*," 76–79; Prandi, "Kindred Spirits," 135–41.

141. Letter of 21 January 1832 to Fanny. Hellmundt, "Arbeit an seiner Kantate," 106.

142. That Mendelssohn saw himself as German and was proud of the fact can be seen in letters such as that of 25 August 1831 to Goethe, where he writes, "I very much want to tell you how especially happy I am these days that I happen to be living at just this particular time and that I just happen to be a German." Ernst Wolff, *Meister-Briefe,* 29.

Chapter 5

1. Jacob (*Mendelssohn and His Times,* 255–57), for example, ends his synopsis of *Elias* with the ascension of the prophet on a fiery chariot, with no mention of the Messianic numbers that follow.

2. Nicholas Temperley's liner notes (11–12) for Paul Daniel's recording of *Elijah* serves as an excellent example: "[A]lthough there is no reason to doubt the sincerity of his Lutheran faith, at a deeper level his inherited Jewishness perhaps craved emotional expression. *Elijah* is in no way inconsistent with Christianity—indeed, the final movements explicitly look forward to the coming of Christ. Yet the story is extremely Jewish." For additional examples, see P. Nohl, *Geistliche Oratorientexte,* 392; Botstein, "Aesthetics of Assimilation," 22; and J. Werner, "Mendelssohnian Cadence," 17–18.

3. Schleiermacher, *The Christian Faith,* 62.

4. Klingemann, *Briefwechsel,* 204; translation after Edwards, *History,* 2–3. Mendelssohn's final suggestion of Og of Bashan was no doubt a jest meant to demonstrate his greater interest in beginning a new composition as soon as possible than in its topic. The story of the destruction of the house of Og, king of Bashan (a district of Palestine east of the Jordan river) by Moses and the Israelites is recounted in Numbers 21:33–35 and Deuteronomy 3:1–3—far too little material on which to base an oratorio.

5. Letter of 18 February 1837. Klingemann, *Briefwechsel,* 211–12; translation after Edwards, *History,* 4–5.

6. Letter of 27 February 1837. Ibid., 212.

7. Letter of 30 April 1837. Klingemann, *Briefwechsel,* 214; translation after Edwards, *History,* 5.

8. Letter of 30 April 1837. Ibid.

9. Schubring, *Briefwechsel,* 109–10; translation after P. Mendelssohn Bartholdy, *Letters,* 117–18. Emphasis original.

10. Forchert, "Textanlage," 64.

11. Letter of 29 November 1837 to Mendelssohn. Schubring, *Briefwechsel,* 112. In the letter, Schubring also mentions that he sent his last letter (now lost) to Mendelssohn in Frankfurt, thus setting its date sometime before Mendelssohn's departure for London on 24 August.

12. Edwards, *History,* 6; Ranft, *Lebenschronik,* 55; diary entries of 30 and 31 August 1837 in Ward Jones, *Mendelssohns on Honeymoon,* 90–91. During his visit, Mendelssohn received

both pleas from *Paulus* admirers for him to write another oratorio, and an offer of a generous stipend from William Ayrton should Mendelssohn allow the impresario to perform the new work. See diary entries of 11 and 17 September 1837 and letter of 4 October 1837 from Mendelssohn to his mother in Ward Jones, *Mendelssohns on Honeymoon*, 104, 108, 195.

13. Letter of 12 December 1837. Schubring, *Briefwechsel*, 116. An entry in Margaret Crum's catalog of the Mendelssohn Green Books of correspondence at the Bodleian Library lists a libretto for a *Petrus* oratorio written by an "M. Strack, Candidat des höheren Schulamts" and annotated by Klingemann (GB-Ob MS. M. Deneke Mendelssohn d. 53, nos. 90–91; Crum and Ward Jones, *Catalogue of the Mendelssohn Papers*, 1:269). However, an analysis of this libretto (no. 90) and its accompanying supplement (91) reveals that it does not represent an exploration into the subject of St. Peter beyond that conducted with Schubring. Indeed, a close examination of the handwriting reveals no involvement by Klingemann; all of it is in Strack's hand, albeit with some segments written more neatly than the others. Moreover, the draft was accompanied by a letter dated 9 July 1840 (GB-Ob MS. M. Deneke Mendelssohn d. 37, no. 189), in which Strack introduces himself as a "complete unknown" (*völlig Unbekannter*) and offers Mendelssohn the text. Since Strack's libretto arrived during the period in which Mendelssohn had temporarily given up on *Elias*, the composer seems to have briefly considered the idea of using it. (He wrote Strack's address in the lower right corner of the cover page to Klingemann's prose draft of *Elias* [Text II, fol. 33r].) The idea seems to have been just as quickly dropped, however, as no further correspondence between Mendelssohn and Strack survives, and Mendelssohn did not mention receiving Strack's libretto or reviving his interest in *Petrus* in his correspondence with the three people he spoke with most about his oratorios: Klingemann, Schubring, and his sister Fanny.

14. According to the preface of the published version of Barry's libretto, Mendelssohn felt that "although this work possessed both literary and poetical merit, it was . . . too long for an Oratorio, but might well be published as a Metrical Libretto." Edwards, *History*, 8.

15. Letter of 9 January 1838. Klingemann, *Briefwechsel*, 228; translation after Edwards, *History*, 7.

16. Klingemann, *Briefwechsel*, 229.

17. The segment of the 2 February letter that includes these statements is not contained in Klingemann's published correspondence, but Mendelssohn reiterates Klingemann's words in his 9 February reply (ibid.).

18. Mendelssohn inquires as to the status of the *Elias* libretto in his letters of 9 February, 12 April, and 19 May 1838. Klingemann, *Briefwechsel*, 229–32.

19. Letter of 19 July 1838. Ibid., 233.

20. Letter of 28 October 1838 from Schubring to Mendelssohn. In the letter, Schubring's mention of "large and small" sheets indicates that he had both the prose draft (which was written on small pages) and the outline (written on large ones) in his possession. See also the letter of 2 November 1838 to Schubring. Schubring, *Briefwechsel*, 125, 135.

21. Letter of 28 October 1838 from Schubring to Mendelssohn. Schubring, *Briefwechsel*, 125.

22. Letter of 2 November 1838 to Schubring. Ibid., 135.

23. Letter of 2 November 1838 from Mendelssohn to Schubring. Schubring, *Briefwechsel*, 134–35; translation after Edwards, *History*, 12.

24. Letter of 1 November 1838. Schubring, *Briefwechsel*, 139; translation after Edwards, *History*, 15. Emphasis original.

25. Letter of 2 November 1838. Schubring, *Briefwechsel*, 135–36; translation after Edwards, *History*, 13. Emphasis original.

26. Letter of 17 November 1838 from Schubring to Mendelssohn. Edwards, *History*, 16.

27. Letter of 6 December 1838 to Schubring. Schubring, *Briefwechsel*, 146–48. For a discussion of the popularity of oratorios on St. Boniface and of Schubring's involvement, see chapter 4.

28. Letter of 2 February 1839. Schubring, *Briefwechsel*, 149; translation after Edwards, *History*, 17–18.

29. Schubring, "Reminiscences," 230.

30. Letter of 9 February 1839 to Ferdinand Hiller. Sietz, *Briefwechsel*, 1:33.

31. Letter of 29 August 1844. Klingemann, *Briefwechsel*, 296.

32. Mendelssohn mentions having begun new work on an unspecified oratorio in his letter of 10 June 1845 to his brother Paul. Todd, *A Life*, 492

33. Letter of 24 July 1845 from Joseph Moore to Mendelssohn. Edwards, *History*, 30.

34. 11 June 1845 resolution of the Birmingham Festival Committee. Ibid., 29.

35. Letter of 24 July 1845. Ibid., 31.

36. Ibid., 32–42.

37. Most of Mendelssohn's drafts are undated, but the approximate date of the least developed one can be reasonably established as being "post-hiatus" by the fact that it is bound with and appears on the same size and type of paper as a draft mailed to Schubring on 16 December 1845.

38. The letter in which Mendelssohn made this request—if, indeed, he made it in writing at all—is lost, as are any letters between Mendelssohn and Schubring written between 17 November 1844 and 16 December 1845. Evidence of the request and of Schubring's new role appears in Mendelssohn's letter to him of 16 December 1845, however. See Schubring, *Briefwechsel*, 204–5.

39. Letter of 16 December 1845 to Schubring. Edwards, *History*, 21.

40. Letter of 16 December 1845 to Schubring. Schubring, *Briefwechsel*, 205.

41. Schubring, *Briefwechsel*, 207–8. Edwards (*History*, 21) incorrectly implies that Schubring visited Mendelssohn in Leipzig; the correspondence clearly indicates the opposite.

42. This hypothesis was first proposed by editor Julius Schubring (II) in Schubring, *Briefwechsel*, 208.

43. Letter of 3 February 1846 from Schubring to Mendelssohn. Schubring, *Briefwechsel*, 218.

44. Mendelssohn's first mention of the *Elias* score appears in his letter of 20 April 1846 to Ignaz Moscheles. F. Moscheles, *Letters*, 268.

45. Letter of 15 May 1846 to Jenny Lind (Holland and Rockstro, *Memoir*, 1:392) and letter of 23 May 1846 to Schubring (Schubring, *Briefwechsel*, 219).

46. Letter of 23 May 1846 from Mendelssohn to Schubring. Edwards, *History*, 22–23, quotation from 23.

47. The few passages from Text XV that appear in either Mendelssohn's final draft of the Part II libretto (XIII) or the Birmingham score had appeared in earlier drafts as well.

48. Schubring, *Briefwechsel*, 221.

49. Mendelssohn, ed. Todd, *Elias*, 459. In addition to serving as the source from which Bartholomew wrote his translation and assembled the solo and chorus parts, Henschke's copy was used by organist Henry Gauntlett, who improvised an organ accompaniment from it during the premiere. Ibid.

50. Letters of 18 and 28 July 1846 from Mendelssohn to Bartholomew. Edwards, *History*, 65, 69. That these three numbers appear in Henschke's copy (Text XVIII) and that the

overture and no. 37 do not, allows us to state with reasonable certainty that Henschke finished the copy on or shortly before July 28.

51. Undated letter (ca. June 1846) from Bartholomew to Mendelssohn. Edwards, *History*, 62.

52. Ibid., 72.

53. The music of the chorus was removed from Mendelssohn's score and eventually bound with a draft of the quartet into PL-Kj MN Bd. 41 (Text XVII).

54. Letter of 9 August 1846 from Mendelssohn to Bartholomew. Edwards, *History*, 72. Mendelssohn's discontent with the original version of *Sei stille dem Herrn* may have been due to the resemblance of its melody to the Scotch tune "Robin Gray," a similarity that Bartholomew pointed out in his 20 July 1846 letter and that Mendelssohn significantly lessened in the new version. For an in-depth discussion of this issue, see ibid., 66–71.

55. Mendelssohn's letters to Bartholomew allow for fairly concrete dating of the chorus parts. Since the parts contain both the pieces Mendelssohn sent to Bartholomew on July 28 and the *Er wird öffnen die Augen der Blinden* chorus that he ordered removed in his August 9 letter, they were most likely completed and sent to Ewer & Co. during the first week of August.

56. Edwards, *History*, 74, 76. With the help of Charlotte Moscheles, Bartholomew probably entered the changes into the printed chorus parts on the night before the performance. As Moscheles records, "After the [Tuesday night] rehearsal . . . I helped Mr. Bartholomew in correcting the text, and so we went on till one o'clock in the morning" (C. Moscheles, *Recent Music*, 325). Since the textbooks had long since gone to the printers at this point, Moscheles must have been correcting the printed chorus parts, which were completed before the textbook was finalized.

57. As for the German text, lack of time prevented Mendelssohn from making any changes; the Birmingham score copy is, therefore, the most definitive source for nearly all of the German text for this first version of *Elias*.

58. Edwards (*History*, 85–91) prints accolades from numerous sources, including the *Times* (London).

59. Letter of 12 October 1846 from Mendelssohn to Lind. Holland and Rockstro, *Memoir*, 1:435.

60. Edwards, *History*, 102–4.

61. Letter of 8 November 1846 to Bendemann. P. Mendelssohn Bartholdy, *Letters*, 371. Although Mendelssohn does not specifically state that Bendemann sent him a textbook from the Birmingham performance, he indicates that his friend wrote his "notes on the margin." The textbook is the only source Bendemann could have taken away from the performance that would have had the complete text for the work.

62. Letter of 8 November 1846. Ibid., 371–2.

63. Letter of 6 December 1846 to Klingemann. Klingemann, *Briefwechsel*, 316–17; Edwards, *History*, 97–98. That Mendelssohn is referring to the text (and not the music) in his discussion of the widow's scene in this letter is most strongly suggested by the fact that he had not yet completed the "*new song* for the Widow" when he sent the orchestral parts to Simrock in early February 1847. Letter of 8 February 1847 from Mendelssohn to Bartholomew. Edwards, *History*, 114. Emphasis original.

64. Although Mendelssohn did not mention having completed Obadiah's plea for rain in his letter to Klingemann, its appearance on the same folio as the widow's scene text suggests it was completed around this same time.

65. Letter of 30 December 1846 from Mendelssohn to Bartholomew. Edwards, *History*, 105.

66. "Unpublished Letters of Mendelssohn," *Musical Times*, 51(1910), 336.

67. Letter of 17 February 1847 from Mendelssohn to Bartholomew. Edwards, *History*, 117.

68. Letters of 8 February 1847 from Mendelssohn to Bartholomew and 12 March 1847 from Mendelssohn to Simrock. Ibid., 113; Elvers, *Briefe an deutsche Verleger*, 260.

69. Staehelin, "On the Aria 'Es ist genug,'" 121–36. While not "Messianic," per se, another Christian symbol frequently noted for its appearance in *Elias*—albeit in a somewhat modified form—is the chorale. See, for example, Feder, "Sacred Music," 264 and Todd, *A Life*, 553.

70. Jahn, "*Elijah*," 368.

71. Jahn, "*Elijah*," 368–71, quotation from 371.

72. Rosen, *The Romantic Generation*, 595.

73. Bartelmus, "Elia(s)," 184. Although Bartelmus believes that *Elias* should be seen as a symbolic work—a *Glaubensaussage* (expression of belief), to use his term—his interpretation differs from the one outlined below. He sees *Elias* as a work which, in part through its extensive use of the Psalms, attempts to be universally relevant to both Jews and Christians.

74. Handel and *Messiah* may well have been on Mendelssohn's mind as he composed *Elias*. As Martin Geck has noted, *Elias*—with its large, full choruses and its lack of narrative recitative—conforms to the Handelian oratorio model and was thus well suited to performance in England, for which it was originally conceived (Geck, "Religiöse Musik," 258). Furthermore, R. Larry Todd has demonstrated that *Messiah* may have served as a musical model: the subject of the "Amen" fugue in the final chorus of the published version of *Elias* appears to have been derived from its counterpart in *Messiah* (Todd, *A Life*, 550).

75. Letter of 14 July 1837 to Schubring. Schubring, *Briefwechsel*, 110; translation after P. Mendelssohn Bartholdy, *Letters*, 118.

76. Letter of 2 November 1838. Schubring, *Briefwechsel*, 135; translation after Edwards, *History*, 12–13.

77. Letter of 15 June 1846 from Schubring to Mendelssohn. Schubring, *Briefwechsel*, 222–23; translation after Edwards, *History*, 25.

78. Jahn, "*Elijah*," 366.

79. In a similar vein, R. Larry Todd has detected a Christological program in Mendelssohn's *Athalie* (op. 74), stemming from its use of Lutheran chorales. See Todd, *A Life*, 505–7.

80. Since we are attempting to gauge Mendelssohn's original intent here, and since Mendelssohn composed the *Elias* text in German, unless otherwise indicated, the English translations of passages from *Elias* used here are my own (after the Revised Standard Version Bible, when appropriate), not those of Bartholomew from the published English edition.

81. Hengstenberg, *Christology of the Old Testament*, 3:327–29. Mendelssohn's letter to his family of 21 May 1830 (Sutermeister, *Briefe einer Reise*, 16–19) tells of how Goethe—whom he was then visiting—asked to hear about Hengstenberg, suggesting that Mendelssohn knew and may have attended lectures given by the theologian, who was teaching at the University of Berlin and preparing to publish his study during Mendelssohn's time there.

82. Hengstenberg, *Christology of the Old Testament*, 3:336–61.

83. Ibid., 3:355–56.

84. Robinson, "Elijah, John and Jesus," 273. Although the clarification "as Elijah did" appears in the Luther Bibles of Mendelssohn's era, it has been omitted from many translations as it does not appear in all of the Luke manuscripts.

85. Klingemann, *Briefwechsel*, 212; translation after Edwards, *History*, 4–5.

86. For analyses of Christology in the other *Elias* scenes, see Sposato, "The Price," 1:351–423.

87. While Mendelssohn undoubtedly knew all of these parallels, his awareness of this last one is documented, as Schubring reminded Mendelssohn of it when he was considering abandoning the scene. See Schubring's letter of 9 January 1846 in Schubring, *Briefwechsel*, 209.

88. In *Paulus*, this same reluctance was likely one of the reasons behind the deletion of a prison scene involving the character Silas, who likewise does not and could not appear elsewhere in the work. For the complete text of that scene, see Sposato, "The Price," 2:140–41.

89. Text X, fol. 1v, also printed in Schubring, *Briefwechsel*, 209.

90. Character names and other titles appear as in the Birmingham score copy, which was sprinkled with bits of English, as seen here.

91. Mendelssohn mentions his desire for *Elias* to retain an Old Testament feel in his letter of 23 May 1846 to Schubring. Schubring, *Briefwechsel*, 221.

92. While the text of the *Sanctus* is also part of the daily Jewish liturgy (the *Kadosh*, which is part of the sanctification, or *Kedusha*), it is questionable whether Mendelssohn would have been aware of this. As argued in chapter 1, it is unlikely that Mendelssohn ever attended a synagogue service, and even if his father had engaged in private prayers at home, it is equally unlikely that Abraham would have recited the *Kedusha*, since it is normally recited only in public (Idelsohn, *Jewish Liturgy*, 94). More important, Mendelssohn would have known that his predominantly Protestant audience would have recognized the text as Christian in nature.

93. Letter of 17 November 1838. Schubring, *Briefwechsel*, 141.

94. Letter of 6 December 1838. Schubring, *Briefwechsel*, 148.

95. Letter of 2 February 1839. Schubring, *Briefwechsel*, 150; translation after Edwards, *History*, 18.

96. Letter of 2 February 1839 to Mendelssohn. Schubring, *Briefwechsel*, 150.

97. Lull, *Luther's Basic Theological Writings*, 139.

98. Letter of 23 May 1846. Schubring, *Briefwechsel*, 221; translation after Edwards, *History*, 24.

99. Letter of 2 November 1838. Schubring, *Briefwechsel*, 135; translation after Edwards, *History*, 12–13.

100. For analyses of the Jewish image in other *Elias* scenes, see Sposato, "The Price," 1:424–47.

101. Smither, *History of the Oratorio*, 4:116–17.

Chapter 6

1. Mendelssohn, ed. Todd, *Christus*, vii.

2. Kurzhals-Reuter, *Oratorien*, 162.

3. Bunsen and Mendelssohn met several times in London, once just before Mendelssohn's departure on 10 July 1844 and then several times during Mendelssohn's mid-March through early-May 1847 visit. Brodbeck, "Winter of Discontent," 30; Bunsen, *Aus seinen Briefen*, 2:358–60. The two may have also met in Berlin before Mendelssohn received Bunsen's libretto in April 1844, since Bunsen was there on ambassadorial business for several months beginning on 24 March 1844, and Mendelssohn was likewise in Berlin fulfilling his duties until his departure for London on April 12. Bunsen, *Aus seinen Briefen*, 2:255–69; Ranft, *Lebenschronik*, 92–93.

4. R. Werner, "Felix Mendelssohn Bartholdy als Kirchenmusiker," 105 n. 138.

5. Letter of 11 November 1838 from Sederholm to Mendelssohn. GB-Ob MS. M. Deneke Mendelssohn d. 34, no. 115. The short excerpt printed here regarding the libretto's content is published in Mendelssohn, ed. Todd, *Christus*, iv. Among some of the other submissions and proposals Mendelssohn received were one for a Luther oratorio and one entitled *Rachel in Ramah*. See Todd, *A Life*, 492.

6. GB-Ob MS. M. Deneke Mendelssohn d. 34, no. 78. The libretto is dated 29 September 1838.

7. Since nowhere else does the title of the work appear with the spiritual locales in this order, Gollmick likely recorded it incorrectly here.

8. Gollmick, *Auto-Biographie*, 2:107. Emphasis original. The autobiography lists only the year of this event (1839), although it almost certainly took place during Mendelssohn's residence in Frankfurt between 1 May and 15 August 1839.

9. Mendelssohn, ed. Todd, *Christus*, iv.

10. Letter of 3 November 1839. Mendelssohn, ed. Todd, *Christus*, iv.

11. Letter of 2 January 1840. Klingemann, *Briefwechsel*, 242.

12. Letter of 11 February 1840. Chorley, 1:309–10 in Kurzhals-Reuter, *Oratorien*, 160–61.

13. Mendelssohn made his appeal in a now lost letter written sometime between two surviving letters from Schubring dated 17 January and 19 February 1840. Schubring, *Briefwechsel*, 151–60.

14. Letter of 19–21 February 1840. Schubring, *Briefwechsel*, 156–57.

15. Schubring, *Briefwechsel*, 158–59.

16. Letter of 25 February 1840. Schubring, *Briefwechsel*, 161.

17. Letter of 26 February 1840. Schubring, *Briefwechsel*, 163.

18. Letter of 19–21 February 1840. Schubring, *Briefwechsel*, 157–58.

19. Letters of 19–21 February 1840 to Mendelssohn, 25 February 1840 to Schubring, and 26 February 1840 to Schubring. Schubring, *Briefwechsel*, 157–63. A second letter of Schubring's from this period is lost.

20. See Mendelssohn, ed. Seaton, *Lobgesang*, iv–v.

21. See Schubring's and Mendelssohn's correspondence from 19 to 26 February 1840. Schubring, *Briefwechsel*, 157–63.

22. Schubring, "Reminiscences," 230–31.

23. A transcription of the folio (GB-Ob MS. M. Deneke Mendelssohn c. 27, f. 48) appears in Sposato, "The Price," 2:471–72.

24. Carl Friedrich Zelter described *Christus der Meister* in his letter of 5 July 1829 to Felix. Schmidt-Beste, "'Alles von ihm gelernt?'" 49.

25. As noted above, the letter in which Mendelssohn told Schubring of *Erde, Hölle und Himmel* and requested information on other Christ oratorios is lost, but the reply (19 February 1840) survives. Schubring, *Briefwechsel*, 155–56.

26. Otto Jahn, *Über Felix Mendelssohn-Bartholdys Oratorium* Paulus: *eine Gelegenheitsschrift* (Kiel, 1842).

27. The complete title, as written on the handwritten copy Jahn sent to Mendelssohn, is *Christus, ein Oratorium aus Bibelsprüchen und Liederstrophen des Schleswig-Holsteinischen Gesangbuchs zusammengetragen, für Solo und Chorgesang mit obligater Orgelbegleitung in Musik gesetzt und mit freien Orgelfantasien verbunden.* GB-Ob MS. M. Deneke Mendelssohn c. 27, fol. 92.

28. GB-Ob MS. M. Deneke Mendelssohn c. 27, fol. 92–101.

29. Letter of 5 April 1842 from Jahn to Mendelssohn. Grossmann-Vendrey, *Musik der Vergangenheit*, 215–16.

30. Letter of Easter Monday (8 April) 1844 from Bunsen to Mendelssohn. GB-Ob MS. M. Deneke Mendelssohn d. 45, no. 227 (partially published in Mendelssohn, ed. Todd, *Christus*, v).

31. Entry of 4 December 1847. Cited in Marek, *Gentle Genius*, 318. Ellipses Marek's.

32. E. Devrient (*My Recollections*, 290) also attests to Mendelssohn's work on *Christus* in 1847.

33. PL-Kj MN Bd. 44. Sketches of the work are found on pages 12 and 59 of the *Christus* score volume, and in GB-Ob MS. M. Deneke Mendelssohn b. 5, fols. 177–8. With the exception of the page 12 sketch, none of the sketches contain any new text or textual variants and will therefore not be considered here. The page 12 sketch contains but a single fragment of new text: "Herr nun laßest du" (likely Luke 2:29, "Lord, now lettest thou [thy servant depart in peace]").

34. See R. Werner, "Felix Mendelssohn Bartholdy als Kirchenmusiker," 106 and Kurzhals-Reuter, *Oratorien*, 163.

35. Mendelssohn, ed. Todd, *Christus*, v.

36. Entry of 1 May 1847. Cited in Marek, *Gentle Genius*, 306. Ellipses Marek's.

37. Letter of 7 November 1847 to Josef Fischhoff. Rychnovsky, "Aus Felix Mendelssohn Bartholdys letzten Lebenstagen," 142, in Mendelssohn, ed. Todd, *Christus*, iv. A similar account appears in an undated letter from his wife's cousin Cornélie Schunck to Mendelssohn's friends in London. The letter itself appears in Klingemann, *Briefwechsel*, 332–36, but is unsigned. Peter Ward Jones identifies the author in "Felix Mendelssohn Bartholdys Tod," 207–8.

38. As Ernst Wilhelm Hengstenberg testifies in his 1829 *Christologie des Alten Testaments*, this prophecy, while fulfilled by David, was commonly believed by both Jews and Christians to refer to the Messiah, primarily because of the reference to the prophesied one's destructive power. Hengstenberg, *Christology of the Old Testament*, 1:63–67.

39. Letter of 2 November 1838. Schubring, *Briefwechsel*, 135; translation after Edwards, *History*, 13.

40. For a summary of Luther's views on this, see Althaus, *Theology of Martin Luther*, 304–13.

41. Ibid., 211–17.

Conclusion

1. R. Larry Todd has interpreted Psalm 114 (op. 51) as a further example of this strategy of dual perspective, an argument that could conceivably be applied to several of the Psalms. Todd, *A Life*, 381.

2. If one ignores *Elias*'s Christological program, even the work's prophetic ending could be seen as Jewish in origin, since the belief that the return of Elijah would precede the coming of the Messiah finds its roots in Jewish theology. Wiener, *Prophet Elijah*, 141.

3. Botstein, "Mendelssohn and the Jews," 213.

4. *Das Judenthum in der Musik* first appeared in the September 3 and 6, 1850, editions of the *Neue Zeitschrift für Musik* under the pseudonym "K. Freigedank" ("K. Free-thought").

Bibliography

Allison, Dale C., Jr. *The New Moses: A Matthean Typology*. Minneapolis: Fortress Press, 1993.

Althaus, Paul. *The Theology of Martin Luther*. Translated by Robert Schultz. Philadelphia: Fortress Press, 1966.

Altmann, Alexander. "Moses Mendelssohn's gesammelte Schriften: Neuerschlossene Briefe zur Geschichte ihrer Herausgabe." *Bulletin des Leo Baeck Instituts* 11 (1968): 73–115.

Alvensleben, Gebhard von. "Über die Idee dramatischen Fortgangs und Zusammenhangs im Oratorium. Bei Gelegenheit der Aufführung des 'Moses' von A. B. Marx." *Neue Zeitschrift für Musik* 16 (1842), nos. 17–22: 65–67, 69–71, 73–74, 77–78, 81–82, 85–86.

Bachmann, Johann Friedrich. *Zur Geschichte der Berlin Gesangbücher: Ein Hymnologischer Beitrag*. Berlin: Wilhelm Schultze Verlag, 1856.

Bartelmus, Rüdiger. "Elia(s): eine Prophetengestalt im Alten Testament und ihre musikalisch-theologische Deutung durch Felix Mendelssohn Bartholdy," *Musik und Kirche* 65, no. 4 (1995): 182–97.

Bering, Dietz. *The Stigma of Names: Antisemitism in German Daily Life, 1812–1933*. Translated by Neville Plaice. Cambridge: Polity Press, 1992.

Bitter, Carl Hermann, ed. *Carl Loewes Selbstbiographie*. 1870. Reprint, Hildesheim: Georg Olms Verlag, 1976.

Blessinger, Karl. *Judentum und Musik: ein Beitrag zur Kultur- und Rassenpolitik*. Berlin: Bernhard Hannefeld Verlag, 1944.

Blumner, Martin. *Geschichte der Sing-Akademie zu Berlin*. Berlin: Horn und Raasch Verlag, 1891.

Botstein, Leon. "The Aesthetics of Assimilation and Affirmation: Reconstructing the Career of Felix Mendelssohn." In *Mendelssohn and His World*, edited by R. Larry Todd, 5–42. Princeton: Princeton University Press, 1991.

———. "Songs without Words: Thoughts on Music, Theology, and the Role of the Jewish Question in the Work of Felix Mendelssohn." *The Musical Quarterly* 77 (1993): 561–78.

———. "Mendelssohn and the Jews." *The Musical Quarterly* 82, no. 1 (1998): 210–19.

———. "Mendelssohn, Werner, and the Jews: A Final Word." *The Musical Quarterly* 83, no. 1 (1999): 45–50.

Brodbeck, David. "A Winter of Discontent: Mendelssohn and the *Berliner Domchor*." In *Mendelssohn Studies*, edited by R. Larry Todd, 1–32. Cambridge: Cambridge University Press, 1992.

Brown, Clive. *A Portrait of Mendelssohn*. New Haven: Yale University Press, 2003.

Bunsen, Frances Waddington. *Christian Carl Josias Freiherr von Bunsen: Aus seinen Briefen und nach eigener Erinnerung geschildert von seiner Witwe*. 3 vols. Leipzig: F. A. Brockhaus, 1868–71.

Butler, Alban, and Kathleen Jones. *Butler's Lives of the Saints*. Collegeville, Minn.: The Liturgical Press, 1997.

Chorley, Henry Fothergill. *Autobiography, Memoirs, and Letters*. London: Richard Bentley and Son, 1873.

Citron, Marcia J., ed. and trans. *The Letters of Fanny Hensel to Felix Mendelssohn*. Stuyvesant, N.Y.: Pendragon, 1987.

Clements, Keith. *Friedrich Schleiermacher: Pioneer of Modern Theology*. 1987. Reprint, Minneapolis: Fortress Press, 1991.

Clostermann, Annemarie. *Mendelssohn Bartholdys kirchenmusikalisches Schaffen: neue Untersuchungen zu Geschichte, Form und Inhalt*. Mainz: Schott, 1989.

Crum, Margaret, and Peter Ward Jones, *Catalogue of the Mendelssohn Papers in the Bodleian Library, Oxford*. 3 vols. Tutzing: Hans Schneider, 1980–89.

Devrient, Eduard. *My Recollections of Felix Mendelssohn Bartholdy and His Letters to Me*. Trans. Natalia Macfarran. London: Richard Bentley, 1869; German ed. *Meine Erinnerungen an Felix Mendelssohn-Bartholdy und seine Briefe an mich*. 1869. Reprint, Leipzig: J. J. Weber, 1872.

Devrient, Therese. *Jugenderinnerungen*. Stuttgart: C. Krabbe, 1905.

Die Bibel, oder die ganze heilige Schrift des alten und neuen Testaments, nach der deutschen Uebersetzung Dr. Martin Luther's. Berlin: Preußischen Haupt-Bibelgesellschaft, 1824.

Dieterich, Johann Samuel. *Gesangbuch zum gottesdienstlichen Gebrauch in den Königlich Preußischen Landen*. Breslau: Wilhelm Gottlieb Korn, 1793.

Dinglinger, Wolfgang. *Studien zu den Psalmen mit Orchester von Felix Mendelssohn Bartholdy*. Cologne: Studio, 1993.

———. "'Die Glaubensform der meisten gesitteten Menschen': Aspekte der christlichen Erziehung der Geschwister Mendelssohn." In *Fanny Hensel geb. Mendelssohn Bartholdy: Komponieren zwischen Geselligkeitsideal und romantischer Musikästhetik*, edited by Beatrix Borchard and Monika Schwarz-Danuser, 288–304. 2nd ed. Kassel: Furore Verlag, 2002.

Dörffel, Alfred. "Statistik der Concerte im Salle des Gewandhauses zu Leipzig." In *Geschichte der Gewandhausconcerte zu Leipzig*. 1884. Reprint, Leipzig: VEB Deutscher Verlag für Musik, 1980.

Dubnow, Simon. *History of the Jews*. Trans. by Moshe Spiegel. 5 vols. South Brunswick, N.J.: Thomas Yoseloff, 1967–73.

Dusella, Reinhold. *Die Oratorien Carl Loewes*. Bonn: G. Schröder Verlag, 1991.

Eckermann, Johann Peter. *Gespräche mit Goethe in den letzten Jahren seines Lebens, 1823–1832*. 3 vols. 2nd ed. 1837–48. Reprint, Berlin: Aufbau-Verlag, 1962.

Edwards, Fredrick George. *The History of Mendelssohn's Oratorio 'Elijah.'* London and New York: Novello, Ewer and Co., 1896.

Elvers, Rudolf, ed. *Felix Mendelssohn Bartholdy: Briefe an deutsche Verleger*. Berlin: de Gruyter, 1968.

———, ed. *Felix Mendelssohn: A Life in Letters*. Trans. by Craig Tomlinson. New York: Fromm International Publishing, 1986.

———. "Frühe Quellen zur Biographie Felix Mendelssohn Bartholdys." In *Felix Mendelssohn Bartholdy: Kongreß-Bericht Berlin 1994*, edited by Christian Martin Schmidt, 17–22. Wiesbaden: Breitkopf und Härtel, 1997.

Elvers, Rudolf, and Hans-Günter Klein. *Die Mendelssohns in Berlin: eine Familie und ihre Stadt.* Berlin: Staatsbibliothek Preussischer Kulturbesitz, 1983.

Feder, Georg. "On Felix Mendelssohn Bartholdy's Sacred Music." In *The Mendelssohn Companion*, edited by Douglass Seaton, 257–81. Westport, Conn.: Greenwood Press, 2001.

Fichte, Tobias. "'. . . don't you think this could become a new kind of cantata?' Rituality, Authenticity and Staging in Mendelssohn's *Walpurgisnacht.*" *The World of Music* 40, no. 1 (1998): 119–34.

Fink, G. W. "Paulus." *Allgemeine Musikalische Zeitung* 39 (1837), nos. 31–32, 498–506, 514–30.

———. "Felix Mendelssohn Bartholdy." *Allgemeine Musikalische Zeitung* 39, no. 52 (1837): 845–51.

Forchert, Arno. "Textanlage und Darstellungsprinzipien in Mendelssohns *Elias.*" In *Das Problem Mendelssohn*, edited by Carl Dahlhaus, 61–77. Regensburg: Gustav Bosse Verlag, 1974.

Freudenberg, Carl Gottlieb. *Aus dem Leben eines alten Organisten.* Edited by Wilhelm Viol. 2nd ed. Leipzig: F. E. C. Leuckart, 1872.

Geck, Martin. *Die Wiederentdeckung der Matthäuspassion im 19. Jahrhundert.* Regensburg: Gustav Bosse Verlag, 1967.

———. *Deutsche Oratorien 1800 bis 1840: Verzeichnis der Quellen und Aufführungen.* Wilhelmshaven: Heinrichshofen's Verlag, 1971.

———. "Religiöse Musik 'im Geist der gebildeten Gesellschaft': Mendelssohn und sein *Elias.*" In *Von Beethoven bis Mahler: Die Musik des deutschen Idealismus*, 256–79. Stuttgart: Verlag J. B. Metzler, 1993.

Geiger, Ludwig. *Geschichte der Juden in Berlin.* 1871–90. Reprint, Berlin: Arani, 1988.

Gilbert, Felix, ed. *Bankiers, Künstler und Gelehrte: unveröffentlichte Briefe der Familie Mendelssohn aus dem 19. Jahrhundert.* Tübingen: J. C. B. Mohr, 1975.

Gilman, Sander. *Jewish Self-Hatred: Anti-Semitism and the Hidden Language of the Jews.* Baltimore: John Hopkins University Press, 1986.

Glasson, T. Francis. *Moses in the Fourth Gospel.* Naperville, Ill.: Alec R. Allenson, 1963.

Gollmick, Carl. *Auto-Biographie nebst einigen Momenten aus der Geschichte des Frankfurter Theaters.* 3 vols. Frankfurt am Main: n.p., 1866.

Graun, Carl Heinrich. *Der Tod Jesu.* Edited by Howard Serwer. Madison: A-R Editions, 1975.

Großmann-Vendrey, Susanna. *Felix Mendelssohn Bartholdy und die Musik der Vergangenheit.* Regensburg: Gustav Bosse Verlag, 1969.

Grove, George. "Mendelssohn." In *A Dictionary of Music and Musicians*, edited by George Grove, 2:253–310. London: Macmillan, 1880.

Hanslick, Eduard. *Suite: Aufsätze über Musik und Musiker.* Wien, Tetschen: K. Prochaska, 1884.

Hecker, Max F., ed. *Der Briefwechsel zwischen Goethe und Zelter, 1799–1832.* 3 vols. 1913–18. Reprint, Frankfurt am Main: Insel Verlag, 1987.

Hellmundt, Christoph. "Mendelssohns Arbeit an seiner Kantate *Die erste Walpurgisnacht*: Zu einer bisher wenig beachteten Quelle." In *Felix Mendelssohn Bartholdy: Kongress-*

Bericht Berlin 1994, edited by Christian Martin Schmidt, 76–122. Wiesbaden: Breitkopf und Härtel, 1997.

Hemsen, Johannes Tychsen. *Der Apostel Paulus. Sein Leben, Wirken und seine Schriften.* Göttingen: Dieterischen Buchhandlung, 1830.

Hengstenberg, Ernst Wilhelm. *Christology of the Old Testament, and a Commentary on the Predictions of the Messiah by the Prophets.* 3 vols. Trans. by Reuel Keith. Alexandria, D.C.: William M. Morrison, 1836–39; German ed. *Christologie des Alten Testaments und Commentar über die messianischen Weissagungen.* 3 vols. Berlin: L. Oehmigke, 1829–35.

Hensel, Sebastian. *The Mendelssohn Family.* Trans. by Carl Klingemann [II]. 2nd ed. 2 vols. New York: Harper and Brothers, 1882; German ed. *Die Familie Mendelssohn, 1729 bis 1847, nach Briefen und Tagebüchern.* 1879. Reprint, Frankfurt am Main: Insel Verlag, 1995.

Heuser, Gustav. "Oratorium und Oper." *Neue Zeitschrift für Musik* 21 (1844): 161–62, 177–78, 181–82, 185–86, 189–90, 193–94, 197–98, 206–8.

Hientzsch, Johann Gottfried. "Über das Musikleben in Breslau." *Eutonia, einer hauptsächlich pädagogischen Musik-Zeitschrift* 3 (1830): 298ff.

Hiller, Ferdinand. *Mendelssohn: Letters and Recollections.* Trans. by M. E. von Glehn. 1874. Reprint, New York: Vienna House, 1972.

Holland, Henry Scott, and W. S. Rockstro, eds. *Memoir of Madame Jenny Lind-Goldschmidt.* 2 vols. London: John Murray, 1891.

Homberg, Herz. *Bne-Zion. Ein religiös-moralisches Lehrbuch für die Jugend israelitischer Nation.* Augsburg: Mathais Rieger, 1812.

Idelsohn, Abraham Z. *Jewish Liturgy and Its Development.* New York: Sacred Music Press, 1932.

Jacob, Heinrich Eduard. *Felix Mendelssohn and His Times.* Translated by Richard and Clara Winston. Englewood Cliffs, N.J.: Prentice Hall, 1963.

Jacobson, Jacob. "Von Mendelssohn zu Mendelssohn-Bartholdy." *Leo Baeck Institute Yearbook* 5 (1960): 251–61.

―――. *Die Judenbürgerbücher der Stadt Berlin, 1809–1851, mit Ergänzungen für die Jahre 1791–1809.* Berlin: Walter de Gruyter, 1962.

―――. *Jüdische Trauungen in Berlin, 1759–1813, mit Ergänzungen für die Jahre von 1723 bis 1759.* 1963. Reprint, Berlin: Walter de Gruyter, 1968.

Jahn, Otto. *Über Felix Mendelssohn-Bartholdys Oratorium* Paulus: *eine Gelegenheitsschrift.* Kiel: n.p., 1842.

―――. "On F. Mendelssohn-Bartholdy's Oratorio *Elijah.*" Trans. by Susan Gillespie. In *Mendelssohn and His World*, edited by R. Larry Todd, 364–81. Princeton: Princeton University Press, 1991.

Jourdan, Paul. "The Hidden Pathways of Assimilation: Mendelssohn's First Visit to London." In *Music and British Culture, 1785–1914: Essays in Honour of Cyril Ehrlich*, edited by Christina Bashford and Leanne Langley. New York: Oxford University Press, 2000.

Katz, Jacob. *From Prejudice to Destruction: Anti-Semitism, 1700–1933.* Cambridge, Mass.: Harvard University Press, 1980.

―――. *Die Hep-Hep-Verfolgungen des Jahres 1819.* Berlin: Metropol-Verlag, 1994.

Keferstein, Gustav Adolph. "Das Oratorium." *Allgemeine musikalische Zeitung* 45 (1843), cols. 873–79, 892–902, 921–26.

Kellenberger, Edgar. "Felix Mendelssohn als Librettist eines Moses-Oratoriums: Erstedition mit Kommentar." *Musik und Kirche* 63, no. 3 (1993): 126–39.

Klein, Hans-Günter. "Abraham Mendelssohn Bartholdy in England: Die Briefe aus London im Sommer 1833 nach Berlin." *Mendelssohn Studien* 12 (2001): 67–127.

Klein, Hans-Günter, and Rudolf Elvers, eds. *Fanny Hensel: Tagebücher.* Wiesbaden: Breitkopf und Härtel, 2002.

Kliem, Manfred. "Die Berliner Mendelssohn-Adresse Neue Promenade 7: Zeitliche Zuordnung und soziales Umfeld als Forschungsanliegen." *Mendelssohn Studien* 7 (1990): 123–40.

Klingemann, Karl, Jr., ed. *Felix Mendelssohn-Bartholdys Briefwechsel mit Legationsrat Karl Klingemann in London.* Essen: G. D. Baedecker, 1909.

Konold, Wulf. *Felix Mendelssohn Bartholdy und seine Zeit.* 2nd ed. Laaber: Laaber-Verlag, 1996.

Kramer, Lawrence. "*Felix culpa:* Goethe and the Image of Mendelssohn." In *Mendelssohn Studies,* edited by R. Larry Todd, 64–79. Cambridge: Cambridge University Press, 1992.

Krause, Peter. "Mendelssohns dramatische Kantate *Die erste Walpurgisnacht:* Ergänzende Bemerkungen zur Werkgeschichte auf der Grundlage von Untersuchungen des Leipziger Autographs der Letztfassung." In *Musik + Dramaturgie: 15 Studien Fritz Hennenberg zum 65. Geburtstag,* edited by Beate Hiltner-Hennenberg, 101–21. Frankfurt: Peter Lang, 1997.

Kupferberg, Herbert. *The Mendelssohns: Three Generations of Genius.* New York: Charles Scribner's Sons, 1972.

Kurzhals-Reuter, Arntrud. *Die Oratorien Felix Mendelssohn Bartholdys: Untersuchungen zur Quellenlage, Entstehung, Gestaltung und Überlieferung.* Tutzing: Hans Schneider, 1978.

Langmuir, Gavin. *Toward a Definition of Antisemitism.* Berkeley: University of California Press, 1990.

Lesser, Ludwig. *Chronik der Gesellschaft der Freunde in Berlin.* Berlin, n.p., 1842.

Little, William. "Mendelssohn and the Berlin Singakademie: The Composer at the Cross-roads." In *Mendelssohn and His World,* edited by R. Larry Todd, 65–85. Princeton: Princeton University Press, 1991.

Loewe, Carl. *Die Zerstörung von Jerusalem. Großes Oratorium in 2 Abtheilungen von G. Nicolai.* Leipzig: Fr. Hofmeister, 1832.

———. *Die eherne Schlange, Vocal-Oratorium für Männerstimmen, gedichtet von Professor Giesebrecht.* Berlin: H. Wagenführ, [1834].

Lowenstein, Steven M. *The Berlin Jewish Community: Enlightenment, Family, and Crisis, 1770–1830.* New York: Oxford University Press, 1994.

Lowenthal-Hensel, Cécile. "Neues zur Leipziger Straße Drei." *Mendelssohn Studien* 7 (1990): 140–51.

Loy, Felix. *Die Bach-Rezeption in den Oratorien von Mendelssohn Bartholdy.* Tutzing: Hans Schneider, 2003.

Lull, Timothy, ed. *Martin Luther's Basic Theological Writings.* Minneapolis: Fortress Press, 1989.

Macmillan, Kerr D. *Protestantism in Germany.* Princeton: Princeton University Press, 1917.

Marek, George. *Gentle Genius: The Story of Felix Mendelssohn.* New York: Thomas Y. Crowell, 1972.

Marissen, Michael. "Religious Aims in Mendelssohn's 1829 Berlin-Singakademie Performances of Bach's *St. Matthew Passion.*" *The Musical Quarterly* 77, no. 4 (1993): 718–26.

Marx, Adolf Bernhard. *Mose. Oratorium aus der heiligen Schrift.* Leipzig: Breitkopf und Härtel, [1844].

———. *Erinnerungen aus meinem Leben.* 2 vols. Berlin: Otto Janke, 1865.

———. "From the Memoirs of Adolf Bernhard Marx." Trans. by Susan Gillespie. In *Mendelssohn and His World*, edited by R. Larry Todd, 206–20. Princeton: Princeton University Press, 1991.

Marx, Therese. *Adolf Bernhard Marx' Verhältniß zu Felix Mendelssohn-Bartholdy in Bezug auf Eduard Devrient's Darstellung.* Leipzig: Dürr'schen Buchhandlung, 1869.

Meiser, Martin. "Das Paulusbild bei Mendelssohn und Mendelssohns christliche Selbsterfahrung." *Musik und Kirche* 62, no. 5 (1992): 259–64.

Melhorn, Catharine Rose. "Mendelssohn's *Die erste Walpurgisnacht.*" D.M.A. diss., University of Illinois at Urbana-Champaign, 1983.

Mendelssohn, Joseph. "Moses Mendelssohn's Lebensgeschichte." In *Moses Mendelssohn's Gesammelte Schriften*, edited by Georg Benjamin Mendelssohn, 1:1–56. Leipzig: F. A. Brockhaus, 1843.

Mendelssohn, Moses. *Jerusalem, or, On Religious Power and Judaism.* Trans. by Allan Arkush. Hanover, N.H.: University Press of New England, 1983.

———. *Gesammelte Schriften, Jubiläumsausgabe.* Stuttgart: Friedrich Frommann Verlag, 1985.

Mendelssohn Bartholdy, Felix. *Hör mein Bitten (Orchesterfassung).* Edited by R. Larry Todd. Stuttgart: Carus-Verlag, 1986.

———. *Lobgesang, op. 52.* Edited by Douglass Seaton. Stuttgart: Carus-Verlag, 1990.

———. *Christus, op. 97.* Edited by R. Larry Todd. Stuttgart: Carus-Verlag, 1994.

———. *Elias, op. 70.* Edited by R. Larry Todd. Stuttgart: Carus-Verlag, 1995.

———. *Neun Psalmen und Cantique.* Edited by Pietro Zappalà and Barbara Mohn. Stuttgart: Carus-Verlag, 1997.

———. *Dreizehn Psalm-Motetten.* Edited by Pietro Zappalà. Stuttgart: Carus-Verlag, 1998.

———. *Paulus, Op. 36 Oratorio: First Recording of the Carus-Verlag Critical Edition.* Royal Scottish National Orchestra and Chorus, Leon Botstein. Arabesque Recordings Z6705. 1998.

Mendelssohn-Bartholdy, Karl, ed. *Goethe and Mendelssohn.* 2nd ed. Trans. by M. E. von Glehn. London: Macmillan, 1874.

Mendelssohn Bartholdy, Paul, ed. *Letters from Italy and Switzerland by Felix Mendelssohn Bartholdy.* Trans. by Lady Wallace. 1860. Reprint, New York and Philadelphia: Frederick Leypoldt, 1865; German ed. *Reisebriefe aus den Jahren 1830 bis 1832 von Felix Mendelssohn Bartholdy.* 1861. Reprint, Leipzig: Hermann Mendelssohn, 1864.

Mendelssohn Bartholdy, Paul and Carl, eds. *Letters of Felix Mendelssohn Bartholdy from 1833 to 1847.* Trans. by Lady Wallace. Boston: Oliver Ditson and Co., 1863; German ed. *Briefe aus den Jahren 1833 bis 1847 von Felix Mendelssohn Bartholdy.* 1863. Reprint, Leipzig: Hermann Mendelssohn, 1864.

Metzger, Heinz-Klaus. "Noch einmal: *Die erste Walpurgisnacht.*" In *Musik-Konzepte 14/15: Felix Mendelssohn-Bartholdy*, edited by Heinz-Klaus Metzger et al., 93–96. Munich: Text und Kritik, 1980.

Meyer, Michael A., et al. *German-Jewish History in Modern Times.* 4 vols. New York: Columbia University Press, 1996–98; German ed. *Deutsch-jüdische Geschichte in der Neuzeit.* 4 vols. Munich: C. H. Beck Verlag, 1996–97.

Mintz, Donald M. "The Sketches and Drafts of Three of Felix Mendelssohn's Major Works." Ph.D. diss., Cornell University, 1960.

Moscheles, Charlotte, ed. *Recent Music and Musicians: As Described in the Diaries and Correspondence of Ignatz Moscheles.* Trans. by A. D. Coleridge. 1873. Reprint, New York: Da Capo Press, 1970.

Moscheles, Felix, ed. *Letters of Felix Mendelssohn to Ignaz and Charlotte Moscheles.* 1888. Reprint, Freeport, N.Y.: Books for Libraries Press, 1970.

Mosewius, Johann Theodor. *Johann Sebastian Bachs Matthäus-Passion: musikalisch-ästhetisch dargestellt.* Berlin: J. Guttentag, 1852.

Müller, Carl Heinrich. *Felix Mendelssohn, Frankfurt am Main und der Cäcilien-Verein.* Darmstadt: Volk und Scholle, 1925.

Nauhaus, Gerd, ed. *The Marriage Diaries of Robert and Clara Schumann: From Their Wedding Day through the Russia Trip.* Trans. by Peter Ostwald. Boston: Northeastern University Press, 1993.

Neukomm, Sigismond. *Mount Sinai, or, The Ten Commandments.* Boston: Handel and Haydn Society, 1840.

Nichols, Roger. *Mendelssohn Remembered.* London: Faber and Faber, 1997.

Nohl, Ludwig. *Letters of Distinguished Musicians.* Trans. by Lady Wallace. London: Longmans, Green, 1867.

Nohl, Paul-Gerhard. *Geistliche Oratorientexte: Entstehung–Kommentar–Interpretation.* Kassel: Bärenreiter, 2001.

Platen, Emil. *Die Matthäus-Passion von Johann Sebastian Bach: Entstehung, Werkbeschreibung, Rezeption.* Kassel: Bärenreiter Verlag, 1991.

Prandi, Julie D. "Kindred Spirits: Mendelssohn and Goethe, *Die erste Walpurgisnacht.*" In *The Mendelssohns: Their Music in History,* edited by John Michael Cooper and Julie D. Prandi, 135–46. New York: Oxford University Press, 2002.

Raff, Joachim. "Aus Weimar. Aufführung des Oratoriums *Mose* von Adolph Bernhard Marx am 3ten Juni 1853." *Neue Zeitschrift für Musik* 39 (1853): 6.

Ranft, Peter. *Felix Mendelssohn Bartholdy: Eine Lebenschronik.* Leipzig: VEB Deutscher Verlag für Musik, 1972.

Reichwald, Siegwart. *The Musical Genesis of Felix Mendelssohn's Paulus.* Lanham, Md.: Scarecrow Press, 2001.

Reimer, Erich. "Textanlage und Szenengestaltung in Mendelssohns 'Paulus.'" *Archiv für Musikwissenschaft* 46, no. 1 (1989): 42–69.

Richter, Arnd. *Mendelssohn: Leben, Werke, Dokumente.* 2nd ed. Zürich: Atlantis Musikbuch-Verlag, 2000.

Riehn, Rainer. "Das Eigene und das Fremde: Religion und Gesellschaft im Komponieren Mendelssohns." In *Musik-Konzepte 14/15: Felix Mendelssohn Bartholdy,* edited by Heinz-Klaus Metzger et al., 123–46. Munich: Text und Kritik, 1980.

Robinson, J. A. T. "Elijah, John and Jesus: an Essay in Detection." *New Testament Studies* 4, no. 4 (July 1958): 263–81.

Rohrbacher, Stefan, and Michael Schmidt, *Judenbilder: Kulturgeschichte antijüdischer Mythen und antisemitischer Vorurteile.* Reinbek bei Hamburg: Rowohlt Taschenbuch Verlag, 1991.

Rosen, Charles. *The Romantic Generation.* Cambridge, Mass.: Harvard University Press, 1995.

Rychnovsky, Ernst. "Aus Felix Mendelssohn Bartholdys letzten Lebenstagen." *Die Musik* 8, no. 9 (1908–9): 141–46.

Schering, Arnold. *Geschichte des Oratoriums*. Leipzig: Breitkopf und Härtel, 1911.

Schleiermacher, Friedrich. *The Christian Faith*. Edited by H. R. Mackintosh and J. S. Stewart. 1928. Reprint, Edinburgh: T&T Clark, 1989.

Schmidt-Beste, Thomas. "'Alles von ihm gelernt?' Die Briefe von Carl Friedrich Zelter an Felix Mendelssohn Bartholdy." *Mendelssohn Studien* 10 (1997): 25–56.

Schneider, Friedrich. *Pharao; Oratorium in 2 Abtheilungen, von A. Bruggemann. Clavierauszug vom Componisten*. Halberstadt: Bruggemann, [1829].

Schneider, Max F. *Mendelssohn oder Bartholdy? Zur Geschichte eines Familiennamens*. Basel: Internationale Felix-Mendelssohn-Gesellschaft, 1962.

Schoeps, Julius H. *Deutsch-jüdische Symbiose, oder, Die mißglückte Emanzipation*. Berlin: Philo Verlagsgesellschaft, 1996.

Schrader, Karl. *Der Apostel Paulus*. 5 vols. Leipzig: Christian Ernst Kollmann, 1830–36.

Schubring, Julius. "Reminiscences of Felix Mendelssohn-Bartholdy." Trans. anonymously. In *Mendelssohn and His World*, edited by R. Larry Todd, 221–36. Princeton: Princeton University Press, 1991.

Schubring, Julius, Jr., ed. *Briefwechsel zwischen Felix Mendelssohn Bartholdy und Julius Schubring, zugleich ein Beitrag zur Geschichte und Theorie des Oratoriums*. Leipzig: Duncker und Humblot Verlag, 1892.

Schumann, Robert. "Aufzeichnungen über Mendelssohn." In *Musik-Konzepte 14/15: Felix Mendelssohn Bartholdy*, edited by Heinz-Klaus Metzger et al., 97–122. Munich: Text und Kritik, 1980.

Schünemann, Georg. *Die Singakademie zu Berlin: 1791–1941*. Regensburg: Gustav Bosse Verlag, 1941.

Schweitzer, Albert. *Paul and His Interpreters: A Critical History*. Trans. by William Montgomery. 1912. Reprint, London: Adam & Charles Black, 1948.

Searle, Humphrey, ed. and trans. *Hector Berlioz: A Selection from His Letters*. 1966. Reprint, New York: Vienna House, 1973.

Seaton, Douglass. "The Romantic Mendelssohn: The Composition of *Die erste Walpurgisnacht*." *The Musical Quarterly* 68, no. 3 (1982): 398–410.

Selden-Goth, Gisella, ed. *Felix Mendelssohn: Letters*. 1945. Reprint, London: Paul Elek, 1946.

Shmueli, Herzl. "Adolf Bernhard Marx (1795–1866): Deutscher Musiker—Jüdische Herkunft (Eine Dokumentation)." *Orbis Musicae* 10 (1990/91): 217–28.

Siegfried, Christina. "'Der interessanteste und problematischste seiner Freunde'—Adolph Bernhard Marx. 1795–1866." In *Blickpunkt: Felix Mendelssohn Bartholdy*, edited by Bernd Heyder and Christoph Spering, 35–44. Cologne: Verlag Dohr, 1994.

Sietz, Reinhold. *Aus Ferdinand Hillers Briefwechsel*. 7 vols. Cologne: A. Volk, 1958–70.

Smither, Howard E. *A History of the Oratorio*. 4 vols. Chapel Hill: University of North Carolina Press, 1977–2000.

Spohr, Louis. *Louis Spohr's Autobiography*. Trans. anonymously. London: Longman, Green, Longman, Roberts, & Green, 1865.

———. *Des Heilands letzte Stunden*. Edited by Clive Brown. New York: Garland, 1987.

Sposato, Jeffrey. "Creative Writing: The [Self-]Identification of Mendelssohn as Jew." *The Musical Quarterly* 82, no. 1 (1998): 190–209.

———. "Mendelssohn, *Paulus*, and the Jews: A Response to Leon Botstein and Michael Steinberg." *The Musical Quarterly* 83, no. 2 (1999): 280–91.

———. "The Price of Assimilation: The Oratorios of Felix Mendelssohn and the Nineteenth-Century Anti-Semitic Tradition." 2 vols. Ph.D. diss., Brandeis University, 2000.

Staehelin, Martin. "*Elijah*, Johann Sebastian Bach, and the New Covenant: On the Aria 'Es ist genug' in Felix Mendelssohn-Bartholdy's Oratorio *Elijah*." Trans. by Susan Gillespie. In *Mendelssohn and His World*, edited by R. Larry Todd, 121–36. Princeton: Princeton University Press, 1991.

Stanley, Glenn. "The Oratorio in Prussia and Protestant Germany, 1812–1848." Ph.D. diss., Columbia University, 1988.

Steinberg, Michael P. "Mendelssohn's Music and German-Jewish Culture: An Intervention." *The Musical Quarterly* 83, no. 1 (1999): 31–44.

Steinthal, P. M. *Nachtrag zur Chronik der Gesellschaft der Freunde in Berlin, vom Jahre 1842 bis 1872*. Berlin: Friedländer'sche Buchdruckerei, 1873.

Sutermeister, Peter. *Briefe einer Reise durch Deutschland, Italien und die Schweiz, und Lebensbild*. 1958. Reprint, *Felix Mendelssohn Bartholdy: Eine Reise durch Deutschland, Italien und die Schweiz*. Tübingen: Heliopolis Verlag, 1979.

Szeskus, Reinhard. "'Die erste Walpurgisnacht', op. 60, von Felix Mendelssohn Bartholdy." *Beiträge zur Musikwissenschaft* 17, no. 2–3 (1975): 171–80.

Teeple, Howard. *The Mosaic Eschatological Prophet*. Philadelphia: Society of Biblical Literature, 1957.

Temperley, Nicholas. "'The world owes good thanks to Dr. Mendelssohn . . .'." Liner notes to Mendelssohn Bartholdy, Felix. *Elijah*. Orchestra of the Age of Enlightenment. Paul Daniel. London compact disc 455 689–2. 1997.

Times (London, England), 17 July 1833, 1.

Times (London, England), 23 July 1833, 4.

Times (London, England), 2 August 1833, 1–2.

Todd, R. Larry, ed. *Mendelssohn and His World*. Princeton: Princeton University Press, 1991.

———. *Mendelssohn: A Life in Music*. New York: Oxford University Press, 2003.

Treue, Wilhelm. "Das Bankhaus Mendelssohn als Beispiel einer Privatbank im 19. und 20. Jahrhundert." *Mendelssohn Studien* 1 (1972): 29–80.

"Unpublished Letters of Mendelssohn." *Musical Times* 51 (1910): 366.

Varnhagen von Ense, Karl August. *Denkwürdigkeiten des eignen Lebens*. 3 vols. Frankfurt am Main: Deutscher Klassiker Verlag, 1987.

Wagner, Richard. *Judaism in Music and Other Essays*. Trans. by William Ashton Ellis. Lincoln: University of Nebraska Press, 1995.

Walk, Joseph, ed. *Das Sonderrecht für die Juden im NS-Staat: eine Sammlung der gesetzlichen Massnahmen und Richtlinien, Inhalt und Bedeutung*. 2nd ed. Heidelberg: C. F. Müller Verlag, 1996.

Ward Jones, Peter. "The Library of Felix Mendelssohn Bartholdy." In *Festschrift Rudolf Elvers zum 60. Geburtstag*, edited by Ernst Herttrich and Hans Schneider. Tutzing: Hans Schneider, 1985.

———, ed. *The Mendelssohns on Honeymoon: The 1837 Diary of Felix and Cécile Mendelssohn Bartholdy Together with Letters to Their Families*. New York: Oxford, Clarendon Press, 1997.

———. "Letter to the Editor." *The Musical Quarterly* 83, no. 1 (1999): 27–30.

———. "Felix Mendelssohn Bartholdys Tod: Der Bericht seiner Frau." *Mendelssohn Studien* 12 (2001): 205–25.

Wehmer, Carl, ed. *Ein tief gegründet Herz: der Briefwechsel Felix Mendelssohn-Bartholdys mit Johann Gustav Droysen*. Heidelberg: Lambert Schneider, 1959.

Weissweiler, Eva, ed. *"Die Musik will gar nicht rutschen ohne Dich": Fanny und Felix Mendelssohn, Briefwechsel 1821 bis 1846*. Berlin: Propyläen Verlag, 1997.

Werner, Eric. "New Light on the Family of Felix Mendelssohn." *Hebrew Union College Annual* 26 (1955), 543–65.

———. "The Family Letters of Felix Mendelssohn Bartholdy." *Bulletin of the New York Public Library* 65, no. 1 (1961): 5–20.

———. *Mendelssohn: A New Image of the Composer and His Age*. Trans. by Dika Newlin. London: Free Press of Glencoe, 1963; Rev. German ed. *Mendelssohn: Leben und Werk in neuer Sicht*. Zürich: Atlantis Musikbuch-Verlag, 1980.

———. "Felix Mendelssohn's Commissioned Composition for the Hamburg Temple: The 100th Psalm (1844)." *Musica Judaica* 7, no. 1 (1984–85): 54–57.

Werner, Jack. "The Mendelssohnian Cadence." *The Musical Times* 97 (Jan. 1956): 17–19.

Werner, Rudolf. "Felix Mendelssohn Bartholdy als Kirchenmusiker." Ph.D. diss., Universität Frankfurt am Main, 1930.

Whaley, Joachim. *Religious Toleration and Social Change in Hamburg, 1529–1819*. Cambridge: Cambridge University Press, 1985.

Wiener, Aharon. *The Prophet Elijah in the Development of Judaism*. London: Routledge & Kegan Paul, 1978.

Wilson Kimber, Marian. "'For art has the same place in your heart as mine': Family, Friendship, and Community in the Life of Felix Mendelssohn." In *The Mendelssohn Companion*, edited by Douglass Seaton, 29–75. Westport, Conn.: Greenwood Press, 2001.

Wolff, Ernst. *Felix Mendelssohn Bartholdy*. Berlin: Verlagsgesellschaft für Literatur und Kunst, 1906.

———, ed. *Meister-Briefe: Felix Mendelssohn Bartholdy*. Berlin: B. Behr's Verlag, 1907.

Zywietz, Michael. *Adolf Bernhard Marx und das Oratorium in Berlin*. Eisenach: Verlag der Musikalienhandlung Karl Dieter Wagner, 1996.

Index